Our Dusty Paradise

Linda Caine

ISBN-13: 978-1505220261
ISBN-10: 1505220262

To our warm-hearted and generous Spanish neighbours.

CONTENTS

Prologue

"Take off your watch, jewellery and belt, please," she said, in Spanish. "You can keep the rest of your clothes on."

I did as I was told, and with some trepidation lay down on the narrow couch with its white, protective paper strip.

"This will take 20 minutes and you must keep very still," the young radiologist explained, as she secured my hands in a sling arrangement that would keep them by my sides.

As she disappeared from my view, an arched cocoon of cream plastic gradually tunnelled its way over my head, coming to rest a mere 20 centimetres above my nose. It hummed like a giant chrysalis awaiting re-birth. I wondered if Egyptian mummies had been given a similar amount of breathing space to get them to the Afterworld. To avoid claustrophobia, I decided to shut my eyes and have a snooze; let my mind wander off to a greener, wilder place where the limitations of the body had no relevance. Where the slow advance of cancer could be ignored.

I knew that Steve would be sitting in the waiting room, trying not to fall asleep over his online, interactive Spanish lesson. Failing that, he might be considering the relative merits of his favourite motorbikes, or which British politician he would most like to consign to a desert island. Although it was November and beginning to feel chilly, he was dressed in his usual attire of T-shirt, shorts, and flip-flops, with a total value of about 10 Euros. Even my old leather belt was worth more than that, but he is not a man to make any concessions to style over practicality - how can you crawl under a car to fix the exhaust if you're dressed in your best suit?

Combining this same practicality with an unlikely degree of patience and fortitude, we had begun to adapt to a new modus operandi: a cycle of blood tests, X-rays, scans, infusions, and injections. Unexpectedly, alongside retirement, my genetic footprint had become visible, a harbinger of death on the dusty stretch of road that took us to our mountain home in Andalucía. There was no point in making a fuss about it; this was just another part of our life together, even though we didn't know how much of that precious time we had left.

Chapter 1

Panjuila

There are at least 8 brooms in our Spanish house. Some are delicate types with red plastic handles and screw-on, soft nylon heads, some are coarse wood-and-bristle yard brooms, with a few long nails clouted in and bent over to hold everything firmly in place. Each one has its own identity and purpose, and usually starts life as a valued and functional object within an invisible hierarchy. Each has its own allocated abode, depending on its status when new; a superior cupboard in the kitchen storeroom for light household duties, a respectable location in the courtyard for serious outdoor work, and an undoubtedly despised corner in the laundry room for removing spiders and sweeping the terrace.

Wherever they start out, all of these brooms end their days in the old stable down below, alongside discarded paint brushes, dustpans and shovels, and several ancient containers filled with rubble. These are the 'untouchables' of our domestic arrangements, once essential but now almost invisible. Yet all have played their part in battling the enemy.

There is no shortage of dust in our Iberian home and no shortage of the means to dispose of it, but, like Sisyphus rolling his boulder uphill, we will never complete our task and contentedly gaze upon a shining whole. This applies to our village, the valley, and indeed the whole of southern Spain. Probably most of the Mediterranean coastline. A combination of heat, wind, soil and stone flows through these regions, as the mountains relentlessly track their way back to the sea from whence they came. The streets can be swept and watered every morning, but by nightfall a fresh layer of dust will have settled on hot concrete, bubbling tarmac, misshapen and dented cars, our tiled bathroom floor, and even my leather sandals, tucked under a bedroom chair.

Perhaps Steve and I will become experts on this aspect of the universe, able to distinguish between dust that has blown in from the wild countryside that very day, and dust that has spiralled downwards from the ceiling timbers, or seeped out of the old stonework over the course of weeks and years. We will know the difference between pure, organic mountain dust and the dross of chemically-constructed building materials, between ancient Moorish particles and more modern residue.

Where the Berbers left iron ore, salt, and dried clay, the modern brigade are leaving plastic, decaying teabags and microchips. Eventually, all will be ground down to the finest grit, yet intermingled with it will be timeless fragments and fragrances of rose, jasmine, pomegranate, and geranium; the sifted powders of red pimentón, orange saffron and green, perfumed thyme. Everything will need to be isolated and identified. We will buy a microscope and 'virtual' vellum notebooks in order to inscribe forensic details for future generations.

One's own life can be just such an accumulation of detritus. Early on in the twenty-first century I had reached a critical moment in my life when it was necessary to stop sweeping, assess the dustpan and its contents, and decide what to do next. With both parents dead, my two sons reaching manhood, and a long-term relationship coming to an end, I had begun to question where I wanted to live in my later years and what I might choose to do. I could go on as a public servant, living in East Anglia and working until I dropped, or I could opt for retirement at sixty and explore some other part of the world. In theory, I had a good eight years to review the options and make up my mind.

In fact, the choice came much sooner. That same year, I had booked myself onto a week's walking holiday in southern Spain, aiming to improve my fitness levels and explore a region well-known to me for its music, fabled place-names and dramatic scenery. Well-known, but never visited. I had reached Madrid as a child, on a family holiday, but as I grew up, the south seemed either too far away or likely to be filled with cheap hotels and expensive golf courses, or sweating, bacon-tinted holiday-makers.

I decided that perhaps this assumption was misplaced, and with Gerald Brenan's *South from Granada* in one corner of my suitcase, leather walking-boots in the other and English clouds in my head, I flew out of Stansted one afternoon in late June, as casually as though I was getting on a bus to Norwich. It had been 25 years since I had taken a holiday alone and it was strange to have no responsibilities except to myself.

Three hours later, Málaga airport appeared, glittering in the darkness, festooned with as many LED jewels as an Arabian princess. The night air on the tarmac was warm and soft, an instant indication of the change from northern to southern Europe. Flight crew wandered about in short-sleeves and thin, fluorescent orange jackets. Cicadas chattered away in the distance and I could smell pine trees, coupled with a waft of sea air.

Five unlikely-looking fellow-walkers were assembled in the Arrivals hall, waiting for transport to take us up into the mountains. Our nationalities included Icelandic and Hong Kong Chinese, our ages ranged from 24 to 67, and we included in our number a Shell company wife with all the latest digital gadgets to hand, and a strange young man from Essex, kitted out as though for an expedition through the jungle: khaki shorts, long socks and a beige Dr Livingston hat. The transport turned out to be a very ancient, wheezing, cream Land Rover. Our kit was piled on the roof, we sat on hard, narrow seats facing one another, and from there we began our slow journey into the invisible foothills, pin-pricked by the lights of isolated farmhouses and small villages. I was conscious of looming cliffs and deep canyons out there in the darkness, yet unaware of the enormous canvas that is Andalucía. By the time we reached our guesthouse a couple of hours later, we were too tired to do more than greet our hosts and fall into bed.

I awoke early next morning to the sweet scent of jasmine drifting in from an open window and the sight of a golden oriole flashing through the grey-green leaves of a tall eucalyptus tree. The air was cool, but I could sense the warmth to come. The yellow light, filtering through the trees, could only strengthen as the day progressed. Some long-subdued signal in me awoke too and my Italian blood, inherited from my grandfather Corrado, responded with delight to all these southern sirens. At that moment, the exact country didn't matter, but the line of latitude did. This felt like home.

* * *

Andalucía is a huge tract of Spain stretching from Portugal in the west, to the Mediterranean in the south and east. It includes historic cities with famously romantic names such as Cadiz, Granada, Sevilla, and Cordoba; also less thrilling places ruined to some extent by tourism and greed, such as Marbella, Torremolinos, and Nerja. It has been the birthplace of many well-known figures in history: Seneca (both the elder and the younger), 5 Roman emperors including Hadrian, Emir Boabdil of Granada, Maria Antonietta of Spain, the painters Velázques and Picasso, Manuel de Falla (composer), Andrés Segovia (classical guitarist), Manolete (bullfighter) and, of course, its own twentieth-century poet, Federico García Lorca. It has achieved long-lasting notoriety for its poverty, its wild flamenco, its resistance to political control, and its instinctive response to all things sensual.

Almost everyone knows something about the Andalucían cultural heritage. Many people have holidayed here and perhaps a few have studied the impact on the region of the Spanish Civil War, of its proximity to Africa and, as ever, allegations of corruption in the construction industry. Economists have a lot to say about Spain and its role in Europe, including the recognition that there is an ambivalence that continues to surround the southern zone, richer now thanks to tourism and joining the European Union, but industrially as poor as it was a hundred years ago. The granting of pensions and the availability of unemployment benefit has eased the life of many, but perhaps it has encouraged a spirit of eighteenth-century gentility as well; surely, it is argued, only the lowest classes have to work manually for a living. A Spanish gentleman should not have to do so.

Some visitors have informed themselves about the sparse territory and frontier spirit that exists in the mountainous area of Andalucía that is known as Las Alpujarras (the high pastures), whose influences include the Romans, the Phoenicians, the Berber Arabs, and more latterly, some modern-day 'alternative' interest groups such as the Alexander Music School and the Buddhist monastery O Sel Ling. Some folk come for the mountain-climbing and horse-riding, others to build yurts and live off the land. Some come here following mystical visions, or so they say, whilst others have simply dropped out of mainstream society.

Steve and I had no such obvious motive, yet this is where we have taken root, like fig trees in apparently barren soil, describing ourselves as independent and benevolent anarchists looking for a quiet life.

* * *

Much of the region's agricultural income is based on olive oil, and the patterns of the olive trees run across the landscape like velvet découpage, the stripes, dots and patchwork squares of soft green clearly delineated against a background of stony terracotta soil. One can drive for many miles and see nothing but these feathery evergreens as they march across the plains, up ridiculously steep hillsides and down apparently inaccessible gorges, preparing themselves for the first frosts and the farmer with his black nets.

Alongside these huge agricultural 'throws' are smaller fields of almond groves, tobacco plants, vines, tomatoes and tropical fruits such as cherimoya, whilst every self-respecting villager has his or her own kitchen garden or *huerto*, with crops of onions, garlic, peppers, and aubergines. Often a mule or a donkey is tethered in a corner, waiting patiently for its master; sometimes a fine horse stands in the shade, its tail whisking away the flies.

This is a landscape moulded by ancient strata movements and glacial action, followed by more recent minor earthquakes. It is still unstable, geologically speaking, and little tremors can be felt quite frequently. The rock has a metallic gleam, tinged with sulphurous orange, and may be exposed as a large formation jutting out on the skyline, or as a coarsely-shaped boulder that has hurtled down from the peaks above. Great slabs bind together to form steep-sided gulleys or *barrancos*, where icy water pours down from the heights above. This rock is always present, just under a surface carpet of wild grasses, hummocks of spring flowers and the thin roots of poorly-developed holm oaks or encina.

In the space of 50 kilometres, the coastal sea-level rises to 3,500 metres, with all types of vegetation contained in the unique biodiversity of southern Al-Andalus, from cacti to nettles, and from kiwi fruit to acorns. It is a thirsty, rugged, and often unforgiving land where the lonely traveller can follow the meandering and sometimes vertiginous roads as they wind their way up into the mountains, overlooked by white villages and a celestial-blue sky, stunned into silence by a burning, summer sun or a fierce and freezing winter wind.

However, wherever water flows there are outbreaks of magnificent chestnut, walnut, mulberry, and fig trees, as well as all kinds of untamed mountain ash, poplar, elder and tall oleander bushes. Birds sing against this backdrop of lush vegetation and every farm, or *cortijo*, has access to this pure and essential liquid. Almost all have an *alberca*, or irrigation pond, located close by, and scattered throughout the landscape are hill-top cisterns and reservoirs.

Where there is water there are animals too, not least goats, sheep, and dogs. Every self-respecting farm, ham-drying factory or smallholding has its posse of canines, barking and leaping energetically at their leashes or racing frenetically up and down the fence line. Some are huge, hound-like creatures who look as though they would take your head off in one bite, but are actually as soft as kittens; others are fluffy mongrels or sharp-eared, fox-brown creatures. The Spaniards are seriously paranoid when it comes to their property and livestock, although one suspects that a good slab of meat would calm down even the most ferocious of their four-legged friends very rapidly.

There are usually dogs loitering around the town centres where, always, there is water. The main drinking fountain in the village square gives relief and sustenance to both animals and humans during the relentless summer days, so naturally that is where the dogs lie down to snooze. In winter, they may choose the middle of the road if that is the only patch of warmth, stretching out there somnolently and heedless of traffic. If they are in your way, you must drive around them as they will not move for you.

Other fountains are located along remote tracks and pathways, often between two villages, bringing cooling water to a strategic point, once upon a time conveniently placed for the thirsty medieval peddler with his well-laden donkey, and nowadays for the modern backpacker, struggling up the hill. Simply bathing one's face in some small, blue-tiled *fuente* in the middle of nowhere can make the heat more bearable.

Contrary to most tourist brochures however, this is not the land of eternal warmth. I have heard it said that Spain is a cold country with a hot sun, which is well-supported for almost three quarters of the year. From November to May, once the sun has set, the cold descends with an intense rapidity. There is little defence against the icy winter nights at high altitude, when the thick stone walls hold no heat and modern radiators are miserable metal boxes that achieve next-to-nothing. Only live flame, hot stew, and a shared bed can get one through to the morning in any degree of comfort. A bearskin or two might help.

My winter bedchamber routine depends greatly on a swift transition from woolly sweater and lined trousers, to winceyette pyjamas, bed-socks and, on occasion, a knitted Peruvian hat. This is reversed in the morning, aided by a cup of tea. Steve, who is made of hardier material than I, acts as a full-length hot water bottle, for which I am pathetically grateful. He deserves a medal.

How did we, or at that point I, end up shivering through the winter nights in the little village of Panjuila? What magnetic force, or ley line, or moment of chance brought us here?

* * *

For me, there is always some special visual element that determines whether to buy a house or not. I have been moved by, variously, a large, elegant beech tree; some delightful Edwardian casement windows; a barn constructed of knapped Norfolk flint; a sinuous, purple-flowering wisteria - and now it was a wrought-iron balcony overlooking a narrow street, in a very small village far away from my native country.

Our walking group had been up in the high Sierras all day, looking down on the well-cultivated land below, dotted with white-washed houses and bisected by wooded ravines, ancient pathways and a few paved roads. Now, we were returning to base camp along the GR7 footpath, the old Gran Ruta that runs from Santiago to Rome. It was mid-afternoon and very warm. Carrying backpacks, we passed through a neat, almost hexagonal-shaped plaza containing a fountain with several spouts and shaded by a silver and green poplar tree, where the only sound was the continuous bubbling and splashing of the water. The whole place was in its own deep sleep, that moment of siesta when the warm zephyr breeze meanders its way over the stones and rustles a few leaves, but most life-forms are lost in dreams. Only Noel Coward's mad dogs and Englishmen were still awake and in motion.

This sleeping beauty of a village had a somewhat grubby presence, like a pretty girl with dirty fingernails, but it retained a mysterious aura of tranquillity. Time had not stopped precisely, but it had certainly slowed down. Narrow, unadorned streets passed beneath timbered *tinaos*, or roof level bridges, which were used in much earlier times to enable householders to socialise with each other without anyone setting foot on the ground. A good defensive strategy as well as a social one, it kept people out of the mud and filth of the streets when the spring rains came, whilst also giving them an opportunity to evade the law by moving unseen from house to house. (In fact, the principle still applies of having stables and cool cellars on the ground floor, living accommodation above and a pleasant terrace at the highest level. In summer, this arrangement can be reversed and, where there are no longer any animals, people sleep in their basements, where it is coolest, reserving the top terrace for the laundry or drying red peppers).

Panjuila's central plaza had a wheelwright's pattern of small slates laid on edge and seemed fairly well-tended, but the backstreets were made of old, poured concrete, littered with dog mess, paper debris and wind-blown leaves. Where exactly was its magic? Was it behind the doorways screened with colourful, striped curtains? Did it find strength in the vermilion-red geraniums sprouting in odd corners, or the luscious green grapes hanging low over private terraces? Did it belong to the bold, black and tangerine cats prowling about on their ceaseless quest for food? Did it exist for the families who lived here? If it had been early evening, might we have seen a few of the locals sitting outside the solitary bar, smiling benevolently at passers-by, but with their daily routine unaffected, their existence shrouded in mystery?

One or two tiny streets led off the square, but a wider route went up an incline with tall houses on either side, then zig-zagged slightly, turned a corner, and finally passed out of the village to the car parking area. As we turned that last corner, chattering and laughing in the sunshine, my gaze was impelled upwards towards an empty, black-barred balcony about 3 metres long. It was my moment of truth, with nothing especially magical about it. Bereft of flowers, neglected and abandoned, the balcony and its triangular, recessed alcove begged for someone to give it attention. A thin piece of white cotton hung over a gaping doorway at the back, and a collapsing chair was perched lop-sidedly against the railing. A small, handwritten Se Vende board hung at a sad angle. My footsteps slowed. What should I do? No one else said anything, or even appeared to notice this architectural waif, but as we reached the car park, I decided that some sort of response was needed.

"Hang on two seconds," I begged and ran back into the village. On a scrap of paper, I jotted down the phone number on the sale board, vaguely aware that I had embarked, impetuously, on a new adventure. This was pretty much in character, although I have tried to moderate my less desirable personality traits over time.

What was I thinking of? I spoke no Spanish, had only visited Spain once before and then as a child, and knew relatively little of its contemporary politics, culture or history. This was like some crazy teenage love affair, all restraint abandoned. Even my return to Britain made no difference; I was back within 2 months to view the house properly and put in an offer.

* * *

When I came back to Andalucía, it was August and Panjuila was transfixed and motionless in the heat. Dogs and cats lay sleeping in the darkest corners, humans remained indoors all afternoon and the ceaseless fountain sang alone beneath its solitary tree.

I moved slowly past the silent houses with their pale walls, violet shadows and shuttered interiors. I relished the concept of a village whose streets were too narrow for more than a pair of mules or a couple of passing wheelbarrows, and whose colour scheme was predicated on the strength of the noonday sun. Beyond, lay the wild greenery and burnt umber terraces of the campo, the raw pink quarry face of El Conjuro to the east, and to the south the arid Contraviesa hills, all set against an intense indigo sky. This was the rich, southern palette of the Mediterranean and I wanted to be a part of it.

Although I had been liaising directly with the vendors over the telephone from Britain, a local estate agent named Jyanna took me under her wing, arranging for a translation service and giving me advice on the house purchase process. A small, intense woman with carefully outlined and painted lips and beautiful Lebanese eyes, she had moved to the area several years earlier with her British artist husband but, tragically, he had contracted motor neurone disease and died, leaving her with a large, new house and all their family still in England. She had found paradise and then experienced hell.

As we progressed matters and I waited for various pieces of legal paperwork to be found, we became more friendly. One evening, she invited me back to her home for supper and I found myself hurtling after her down a steep hill into a pitch-black Alpujarran valley. My little hire car bounced over potholes and round the hairpins as though it had been designed specifically for that purpose. We ate a sparse meal in her large and chilly dining room, where I longed to see a few books or a comfortable settee. The air conditioning and the stripped-back summer furnishings combined to make the house feel unlived in and cold, even though it was August. It was just a place to sleep before she went back to work in the morning.

"While you're here, why don't you go to the ballet in Granada?" she asked.

"Ballet? What ballet?"

"At the Alhambra, they're putting on an open-air performance of Lorca's Blood Wedding. There's flamenco dancing as well."

11

Although I had been to Granada before, that had been part of an organised group visit in daylight. To drive there on my own, find my way through the city and get back safely to my rural hotel, was a scary prospect. However, this seemed like an occasion not to be missed and at 12 Euros, about £7 then, it was very tempting. Jyanna assured me that the road system would take me where I needed to go.

She was quite right. By 8pm I was in my seat, surrounded by the sweetly-scented gardens of the Generalife and overlooked by gigantic magnolia grandiflora with their creamy, plate-sized flowers. Next to me sat several Granadino matrons, immaculately coiffed, beautifully dressed and all of them very disapproving of the fact that I had come there '*sola.*' This bothered me not at all.

We saw spectacular dancing, accompanied by gypsy *bel canto* singing, and as I already knew the Lorca play in English, I was able to follow the action of the ballet closely. Based on actual events that Lorca chose to dramatise, it spells out the fatal consequences of arranged marriages and jealous hearts, metaphors for the political rigidity and reactionary morals of the 1930s. No wonder the authoritarians of Franco's Spain wanted to destroy not only the play, but also its author, since he had his work performed in the village squares as well as the great theatres, sending out revolutionary and destabilising messages to ordinary peasant communities.

Once more, despite the heat of the day, by about 11 in the evening it began to cool down rapidly. Granada is a city set high on the Sierras and the Alhambra looms another 200 metres or so over the city. The matrons next to me pulled elegant shawls out of their capacious handbags and wrapped them around their shoulders. I had nothing with me and my bare arms were soon goose-pimpled, so I learnt a valuable lesson. The mantilla is an essential part of one's evening attire all year round, even if it has evolved nowadays into a cardigan or a jacket.

* * *

The next day, Jyanna arranged for me to view the house more thoroughly, with a translator in tow - a young woman named Zara. One of the owners, Basilio, would show us round. As we drove up into the mountains, Zara told me a little of her life growing up in a 'tepee village.' Her parents had come over from England when she and her brother were babies and they, *los padres*, still lived a precarious existence in a yurt, hidden away in one of the valleys. Now, Zara shared a tiny house with her New Zealand boyfriend and was keen to emigrate; her brother had rebelled against his parents' alternative lifestyle and worked in a bank in Granada, having exchanged his T-shirt and jeans for a business suit, a tie, and some security in his life.

When we got to the village it was getting close to lunchtime, about 2pm. Zara knocked on the door of the first house we came to.

"Can I use your bathroom?" she asked the woman who answered the door.

It seemed that this was normal behaviour for women 'caught short' in the countryside and Zara vanished briefly into the cool, dark interior. Next, we went to find Basilio. He was a man in his late fifties, very polite and pleasant, wearing a well-pressed, light pink shirt. He was unperturbed by the complete state of dereliction that the house was in and as he showed us around, I realised that only I could see its potential. Zara went through the motions, doing her job, and Basilio seemed to think that I could not possibly want to buy such a wreck, but was too polite to say so. As he lit a cigarette, I tried a bit of humour.

"You should give that up," I said. "It might warm up your lungs too much on such a hot day."

He took me very seriously.

"You're right," he said, "I keep trying to stop."

I ignored the mess that the house was in and made an effort to examine the basics. How sound the walls were, whether the timber looked worm-ridden, and if it had electricity and running water. Steve always accuses me of a 'load, fire, aim' approach to life but at this point I was trying to be practical and objective. Just looking at something and making assumptions about its quality does not always equate to actuality. The trouble was that I was already committed. I had fallen in love and could not see anything beyond my heart's desire. Once back in Jyanna's office, we began the process of haggling over the price. I agreed to buy it at, it seemed to me, a very reasonable price compared to equivalent costs in the UK, and I arranged to make a third trip in the autumn to complete the purchase.

When I returned in late October, the tourists had gone home, yellowing leaves were blowing down the dusty streets and early snow graced the tops of the Sierra Nevada mountains. I was enchanted. I felt like the heroine of a novel by Marquez, wandering dreamily through a remote backwater of the world, far from reality. Life was lived at a slow and charmingly disorganised pace, everything slightly unkempt yet immensely relaxing. I ate my lunches in the orange grove of an end-of-season restaurant and took long baths in my hotel in the evening, sipping cheap wine and nibbling on salted almonds.

But I did not lose my sense of reason too much. I was sufficiently sane to use a proper lawyer and ensure full legal title, checking that all debts against the property had been paid and insisting that the house be cleared of rubbish prior to taking possession. Luckily, as it turned out, this was interpreted to mean that the bedsteads, ancient stable doors, beer bottles, and straw could be thrown into the little barn at the back, out of sight, rather than taken to the rubbish dump or *basura voluminosa*. Later on, I discovered some real gems among the debris.

On the other hand, I was very naïve about getting the property surveyed, transferring the money cost-effectively and then locating a good builder. My knowledge of barn conversions and a willingness to put in solid physical work was useful, but I was lucky not to be the fool whose money was taken from her all at once, at the very beginning. In fact, it would take several years before that particular result was achieved.

My purchase turned out to be half of a bigger house, originally belonging to Basilio's grandparents, then shared between a brother and sister in the 1960s. I had bought the outer, street-facing half, comprising a couple of stables on the ground floor, several rooms on the first floor along with the neglected balcony, a small barn or *granero* at the back and, it seemed, half of a secluded *terrazza*.

No one had lived there for years, so the kitchen was a mess of ancient plaster and sagging electrics, a precariously hung water-heater, and a sloping cement floor. What had once been the shower room was in a similar state, and the loo had long since been blocked up with debris and brick dust. On the plus side however, there were 'reception' rooms with high ceilings supported by chestnut *vigas* (whole tree trunks), and chestnut *alfajillas* (smaller joists), adze-cut and roughly-shaped. Each *viga* and *alfajilla* varied in tone and colour, from pale auburn to walnut-brown. These timbers held up the grey stone slates and flattish rocks of the roof, which in turn was 'topped off' with an impervious, grey river-sand called *launa*. Impervious to rain but not to weeds, as it turned out. Many openings in the house had exposed chestnut lintels above them and there were recesses that echoed old Moorish doorways or sleeping alcoves, long since blocked up.

Some of the stable walls down below were built in the traditional method of straw, red mud and tiny slivers of stone, mixed to a solid paste and reinforced with lengths of wood. Wattle and daub, more or less. These stables had been divided up for various animals, each one with their own feeding trough; a cow in one corner, the chickens in another, a fat pig and a donkey somewhere in the darkness. The stable partitions consisted of wooden half-doors, old metal bed bases and wire netting, held together with baler twine or rope. Underfoot was the accumulated debris of fifty years: straw and dried manure, crates of empty Alhambra beer bottles, abandoned rope halters, and horseshoes. Yet, incredibly, there were also hand-cut stone feeding basins and the remnants of a flagged stone floor. This part of the house was dark and gloomy, with no lighting, but as soon as I looked closely I knew that I was peering into history.

The horse, mule and donkey have all been significant elements of Spain's past, and one can still see them in use today. Until the mid-1960s, almost every house had its stable and every village its *posado*, or hostelry, and of course, a blacksmith. The horse in particular was given preferential treatment. Sweet-smelling alfalfa, oats and fresh water were provided daily, since this proudly-owned animal (*caballo noble*) provided transport, status, an income through foaling, a degree of heating for the household above - and the family toilet facilities! Sadly, the advent of the motor car means that except for breeding or fiestas, the horse has ceased to have a significant place in mountain village life, but we have friends who still use mules and donkeys to work their land, especially in inaccessible places, or to carry large loads along the tiny hillside *caminos*.

The *granero* had been used as a stable on the ground floor as well, but the upper level had a smoothly polished cement floor, a window with a magnificent view of the hillside known as the Elephant across the valley, and an old fireplace with a chimney. It had been used for drying pimientos and other vegetables, and perhaps as a winter living quarters for a shepherd. It was attached to the house and had its own entrance, but on the north side abutted a ruined smithy. Standing on the roof on a clear day, I was thrilled to locate a tiny piece of the Mediterranean Sea 50 kilometres away, caught like a turquoise jewel in the 'v' of the distant mountains.

I had bought a house in serious need of restoration and modernisation, but it had good, thick stone walls, shelter from the extremes of Andalucían weather, and plenty of opportunities for me to return to the world of my childhood, growing up on a Lakeland hill farm. I recognised the essential features and sensed that here was something of intrinsic value. The question was, could I do it justice?

* * *

Almost as soon as I had acquired the house, I had a run-in with my nearest neighbour, who turned out to be not a Spaniard, but a young Scots woman with the dangerous, pale-grey eyes of a wolf. She was renting the 'inner' half of the property and was keen to assure me that although I could look out over the supposedly shared *terrazza*, I had no right to set foot on it. I disagreed.

"It belongs to Jack, my landlord, all of it!" she yelled, scooping up some puppies that were running around in hysterical and incontinent joy. "You know nothing about this place and how things work."

With the second part of this, I could not disagree, but on the first point I was intentionally cool and clear. "You are wrong," I said, "and my *notario* can prove it."

Her young daughter arrived and looked at me wonderingly. I decided that this irate verbal altercation was not fair on a child, so I decided to go back to my lawyer to seek clarification. I jumped in the car and raced back down the mountain to the main town, to see Señor Montez. He, a charming man of old-style courtesy, clicked his heels as he shook my hand, assuring me that I had 50 per cent ownership of the terrace and that Jack would have to prove otherwise in a court of law if he disagreed. My heart sank. I had not planned for a new life that would include legal wrangling. I decided that as I was due to return to the UK within 24 hours, I would wait and see how things developed on my next visit before taking that step.

When I got back a couple of hours later, the enraged tenant was out, the puppies only in evidence by the amount of mess on the tiles, so I simply positioned a large log of wood across a 'virtual' dividing line, swept my side of it and got on with the huge task of clearing the house. So my first broom was used in anger, an unlikely and undesirable beginning. Fortunately, the neighbour left the property within a year, taking her puppies with her, and as events unfolded I had no need for legal proofs.

Over the next two years, I returned several times to the house, trying to progress its repair, meet local people and have a holiday at the same time. I stayed near the village in a little self-contained *casita* owned by a gifted artisan and his wife, both originally from Madrid, who offered a swimming pool and much kindness. Most days, I worked long and hard, scraping peeling paint off the walls and beams, taking out debris by the barrow-full and attacking hideous 1950s tiled floors with a lump hammer and steel chisel.

The usual working day in the summer in Andalucía runs from 9 a.m. to 2 p.m. and then 5 p.m. to 8 or 9 p.m. I tended to observe these times too, going back to the *casita* and pool for a lunch of salad and cheese, a swim and a siesta. We have since realised that the *campesinos* are often out in the cool air by 7 a.m., and nowadays Steve is frequently down on the land at that hour too. In Seville in August it is not uncommon to advise children and the elderly to stay indoors between 11 a.m. and 5 p.m., and most people find it hard to continue working through the hottest part of the day.

One April I came out with my younger son, Cameron, then aged about 19 and in his first year at university. We both expected some warm weather and were taken aback to see the temperature gauge in the car drop to only 3 degrees centigrade as we climbed into the mountains. There was a thin scattering of snow on the ground and our kindly hosts had to lend us some firewood to supplement the electric heater. I think Cam, with his very short, peroxide hair, rugby-player build, and complete lack of Spanish, was disappointed not to be able to acquire a tan, but he soon learnt the most essential words: *cerveza* (beer) and *servicios* (toilets). But where were the señoritas for him to impress?

On one of our shopping trips to Orgiva we were brought to a standstill by the Guardia Civil. Two pairs of stern-faced and fully-armed policemen, dressed in dark green, seemed to be stopping almost everyone and we wondered if this was normal. Luckily, I had my passport with me, and one of them spoke a little English, but they took a very dim view of the fact that the car hire company had not provided any insurance documents. "You go where?" they asked. "You stay where?"

All became clear a couple of nights later when some local lads took Cam off to a spring festival, armed with beer, marijuana, and much good humour. They too were stopped in their beaten-up old vehicle, but managed to convince the police that they were on their way to Alicante. Cam kept quiet in the back and hoped that his artificially Nordic appearance would count in his favour. It must have done, as they returned him without mishap at about four in the morning after a long session of music-making and hilarious attempts to communicate in Spanglish. I had long since gone to bed. I had not worried about my two sons' whereabouts for quite some time; they seemed to live charmed lives and were both over 18, so my maternal responsibilities were at an end, theoretically speaking.

While Cam enjoyed his all-night rave, I was invited for supper at a nearby hotel by a large Dutch woman and her leather-jacketed son, Donni. There must have been a dozen of us seated around a long banqueting table under some exceedingly bright lights (a noticeable feature of most restaurants and bars, to the extent that one wonders why the Spanish seem to despise any attempt at 'atmosphere'). Who this woman was and why I was invited remained a mystery for some time, but I found myself placed between the local Alcalde, or Mayor, and a young woman doctor from Medecin Sans Frontières, taking a break from her strenuous and emotion-sapping work in the Sudan.

"How do you organise your waste disposal in England?" asked the bearded Alcalde, in excellent English.

"Each household has at least one dustbin," I replied, somewhat mystified, "but also we can use a neighbourhood or regional centre for bigger items. Recycling is pretty important now."

"We can do nothing regionally," he complained, "and the villagers in one town will not share their rubbish with anyone else. Even adjoining villages want their own bins. As for recycling..."

"Perhaps you should do it slowly, by stealth," I suggested. "First a communal village collection point, then something bigger and more central later on. Almost everyone has the use of a car these days, to transport bags and sacks."

Something in this must have made sense to him as, 10 years later, we all have free recycling bags, a village waste-disposal building with several large bins, and two *basura voluminosa* yards in the locality. People are cynical about the reality of recycling, and getting them to actually use the bins properly is a less successful concept. Often the box or bag of rubbish is dropped inside on the concrete floor, just waiting for a passing swarm of wasps or a herd of hungry cats. I have seen a man walk past the saloon-type doors of the village bin-store and simply toss his rubbish bag over the top. Why bother to open a door, then a bin lid, and then put his bag inside the bin? Cats? Rats? Who cares?

Even folk who drive right past the *basura voluminosa* on their way to the shops often cannot be bothered to take an old TV or mattress so far. They leave these things outside the local bin-store and hope that someone else will want them. Idleness disguised as benevolence perhaps, or the other way around. Often it works, as any item of use will disappear within a day; we too have benefited from the scheme, collecting up slightly damaged, traditional cooking pans (potential flower-pots), a bicycle wheel (spokes for a camping stove), and lengths of plastic pipe (garden watering aids).

About a year after this dinner party, I discovered that the large Dutch woman had been trying to 'soften up' the Alcalde so that she could get planning permission for an extension to her house and for a swimming pool. I am not sure whether her idea worked or not, but he was a well-rounded man who looked as though he had had many such dinners thrust upon him.

One evening in England, I received a phone call from Donni.

"I hope you don't mind me ringing," he said, "but we have a problem here with our English builder, who has become seriously ill and is in the main Granada hospital. We are wondering whether he should be flown home to England. With your contacts, perhaps you can advise us."

He went on to explain that the 50 year old man had had some kind of stroke and would need an emergency operation.

"I'm not a doctor," I said, "but I doubt if any airline company would fly him back, at altitude, with a brain injury such as a stroke. Furthermore, the English hospitals are so over-stretched, there might not be a bed for him. If he has a bed in Granada and they can give him the right care, I would advise you to keep him where he is and let them go ahead with the surgery."

"Do you think they know what they're doing here in Spain?" he asked.

"I can't say for sure," I replied, "but many European countries have a better record of stroke survival than Britain, so his chances of a swift recovery are probably just as good in Spain as in England."

How that worked out, I don't know. We never discussed the other key issue of long-term rehabilitation, but I hope that the same builder is still functioning, happily plastering walls and fitting out kitchens, thanks to excellent Spanish healthcare. I did not know that within a decade I would be testing the system also, on my own behalf.

* * *

On my next solo visit, as I came back to the village with my first day's shopping, which included a long *barra* of bread, I was greeted by a young, dark-haired woman with her little daughter. She spoke some English, saying her name was Esmé, and asking me how the house was

19

progressing. I explained that I really needed to find a reliable local builder and asked if she knew anyone. She nodded enthusiastically and invited me into her house so she could write down a name and phone number. As I loitered in her hallway, smiling at the little girl, I made the fatal error of putting down my bags. Within seconds, a honey-coloured, sharp-eyed dog appeared, grabbed the end of the *barra* in its jaws, and dashed off down the street. I gave chase but only in time to see the dog, and my bread, disappear down into the campo, leaping over low walls and hedges, well away from humans. It was so ridiculous I had to laugh, but I never put my shopping down on the ground again, in any part of any village.

Esmé's building contact turned out to be Paolo, who appeared one day at my door wearing striped cotton trousers, a cotton kaftan top, and tied-back hair. He said he could help to restore the house. Gazing at me with brown-eyed sincerity and speaking in stumbling English, he assured me of his craftsmanship, his honesty, his reliability. He knew a plumber, an electrician, a friend who was also a builder and how to hire *el dumper* to remove the debris. He could show me work that he had previously undertaken; I should come down to his *cortijo* and see the progress he had made there.

So, late one afternoon, when it was too hot to do more than wander slowly through the countryside, I meandered my way down to his newly constructed, ochre-yellow house. There were hoops of black hosepipe coiled like snakes under drooping almond trees; tottering piles of paper-thin bricks and hefty concrete blocks butting up to the house wall; interesting doors and window shutters lying in the corner of a future patio; and an ancient pram containing a bucket or two accompanied a pair of exotic knickers which were hanging above it on the end of a twiggy branch. I knocked tentatively at the back door. A very pretty girl appeared, paint brush in hand, followed by Paolo, who smelled suspiciously of marijuana.

"Come in, come in," he smiled, "this is my girlfriend, Narina. Let us show you our house."

Together they made a good-looking couple, and their adobe-style, single storey home looked solid enough, although there was still much work to be done. On the hearth in the main room was a random collection of bleached wood and bone, while bunches of (legal) herbs hung from the beams.

"You can see," said Paolo, "that we are getting this done very well, very traditionally. We are mixing our own paint using soil from the ground and olive oil; this is how it used to be done many years ago."

Much later on, I located the source of this magically coloured clay soil and wished that it had remained undiscovered. Many other people, it seemed, were intent on removing something that needed a preservation order slapping on it; soon, it would all be gone.

I agreed that Paolo should undertake some work for me, starting as soon as possible. As he didn't seem to have much of his own equipment, I purchased a ladder, buckets, scrapers, a shovel… sand, cement, plaster… more buckets… more cement. The work only got started just before I departed again, but we agreed on an hourly rate and what he should do in my absence. Naively, I imagined that because he had a partner, and a baby on the way, he was in need of work and would make good progress, but this was not the case. From time to time he would ring me in England to tell me what had been done, and I would send more money, yet when I came out, activity seemed to have progressed very slowly. I could not equate the cost with the outcome and said so. That was pretty much the end of his 'contract'.

Other irregularities followed. I had electricity, illegally accessed straight off the street lighting, just like many other householders at that time, and I had water courtesy of my now less aggressive, because of the pecuniary advantage, Scots neighbour, to whom I gave the occasional 10 Euros, but none of this was assigned to me officially. I wanted to regularise everything, but when I investigated the processes, it turned out that Paolo's electrician could do most of the work but was not qualified to sign it off and the plumber was as difficult to get hold of as a snake in oil and just as useless, even if he did have a unique knowledge of the village drainage system. There seemed to be no official paperwork on which to base a legitimate and legal request. I felt like a complete beginner and very gullible to boot.

But I began to meet some interesting folk. There was Hannah who, with her pretty teenage daughter and bicycle-mad 10 year old son, had long since abandoned a good British job for the vagaries of selling raspberries and providing food at hippy festivals; Marianne from Belgium whose self-interest made conversation very one-sided but who helped me as much as she could with useful contacts and delicious gazpacho. Also, the ebullient and creative Salva, who was building his own wattle-and-daub hut out in the campo on a secret site hidden from view. This interesting creation slowly evolved into a stylish hut about 7 metres long by 3 metres wide, all curved walls and hand-smoothed plaster. He took his mud straight out of the earth, mixing it with the straw and grasses growing round about, and fashioned his main 'picture window' from an abandoned car windscreen.

As I have mentioned before, rescuing and recycling are key features of Alpujarran life. Anything useful left out at the village bin-store is snapped up within hours. Old chairs, reject washbasins, a coat-rack, rusty tools - someone in the village can always find a use for them. Recently we heard of a couple who wanted to extend their newly acquired and very small shepherd's hut, but were too far from any road to carry materials to it. Fortunately the shepherd had had a serious drink problem and left behind hundreds of empty wine bottles in a pit nearby, which have now been laid end-on and rendered over with cement, providing an extension wall with excellent insulation properties.

On one of our visits, Steve and I were embarrassed to discover that we ourselves were contributing to local landfill, but in the wrong way. As the rubbish from the stables came out, shovelled into old feed bags, Paolo's dumper man would take the bags away for a small fee, we assumed to some remote and organised site, we assumed. We did not worry about the mixture of rubble, plastic and metal as they had no recycling distinction at that time. However, we were accosted one afternoon by a slim, bearded man leading a fine, grey mule.

"You are filling up the countryside with your horrible rubbish!" he exclaimed angrily. "What right do you have to come here and do this?"

"But it goes to the tip," I said, "in the dumper."

"No it does not. It goes right here." He led us to a steep drop out on the edge of the village. "Look!"

We saw immediately that our recent bags of debris were scattered down a 15 metre avalanche of building mess. We were not the only ones doing this, but we were the most recent. We were cross about it too, and did our best to explain that it was not our fault. No one had told us where the dumper man went with the rubbish. That didn't wash and we were left with a sense of guilt that lasted several weeks. It is now forbidden by law to tip there, and the fast-growing plant life of the ravine has covered up our secret.

Another expert in the art of recycling turned out to be Francesca, an Italian who has spent much of her life in the Caribbean. Petite, clever, and friendly, she and her partner José contribute a more cosmopolitan aspect to the village but are an unlikely pair. She is a painter and business woman, speaks several languages fluently, owns more than one house, and admits to having paid no taxes in any country in her entire life. He is a wiry, somewhat ragged 50 year-old urchin, often to be spotted meandering through the village, checking out what's going on, or sitting at midday outside the bar, having his first beer of the day. He could be described as a prince of vagabonds - a free-thinker but also an idler, an occasional craftsman but also a nihilist, an irrepressible spirit with whom we laugh a great deal but who, privately, in all likelihood pours scorn on us, the foreigners.

In the early days, when neither he nor Steve could communicate in each other's languages, they soon established a rapport through extravagant gestures and mime. Within a single evening they had worked up a plan to go wild boar (*jabelí*) hunting. Men seem particularly adept at dispensing with language skills, especially after a couple of beers; the hunt is yet to be accomplished.

In addition, we met a gap-toothed Welshman and some of his sons, a tweed-jacketed Dorset farmer, and an adventurous couple from Valencia, Beth and Dave. But getting to know the local Spaniards was a different matter. Limited to "hola," or "buenos días," and any true understanding complicated by the strong Alpujarran dialect, I began to wonder if we would ever get beyond the superficialities. Our neighbours smiled frequently and were often gallant, carrying one's shopping or offering gardening advice, and seemed well-disposed to *los extranjeros*, but we weren't quite sure how we were viewed. Gradually we came to understand that everyone was related and almost the whole village belonged to four or five families, no more. Some of the younger, working element lived in Granada and came 'home' at weekends, others were based in Almería or Barcelona and only visited for the fiestas. When that happened, children, grandchildren, even great-grandchildren, would appear overnight and race around the village, treating it as their own private playground.

Amongst the men, we grew accustomed to the unintelligible Spanish of the bar owner, another José, and the warm friendliness of Antonio-with-the-beard, his brother-in-law Sancho and, eventually, that of Carlos, who definitely had right-wing political leanings and was not too sure about any stranger in 'his' village. There was also 'the man who never smiled' as we dubbed him. Despite his bubbly and joyful wife, he gazed at the world with indifference, morosely taking up his hand in the card games in the bar and saying little. One warm evening however, as we strolled past his kitchen garden, we commented to him on the maturity of his tomatoes compared to ours and how good his aubergines were looking. A huge grin spread across his face. "Lots of fertiliser in the winter," he said, "and lots of water in spring. That's all."

"What about the raised rows?" asked Steve. "We usually put tomatoes into flat ground and then tie them up."

A long conversation followed about the respective merits of different types of tomato growing and by the time we left, we felt that real progress had been made. And so it turned out. Now he is 'the man who smiles a lot,' a retired policeman of great warmth and character and charm.

José's little bar appeared to be a bastion of male exclusivity, but this has changed quite markedly over the years. Now we are a mixed group and single ladies are as welcome as anyone else. It is open when José chooses, and in winter that might be only twice a week or just for Old Year's Night, but in summer there are many backpackers passing through during the day and sales of fizzy drinks or *resfrescos*, shoot up. In the evening it becomes the social hub for all ages and nationalities, from the elderly Angelina to some scampering two year-old hunting for beetles in front of the fountain. Chairs are brought outside, music blares, dogs wander around and the cats prowl in the shadows.

The daily gathering of the local ladies used to be far more terrifying than the male gatherings at the bar, and I have yet to count myself as a regular with them, although I am sure that I would be made welcome. At least 4, and often 6 or 7 señoras sit to chat in the shade at the entrance to the village, after their morning's housework. Everyone coming or going passes in front of them and if the men join them, they often remain standing, perhaps for a quick getaway! Conversation seems to focus on domestic issues and in the early days I wondered what comment they might be making as I toiled past with wheelbarrow and shovel, dressed in blue overalls and heavy boots. Now, I flatter myself that they look with tolerance on my various other costumes: horse riding kit, backpack and trainers, tango dress and stiletto shoes.

When Steve arrived on the scene and they established that I had children and he, children and grandchildren, we must have overcome some invisible barrier. We were not hippies, we lived a fairly well-regulated and normal existence, kept our part of the street clean, and did as little as possible to disturb the pattern of village life. Perhaps the motorbikes were a bit unusual and my enthusiasm for dancing somewhat undignified for a woman of a certain age, but, gradually, we seem to have become part of the local scenery. Living here permanently and growing our own vegetables has made us 'family' rather than off-comers.

The two women with the most influence appeared to be two sisters, the wives of Antonio and Carlos respectively. It was their family from whom I had bought the house, but I was told that they could be vindictive and untrustworthy if they didn't like you. None of this was ever proved to us. Their concern for the stray cats, their generosity with vegetables from their gardens and, eventually, their almost maternal support for me when my health threatened to collapse, reinforced our view that one can only use personal experience as a guide in such matters. Gossip, animosity and other people's agendas are no basis for forming an opinion about someone.

Chapter 2

Lovers Old and New

One day, Marianne, a Belgian, suggested to me that we should make a trip to Granada, as I wanted to locate a traditional window for the kitchen and she was hunting for a garden table. We set off in my little hire car, driving through Orgiva and Lanjarón, then northward on the new motorway to Granada. Lanjarón is a well-tended town, bisected lengthwise by its one main street, with a reputation for health-giving spa waters. It seems to be frequented by middle-aged Europeans, mostly British, and springs into life only during the summer months. In the 1950s it suffered badly from outbreaks of typhus, especially in the gypsy quarter of the town, so I am not sure how reliable its reputation for good health may be, even now. In the little back streets are many small houses with neon-lit Madonnas embedded in the walls, surrounded by artificial flowers and often behind glass. We have also discovered extraordinary, newly built mansions, painted in violent pink or terracotta and enhanced with excessive quantities of white balustrades, balconies and roof decorations.

On our journey, Marianne pointed out the *carpinteria* workshop and we agreed that at some point she could arrange for someone to come and replace my ancient, dilapidated, terrace door with a new one. As we passed an expensive tourist's café, with many stylish umbrellas and empty tables, she commanded me to stop.

"We will have a coffee 'ere," she gestured. "They do very good coffee."

It was not at all my style of place but one did not get much chance to oppose the grande dame when she issued her orders. Besides, she had a bad cold and her little dog made me sneeze from some kind of allergy, so it seemed a kindness to both of us to stop. Together, we spluttered and snivelled our way through our drinks. She told me about her life in Brussels, Paris, and Spain as a young woman, the many 'rough' lovers she had had, and her thriving tourist business near the Champs-Elysées. Many years ago, she had married and divorced a feckless South African with whom she had a son, but she was now in the process of retiring and moving from the Costa del Sol to our remote mountain village.

Once very good-looking, she still had the bone structure and lively eyes of a younger woman and knew how to dress well. Even in her seventies, she could make quite an entrance and at one of her small dinner parties she wore a shimmering, yellow Issy Miyake pleated pinafore-apron dress with a sun-ray yellow and grey bra underneath - very modern, very daring, very elegant.

When we first met, she had acquired a steeply-sloping piece of land on the edge of the village and was having a house built at the top. The idea was good, the execution of it a nightmare, but the end result proved impressive. She got through quite a lot of builders en route, often it seemed, because of arguments about cost and quality of workmanship. Sometimes a young man would arrive and work on her kitchen garden or help set up internet access, sleeping in her little garden hut, but often she spent more on feeding him and providing some home-grown cannabis, than she ever got in return. Of course, everyone assumed that these young men provided other services too.

The local ladies of the *pueblo* took a dim view of such goings-on and later I heard a curious tale of their 'revenge.' Marianne had difficulty getting a regular supply of drinking water, particularly as she was situated outside the village envelope at the time. She appealed to the Alcalde (my waste disposal friend), and was granted the right to access the water supply allocated to her nearest neighbour, which happened to be our small church. The water meter box was opened up and a *grifo* (tap) and *tubo* attached. Water flowed. However, the very next day the *tubo* had been disconnected and the meter box padlocked shut. Marianne appealed again to the Mayor and two men appeared with bolt cutters to remove the padlock. The flow of essential water was resumed. But by the next day, a new padlock had appeared and the Alcalde had to be summoned again. A great deal of dispute, slanderous accusations and bad relations ensued, some of which seem to be ongoing today.

On our trip, however, as we reached the outskirts of Granada and a suburb named Armilla, we soon found a dark shop full of reclaimed items, mostly junk, and a fat, sweating owner who left us entirely to our own devices. What a blessing. We were able to peer into boxes and pick over pieces of horse tack, antique door-knockers and ugly tiles. We measured doors and wrestled with huge old wood stoves. Marianne found the table top that she was looking for, something that could be cleaned up, re-laid with small tesserai and placed on her terrace. I spotted a woodworm-ridden but splendid window, complete with little shutters and the slightly bent, metal grillwork or *reja*, that used to be in place to keep young girls in and young men, or thieves, out. It was about the right size and I was hopeful that it could be repaired and placed in the wall just as it was. The *reja* would give some security too, as my kitchen was at ground level and facing a secluded backstreet.

Through Marianne I asked the price - 90 Euros or about £75. This seemed reasonable and the fat man did not look as though he had any interest in haggling. Later on, I wished I had offered him half that, as most of the wood was too rotten to be used and all I had acquired was an expensive frame and a delightfully lop-sided *reja*. On the other hand, once in place it looked as though it had always been there, and three years later a talented local carpenter, Isse, made up new chestnut casements and fitted the glass. In the interval, we lived with superior ventilation in summer and an icy draught, to keep us decently refrigerated, in winter.

When I returned to England, Marianne arranged with the Lanjarón *carpintero* to make the new terrace door. The original was a masterpiece of ancient, bleached chestnut, a stable door hanging loosely on its bent-nail hinges and as full of character as an old sea-dog. I felt sure that it could tell many a tale of star-crossed lovers, bickering women and whining dogs. Surely the last incumbent of the house had leaned on it on starry nights and looked up through the vines towards the heavens? I would have liked to have kept it, but it was in a worse state than the recently-acquired window *reja* and it had to go.

The replacement was - is - a marvel in another way. It is not a street door but just a means of access onto a private, first floor terrace about 25 feet long and 8 feet wide. The *carpintero* has left nothing to chance however - the new version is also chestnut, but could keep out a whole platoon of invading Moors or Christians, even if they were armed to the teeth and desperate for entry. It is about 4 inches thick, has a quadruple lock and no external door handle. Goodness knows what it weighs. I hope it is in place for the next 100 years and ends its days with similar character and charisma to the old one.

* * *

Another old sea-dog and novelty in my life at this time was Steve. We met on the internet, through one of those dating sites which compel you to be as honest as possible about the sort of person you are, and the type of person you are looking for. Succinctness is an advantage. I think I said something about my own self-reliance and independence, and that a man's sense of humour was important to me, the latter being a quality most women crave in a partner. Steve stated that he had no vices, still sported his own teeth, and 'had his life sorted and liked to live it quietly.' In his photo, he looked straight out of the frame at the viewer, bearded, unsmiling, slightly challenging. I found that intriguing. A bygone hippie, I thought.

We arranged to meet for lunch in a café in Norwich, where, as he put it "we can find out if we hate each other." That suited me fine. I had already had occasional cups of coffee and glasses of wine with a few other men, and discovered that one knew almost immediately whether there was any chemistry or point of interest at all. For me, the reaction ranged from: "You call that slim?" to "Where did he get that awful medallion?" and "This man needs a mother, not a partner". Plus I could see the disappointment in their eyes because I was not Julia Roberts or Andie MacDowell or some other auburn-haired, fantasy beauty.

It was a chilly Norfolk day in early December, his birthday in fact, and he had sat himself in the farthest corner, alongside a small artificial Christmas tree and just below the wall-mounted speaker system. Both of these elements were disadvantages. I managed to sweep most of the baubles off the tree and onto the floor as I removed my jacket, and he was more or less inaudible throughout our lunch, owing to the volume of the music. Only later on did I realise that he was often inaudible, due to a tendency to mumble quietly into the back of his throat; so on this particular day I was entranced more by his smiling eyes and quiet calmness, than any intellectual discourse. Later on, he said that he was tempted to simply pick me up, throw me over his shoulder and run around like a crazy idiot. Ah, such an eloquent cave-man response! Yet when we got up to go back to our respective jobs, I think we were both pleased to have found, at the very least, a friend.

Just before Christmas, I went with my younger son on a 3 day trip to Barcelona. We had a great time, but as I wandered through the Parque Guell, I felt bereaved, with a chilly breeze running through my mind. I wondered whether I would see or hear from Steve again. I had sent him an email, inviting him to join a small group of us for Christmas lunch, but the airways were silent. No reply. I thought that perhaps I had been a disappointment to him, just like the others had been to me.

In fact, he was driving through Italy, loaded to his 40 ton gunnels with Scotch whisky and trying not to attract the attention of the Mafia; this was honest cargo, destined for honest shopkeepers. He only managed to visit an internet cafe as he docked in Dover, 2 days before the holiday, and rang me in some haste. He was on his way.

In the end, due to the 'flu, there were just the three of us for Christmas lunch, he and I and Cameron. My other son, Duncan, was in Thailand. Steve brought me a rather sad-looking bunch of flowers, clearly picked up from the only petrol station open on Christmas morning in the whole of East Anglia. However, he was wearing a jacket, trousers, shoes, and socks, which, I realised later on, was a huge compliment. Even now he rarely dresses for the occasion. We pecked each other on the cheek and walked into the house. He and Cameron gave each other manly handshakes, then we all headed for the kitchen. I had bought the ingredients for paella and together we set about cleaning squid, shelling prawns, and dicing onions. I hoped we could produce something moderately edible.

"Have you got any sharp knives?" he asked, looking anxiously at the miserable assembly in the kitchen drawer.

"Not really," I replied, perhaps a little defensively, "but I have a steel."

In minutes, my pathetic collection was sharpened and gleaming; ingredients were cleanly sliced and diced and set aside into their respective piles. It seemed that there was the chance of a decent meal after all. We were three happy people on our way towards an excess of food and drink, some silly games, and a James Bond film on TV. There was no dissimulation and no hidden agenda. We managed a short afternoon walk in the usual dismal Yuletide weather and in the end, Steve stayed the night in the spare bedroom on the ground floor.

I took him a tray of tea in the morning, waiting until nine o'clock so that he could have a good lie-in. Little did I know then, but this was a man who only slept in 4 hour shifts, but his good manners prevented him from roaming into my kitchen at first light. He must have been awake, bored to death, for a long time. As it was, all I was aware of was his handsome, naked shoulders above the sheets and my own instinct to chuck the tray aside and climb in beside him. As it was, I made a bit of a run for it, escaping temptation as rapidly as possible. That fine resolution only lasted until New Year.

Time zipped by, life continued, and within 3 months of meeting we were on our way to Madrid in an enormous pantechnicon, courtesy of, I think, Sony. What Steve referred to as 'just everyday work,' involved transporting the sound equipment, display material, lighting and electrical gear for a large business conference being held in a medieval *parador* on the outskirts of the city. All we had to do was unload the kit, vanish for 5 days, and then drive it all back again to the UK. It was an opportunity to find out how we got along in a confined space for several consecutive days. I think I had already decided that here was a man I could live with, even in a tent.

Driving around and living in a large truck has many advantages, but also its downsides. It is your home-on-wheels but space is limited, and there is no toilet or wash-basin as in a caravan. The two bunks behind the driving area are generous and, as we discovered, each one can accommodate two people sleeping head-to-toe. So we used the top bunk for spare bedding, clothes, extra kit and a holdall full of maps and hung onto each other's fairly clean feet as a child might hold onto its teddy bear. In the mornings, just like a sleepy marsupial, I would turn around and crawl up to Steve for that essential early-morning cuddle. The next trip would see the maps in the dustbin and a neat Sat Nav perched on the windscreen, but we still shared one bunk.

The front seats in modern trucks are immensely comfortable, with plenty of adjustable elements, but if you lean on the wrong handle when you're getting dressed, you can find yourself compressed into a sandwich very quickly, with all extremities waving around helplessly - as I discovered quite early on, and which still makes Steve laugh. I was almost naked at the time, with one foot in my knickers and one out. Very graceful.

We depended on autoroute stops for loos and showers, but not for food. Steve, ever-resourceful, had his own fridge, cool box, and fresh produce, as well as a cooking stove and pans. We could make various types of salad for lunch and have couscous with fried peppers in the evening, buying fresh bread as we went. As an inveterate tea drinker, I was delighted to be able to plug the travel kettle into the cigarette lighter whenever I felt like it. Also, we discovered that although France still produces excellent service station breakfasts, Spain trounces it completely with its spotless toilets and showers. If you can, hold it in until you cross into España. Compared to Britain, where drivers have to pay even to park up for the night, European facilities are excellent, and free. It is strange that although drivers are compelled to stop as soon as their legal hours are done, the British system does little to give them a restful and cost-effective night's sleep.

Very late one night we found ourselves high on the Sierras, north of Burgos, looking for a shower and a hot meal cooked by someone else for a change. Turning off onto a service forecourt, we realised that not only could we get these simple facilities, but there was also a nightclub next door. I was mystified. Steve educated me (at the age of 54) on the meaning of 'nightclub' out in the wilds of Spain, and I had my first, and probably only glimpse of the interior of a brothel. We briefly entered the bar where the women, looking jaded and pale, waited around in a pink neon glow for some potential business. They stared in amazement at me, and I stared back. I thought it was a pretty miserable existence for them.

When we awoke the next morning in the truck, it was icy cold. Early March up on the central plateau is challenging until the sun has done its work. I ran for the *servicios*, hugging myself and hoping for hot water to wash in. The last time I had lived in this way was in the mid-1970s, as an art student roaming through France, but youth and ambition had given way, not only, as it is said, to old age and treachery, but also to a preference for central heating and thermal underwear. When I got back to the truck, the kettle was boiling and there was Steve, blithely carrying on as usual in T-shirt, jeans and flip-flops, checking the load to make sure all was secure.

The first couple of days in Madrid were uneventful. We off-loaded the conference materials in a large, sand-red car park surrounded by monastery towers and high walls, watched closely by long-legged storks, perched on their twiggy nests on the highest pinnacles. The extraordinary principle of constructing a vulnerable, bushy nest on top of a church spire, then standing on it on one leg, just goes to show how bizarre Nature can be in achieving its aims.

On our first free day, we decided to take the suburban train to the Atocha railway station and then go to the Prado art museum. As we planned our routes and checked timetables, a ticket man at Atocha made exceptional efforts to tell us how to travel cheaply around Madrid. We struggled with his Spanish, so he left his desk and came out to us, locking his office behind him, to explain yet again that it was cheaper to buy a book of tickets for the week than to buy returns every day. Once we understood, we were delighted, but also amazed. We were not sure that anyone at Victoria Station in London would make such an effort and certainly not at a suburban spot like Bethnal Green or Clapham. We thanked him profusely and went off to make our way to the city centre.

We enjoyed the Prado and I was thrilled to gaze once more at the Velazquez masterpieces, although Steve was not sure about his 'skanky horses' as he referred to them. I just thought that they were rather fat. The Goya portraits were as sublime as ever and we appraised the violence of his Saturn Devouring His Son and the mystery of The Colossus, perhaps a metaphor for the aftermath of the Napoleonic wars of the early nineteenth century. In purely painterly terms, has any other artist used black pigment so effectively? Neither of us had much time for the many lesser paintings by minor artists, depicting the bleeding souls of religious martyrdom, but it was a treat to pass through the galleries nonetheless.

The next day, Thursday, although we had planned to take the train again, a bus stopped right next to us on its way to the city centre, so we jumped aboard, only getting off when we reached the Naval Museum in the Gran Via. As we wandered around its wood-panelled display rooms, with just a handful of other visitors in our company, we heard the odd siren going off in the street, but thought little of it. All major cities endure ambulances, police cars, and fire engines racing through their streets.

As it neared lunchtime, we found ourselves in one of the main galleries, hung with long, red-velvet drapes and a rather gloomy atmosphere. Unexpectedly, two museum officials entered, threw back a pair of these sumptuous curtains and opened tall, double windows onto a small balcony overlooking the street. There they took hold of some ropes attached to a flag-pole and, to our surprise, lowered the Spanish flag to half-mast. What was this all about? As we left the building we speculated on whether they did this every day at two in the afternoon, or had the King died or some other member of the Royal Family?

Crossing over the Gran Via and walking towards the city centre, we became even more conscious of strange activity. Large limousines were driving in and out of palatial edifices at speed, ambulance sirens were still sounding and everyone looked very grave. Steve found a peak-capped chauffeur waiting beside a gleaming Mercedes, who happened to speak English, and asked him, "What's going on?"

"There's been a bombing," the man replied sombrely, "at Atocha railway station. Hundreds are injured."

We were horrified. Walking on, we saw mobile blood donor vehicles with queues of people waiting to contribute, their lines stretching right around the block. Most of them were young, many of mixed race. Madrid is a cosmopolitan and tolerant city, yet intolerance and extremism had chosen it as a target. We thought of the kind ticket officer: was he on that fateful train, on his way to work? Had he lost colleagues or family in the devastation? Was it right that those who felt themselves to be persecuted or ignored or even morally superior, should make their point by attacking innocent and well-meaning members of the public? We passed the rest of the day quietly, visiting gardens and public squares, sharing in the city's shock. 191 people died that morning and 1,800 were wounded.

This was not the only bombing at which we were present. Steve was in Athens when they received similar treatment in early 2010, but before that, on 7 July 2005, I had a close shave in London. I had been asked to visit a large London hospital to advise them on one of their strategic policies and planned to catch the 07:55 train from Norwich. Running slightly late, I missed this by a few minutes, but did not panic. I could catch the 08:05, jump on the Underground from Liverpool Street to Aldgate, change trains there and soon be at my destination. It was a beautiful sunny morning, too nice to cause any anxiety.

At Liverpool Street, I got out and walked across to the Underground access. As I arrived there, solid steel shutters were brought down right in front of me.

"No service!" shouted one of the staff, "Underground closed."

People were stupefied. How could the Underground be closed, just like that? At rush hour too. There was a lot of milling about and confusion, but I headed straight for the suburban line office and bought another ticket. Though I did not realise it at the time, I probably caught the last train out of Liverpool Street for the next 24 hours. Certainly I had to run down the platform and leap aboard, just before the guard's whistle went.

Twenty minutes later I was exiting another station and witnessing more confusion, but without any clear knowledge of the reason. I caught a bus to Whipps Cross Hospital, walked calmly through the main doors and down the mile-long corridor that forms the building's spine. My mobile rang. It was Steve, calling from the M20 on his way to a gig in Hyde Park with a cargo of music equipment.

"Where are you?" he asked. "There's been an explosion, a bomb, on the Underground."

He had heard about it on the radio, but had no details.

The gravity of the event did not sink in until my meeting was about to start. We were all gathered in a small conference room, drinking coffee and eating croissants, waiting for more arrivals, when someone rushed in and set up a TV screen and temporary aerial. The room filled up with passing doctors and nurses. We could see hazy images of Aldgate Station and then Tavistock Square, with people wandering about in bandages and blankets.

The Chair of the hospital Board arrived. "Everyone to their stations," she announced, "this is a red alert."

It was clear that the hospital might need to take in casualties, and managers disappeared at speed, like beads of oil rolling effortlessly across a glass table. No panic, just well-rehearsed action.

"Is Linda Caine here?" asked the Chair, looking round.

"Present," I answered.

"We need to get you back to Norwich," she said, "so we've ordered you a taxi."

"That's OK," I replied, "don't worry about me. You have more important things to attend to. I'll get a train back."

"You don't understand," she replied, "there are no trains."

Two hours later, I was back in Norwich, having listened to the radio with the taxi driver all the way up the M11. It seemed that I was lucky to have missed that first morning train; I could easily have been at Aldgate at the wrong moment and been caught up in the mayhem and horror, along with many others.

Chapter 3

Building Works

Our next trip to Spain was less dramatic, though also eventful. In late May we flew to Granada so that Steve could have a look at my future 'retirement home.' We arrived late at night and, as he remembers to this day, his first few glimpses by the car headlights of the remoteness of the area, the rough road down to the village and the state of the house, convinced him that he was, as he put it, in tow with a madwoman. In the morning, not a lot had changed this conviction, but the sweet smells of thyme and broom, and the huge green landscape at the end of the street, encouraged a tiny flicker of optimism. He kept his negative thoughts to himself at the time, for which I was very grateful, as I was full of excitement and enthusiasm.

I had booked us somewhere respectable to stay just outside the village, a little stone-built *casita*, or holiday cottage, but for the first 3 days we were camping in the house. It was still a shambles, without running water or toilet facilities although we did have a key for a house around the corner, where we could use the bathroom. Otherwise things were pretty basic - our bed was an inflatable mattress on the floor and we had only a single primus stove for cooking on. Candles supplied the lighting. Dust lay everywhere, as well as bat droppings, evidence of visiting cats and a variety of creeping insects.

Over the next few days, we spent much of our time continuing to clear out debris and cleaning doors and windows. Paolo was not about, but the abysmal plumber was. Steve despaired of his handiwork and on this occasion was happy to say so, using one of our friends as an interpreter. It was mutually agreed that he should pack up his toolkit and depart, never to be seen again, and we were left with a drainage pipe hanging loosely from some rafters and a leaking kitchen tap.

Steve also looked sceptically at the ceilings where, in places, sagging timbers and disintegrating slates threatened collapse, and said that he thought the entire roof needed to be re-laid. Thinking of the cost and being the eternal optimist, I said I was not sure he was right. Again, he kept his counsel.

However, this part of the building had other interesting features. One of our first tasks was to get some weed killer and sort out all the greenery which was growing on the outer, top side, exposed to the wind and sun. Clearly, no one had bothered to do this for years and the weeds were well rooted in about 20 centimetres of *launa* and soil, encouraging insects and water retention whilst gently destroying the impermeability of the surface.

An unplanned, organic roof garden was not on our agenda, so off we went to the nearest *ferretería*, or hardware shop, to see what we could buy, forgetting to take a dictionary with us (I usually carried one with me, or at least a small phrasebook). We saw nothing suitable on the shelves; plant food, bleach, ant killer and kitchen cleaner were there in quantity, but not a glimmer of what we were looking for. We struggled to communicate with the shopkeeper and other customers, despite their best efforts and began to despair of getting what was needed, when in came a youngish man with a shaved haircut, a glimpse of a tattoo on his right shoulder and a nose ring.

"Can I help?" he asked. "What do you want?"

We explained.

"My Spanish isn't brilliant," he said, "but I'll see what I can do."

He turned out to be Martin, whom we got to know much better over the years, and although his translation wasn't fluent, comprehension soon dawned on all faces.

"*Saquen los hierbos!*" they chorused.

Sacar means to pull out or remove, not necessarily to kill, but as in English, unlikely words are often used in different contexts. It also means to photograph, perhaps in the traditional sense of stealing or removing one's soul, and in the hardware shop it seemed perfectly obvious once we heard the phrase.

So, then, did they have this chemical? No, for that we would have to go to the shopkeeper's brother-in-law, the butcher in the next village. This was a bit like playing Happy Families, so off we trooped to the *carniceria*. Meat and weed-killer in the same place? Surely not. But there, secreted in his back room and, we hoped, well away from the animal carcasses, was a chemical of a type long since banned in the UK, plastic-bottled and ready to go. We were given advice on the dilution, and told always to wear protection, gloves and so forth. Did we want to buy some *morcillas*, black pudding sausages at the same time? The best in the Alpujarras? Of course!

Although we were managing well with our little primus stove for cooking, it did not give us any warmth. The nights were still quite cool at 1100 metres above sea level and Steve had found a small, abandoned wood stove in the rubble of the old smithy at the back, and was keen to get it going. Made of cast-iron, with fins like an old-fashioned radiator, it boasted a removable, circular top-plate for cooking on and a little door at the bottom. After some diligent searching, we found a short, right-angled piece of chimney pipe that fitted the smoke-hole at the back, but nothing to take that smoke away. If we had a reasonable length of chimney pipe, we could place the whole thing inside the old fireplace in the kitchen and guide the fumes and smoke away.

It was after dark when we went back into the smithy, clutching candles and a torch and picking our way carefully through collapsed walls, broken timbers, piles of horseshoes and heaps of charcoal, but eventually we found a long length of metal pipe. Perfect. Or nearly perfect - both pipes were of the same diameter and could not be fitted together. We needed a third piece, something slightly smaller or slightly larger, to act as a connector. This seemed an impossible task, but as Steve continued to search the smithy, I wandered off into the rest of the house. There was nothing in the dark pit of the cellar and nothing in the heap of rubble waiting for the dumper truck. Back upstairs, I gazed at our small stock of tinned food. Perhaps a solution lay there.

My eye fell on a likely candidate. Opening a tin of sweet corn, removing the contents and then levering off the base, I soon had a neat metal tube that, miraculously, fitted tightly inside the other two. I rushed to find the man.

"We have lift-off!" I announced with pride.

Positioning the stove under the old mantelpiece, with its pipework disappearing up towards the sky, Steve opened the little door at the bottom and put in chips of wood and balls of newspaper. Then he put match to paper and we waited for a result. At first it all looked positive and the dry paper and wood burnt brightly, but for some reason, despite much fiddling, blowing and cursing, the wretched thing simply would not stay alight. What could be the problem?

"Hang on here," he said, and vanished into the darkness, returning two minutes later with a small bucketful of charcoal. "Perhaps it's a charcoal stove," he speculated.

Lying on the stone floor, ignoring the cold and the dirt, he fed in straw and more wood, then added the charcoal, blowing it into life. Removing the top lid, he dropped in some bigger pieces of wood (the correct way to fill it, we realised later on) and soon a glowing red indicated that the desired miracle was occurring. Within half-an-hour we had a sizzling pan of sausages on the go. I was filled with joy and love. By candlelight, in a cosy kitchen, with a glass of cheap red wine, we toasted our first hot meal in *la casa*.

The next evening we were tested again, this time with water rather than fire. The angry neighbour having disappeared temporarily, we were able to roam freely across the terrace, discovering that a little tap above an old cement washbasin actually functioned and that we had access to running water without going to the fountain in the square. These old, wash-boarded constructions appear individually on a few of the balconies belonging to traditional properties; more often nowadays they can be found in a group on the perimeter of a village, either in a shady spot or under a tiled roof, as that was where the women went to do their washing together. Some *lavaderos* still have running water but no one uses them for their original purpose. They have been superseded long since by the washing machine, and the village gossip carries on in other settings. The basin on our terrace was half-filled with dirty water, cement debris and dog-hair. The tap was a very small brass spigot with a T-shaped top.

It was about nine o'clock in the evening, with the heat going out of the day, the light fading, the village silent. I took a plastic washing-up bowl, put in some squeezy and a bit of boiling water, and wandered out onto the terrace to top it up with cold water. I could wash up our supper plates out here. I held the bowl under the tap and reached for the little spigot. As it turned anti-clockwise, it came away in my hand, and a plume of water shot skywards, geyser-like, propelled by a significant amount of pressure and dousing me in an icy shower. I shrieked and dropped the bowl, the little spigot top disappeared somewhere in the jet and Steve came running.

In a few mesmerising seconds, water was hitting the floor, pouring over the cracked tiles and running out of a gulley into the street below. We could hear it splashing onto the concrete one storey down. The slope of the little *calle* meant that it would run down past other houses and out towards the campo. It was not a trickle but already a small river.

Several thoughts careered through my mind at once: this was valuable water straight from the mountain, not to be wasted; the villagers would appear and want to know what was happening; we couldn't speak enough Spanish to explain or even call for assistance; we didn't know the plumber's whereabouts or his phone number and had just sacked him anyway; it was getting dark. Critically, where was the stop-cock?

Steve must have had similar thoughts and we looked at each other in some panic. "Put your thumb over the tap," he said, "and give me a moment."

He went off into the house, leaving me standing there like the little Dutch boy, with my thumb rapidly losing all sensation. Some water was still escaping. Perhaps he had gone to find the car keys and would simply drive off to Granada airport, never to be seen again?

I had underestimated my man. Two minutes later he returned with some silver foil that had contained part of our lunch and that I had failed to throw away. Having created a bung shape, he advised me to wait for the word, then take my thumb off the water jet.

"Now!" was the word, and as soon as I removed my frozen thumb he wedged in the bung and began to turn it.

The adaptability of the foil meant that it took on the internal thread of the tap, filling it completely and blocking the water. Everything stopped except for a continued sploshing into the street below, then that too ceased. I was wet and shivering, but greatly relieved. We began to laugh, knowing that we had been saved from a ghastly situation. In due course, as I cleaned out the foul water of the sink, I found the spigot top and we were able to put everything back together as it should have been. The neighbour must have been pleasantly surprised on her return the next day, to find that her sink was clean, the spigot screwed tightly together and the terrace well-washed.

Later on, Steve admitted that had I become hysterical and run around screaming, 'the deal might have been off.' I am not sure that I have ever told him that I too thought he might abandon me then and there. As it was, we agreed that there were now three essentials to life: WD40 (to get things moving), gaffer tape (to stop things moving) and silver foil (to plug the gaps). Perhaps human relationships require similar, if psychological, repair kits in order to survive?

* * *

During that visit we met up once again with Martin and discovered that he was of Lithuanian descent, had been to the Royal College of Art in London and was married to a clever girl called Lorraine, who was an architectural technician. They had two small children and Lorraine's mother and stepfather often visited the area; they were in the process of buying a house here too. Sitting on our kitchen doorstep, Martin and I discussed Modernism and the influence of the American artists Mark Rothko, Frank Stella and Barnett Newman, and how we thought some of the concepts of post-Modernism might develop in the 21st century. This conversation did not seem strange, despite the fact that the doorstep under our bottoms was at least 200 years old.

Martin had noticed our exceptionally tall, white chimney on the roof and, carefully rolling a cigarette between paint-stained fingers, asked if he could decorate it with a colourful, abstract design. I agreed, providing the paint was water-based and could be washed off again, and that he did it alone, as the roof might not take the weight of too many people up there. These distinctive chimneys are conical in shape with small 'hats' of slate and although his idea never bore fruit, I was keen to support the arts where I could. I don't think Steve minded either, even though modern art is not his favourite subject. However, he was proud to be associated with *'la chimenea lo más grande del pueblo,'* whatever design it acquired. A year or so later, and sadly for his male ego, the chimney had to be reduced in both height and weight for the sake of the roof.

Martin was struggling to make a living out in Spain, with little demand for chimney art, and was taking on building work to make ends meet, so we agreed on some jobs he could do for us while we were back in England. The tiled stairs needed to be re-laid with chestnut 'nibs' at the front of each step, and both of the ground floor stables were ready to be power-cleaned, concrete-floored, and the walls rendered. He was happy to do the stairs, but "I know just the man for the stable work," he said, enthusiastically. "You need Emilio."

Emilio turned out to be the kind of stalwart Spaniard that you want on your side in the Alpujarran construction world. Physically bulky and strong as an ox, with a roundish, clean-shaven face, he turned up wearing a loose shirt, baggy shorts and climbing boots, and carried his money and papers in a useful shoulder bag that adapted itself comfortably to his embonpoint. He drove a dark green 4x4 which we soon learned to recognise and was a member of the Independence Party at the town hall. He had a tendency to look only at my bosom area while he spoke to me and this has not changed over time, despite the fact that cancer has robbed me of anything feminine enough to be termed 'breasts.' Even the local supermarket *pollo* has more flesh in that area than me.

Emilio had no hesitation in condemning some of the workmanship previously done by Paolo, picking at pieces of flaking plaster with stubby fingers, tapping his knuckles over hollow or thinly-covered areas, staring gravely at the poor grouting of the floor tiles and shaking his head as he ran his eye over a door lintel that was too weak. At the same time he was reassuring about what could be done to move us along. His English was limited, but with Martin's help and our own efforts we managed to get some ideas agreed.

That was over 6 years ago. Since then, along with his handsome and hard-working Belarus colleague Miguel (perhaps Mikhail once upon a time), his own brother Francisco, his stepson Plato, and some other local men, he has done all the major jobs for us and we are not finished yet. He has adopted us to some extent and successfully dealt with irritated neighbours (the cement mixer running all day or the angle-grinder causing clouds of red dust to float through the village and ruin the washing), difficult technical problems (putting in big, new timbers without the roof falling in) and fixing our recalcitrant hot water system (at last I can have a steaming bath in the winter).

We have met his artistic Russian wife Olga, who is built not like a potato farmer but like a blonde fairy, and witnessed his youngest son 'Ivan el Terrible' racing around the plaza when Spain won the 2010 football World Cup. Without Emilio in particular, our house would never have become our home. We have had to restrain his ardour for fake plaster stones and translucent wall bricks, but as well as doing a lot of mundane building work, he has rebuilt the stone terrace, enhanced the existing fireplace, delicately restored whole ceilings and found antique terracotta roof tiles to act as wall lamps. The phrase '*nuestra casa es su casa*' (our house is your house) applies very well in this instance, although he would never take advantage of it.

* * *

On our next visit, about 6 months later, we noticed that the neighbour was still absent, the inner house looked even more neglected and its outer courtyard wall, facing the street, was a deteriorating mess of flaking cement render, loose stonework and clusters of weeds. The timber lintel above the still beautiful, planked door looked fragile too, as though it would not take the weight above for much longer. One evening, going out for a *paseo* and to listen for transient nightingales, we bumped into a forthright woman called Diana. She is an English schoolteacher who comes out here during the holidays in her stalwart VW van, visiting the haunts of her youth and catching up with friends. She lived here over 30 years ago and knows all the previous generation of expatriates, including, by good fortune, the owner of the house next door.

On this occasion she did not mince words.

"Jack wants to sell," she announced. "Are you interested?"

The angry tenant, together with her children, dogs and lover had left the village and the house was empty.

We knew that many years ago the two houses had been one, with a relatively grand courtyard at the front, the *granero* at the back and a good location close to the village plaza. Here was an opportunity to put these houses back together, although the valley view had been lost, thanks to some unfortunate 'high-rise' building work in front of us that should never have been allowed (we joked that if we won the lottery we would acquire this blot on our landscape and then demolish it). Jack's house was almost completely enclosed by mine, so we were the obvious potential buyers.

His property had another significant advantage, namely land. Down below the village, he owned a hectare of fairly level *terreno* with a water channel or *acequia* running through it. On the other side of the village he had another, smaller piece featuring two big chestnuts and a dried-up stream. Steve and I had a yearning to grow our own vegetables and I had often considered having a couple of pigs. This part of the Alpujarras has the reputation of being an area where 'anything grows' providing you give it enough manure and water, so this was a deal that we did not want to miss. According to Diana, it seemed that other people were interested in the house but, surprisingly, did not want the land. We wanted both.

We tried not to appear too excited and Steve, looking as rich as a church mouse, asked for a key so we could have a proper look round. As it happened, he was anxious about the stock market at the time, a good two years before the 'crash' of 2007, so investing in property made sense. We wondered what lay next door and how we could make the most of our opportunity.

Many of the old Moorish houses have complex interiors, with rooms added on at different levels, recesses created in the walls for sleeping and stairways that lead to the rooftop. Jack's house, like mine, had been renovated in the late 19th century, then he had put in some internal walls, so that there was a combination of high ceilings and old vigas with small and rather airless bedrooms. It did, however, have the advantage of a magnificent 'King' fireplace with a deep mantelpiece, a beautiful built-in wall cupboard with a small, fretwork chestnut door and yet another ground-floor stable leading off the courtyard.

As a disadvantage, there was a dingy back room in which we found a disconnected gas heater, some empty plastic flowerpots and a mattress. We decided that this room had been used for illicit cannabis growing and called it 'the pot room' for obvious reasons. Later on, we took down its non load-bearing wall and it became part of our *gran salón*. This main reception room had floor levels that equated to the other half of the house and we could see exactly where the original connecting doorway had been. We could open it up again. All the walls were hand-built, without right angles or straight lines. Some doors were ancient originals and some were hideous modern pine - "These will have to come out," Steve muttered.

By curious coincidence, in the late 1980s in Norfolk, before I met Steve, my previous partner and I had bought a pair of semi-detached houses in a very ordinary street, which also appeared to be completely separate. Only when we decided to do some renovations did we discover a doorway on the first floor that linked the two together. I wonder how many houses around the world have these secret connections, through attics or hallways or corridors?

Almost immediately we could see that Jack's house could be opened up and made beautiful. The courtyard would be very useful and there was a cubby hole off the stairs, suitable for a laundry room. Then we went to view the land. We were given some vague directions and having put on sensible boots, we set off out of the village along a stony footpath. It took several false turns and a bit of battling with brambles, thistles and overhanging fig trees, before we found the place we were looking for. The figs delayed us because they were ready to be eaten and we could not resist. At the right time of year it is possible to wander along the mountain paths and breakfast off mulberries, lunch off figs and dine off plums. Or other combinations such as almonds, walnuts and chestnuts, accompanied by the fabled saffron milk caps that emerge in abundance in November. All fresh, organic and delicious.

Jack's land was shaped like a wide crescent, with the *acequia* running parallel to the inner, shorter part of the curve and a vertical drop of about 15 metres on the outer, front edge. At both points of the crescent, the land dropped less severely, in part consisting of overgrown terraces stepping down towards a rushing torrent of water. There were large trees growing on the perimeter and down on these neglected terraces, but the main *parcela* was bare, sunburnt and uncultivated.

We walked slowly across to the outer edge and realised that we were looking westwards, straight down the valley towards waves of blue hills and, not too far from view, the distant sea. Small white villages clustered below us, their church towers giving them identity and purpose. Higher up, to the east, was a rocky promontory jutting out into the landscape with the remains of a *mezquita* still visible. Not only were these Islamic mosques created to call on the faithful to put down their tools and pray, they were also in excellent defensive positions and usually located on sites of even greater antiquity. Advancing soldiers or marauding guerillas could be spotted long before they reached the high valleys.

The Moors have left many impressive structures in the agricultural landscape. Exquisitely engineered dry-stone walls, often 3 or 4 metres high, dovetail neatly into natural rock. Where mortar was used, it was made of river sand and lime, but the overall impression is of strength and beauty. Water cisterns or *aljibes* occur alongside remote pathways or mule tracks, whilst the *acequias* run for many kilometres along the valley walls, taking essential water from the high Sierras to the terraced fields and gardens below. These channels, once carved out of rock or built up from stone, and nowadays cast in concrete, are maintained by a posse of men who walk their designated routes every day, clearing out twigs and leaves. Occasionally a dead mountain goat or fallen tree has to be cleared and, horribly, there are some waterways that are being used as open sewers. In places, plastic pipes, or *tubos*, have been put in, to prevent leakage and loss of water, but it is sad to lose the sound of running water and the accompaniment of birds, dragonflies, and small, harmless water snakes.

Everyone with land is entitled to a specified number of hours of water, but must generally stick to their allotted time, so that the next smallholder along can get his or her plants watered too. Slates and rocks are positioned in key places, where water routes divide, acting like the locks in canals to divert water from one terrace to another, and the *acequeros* may have to open and close these by hand at specified times of day. Later on, we discovered that we were entitled to 4.5 hours of water, to be taken on a Friday between midday and 5pm. Not very auspicious in summer, when all sane people have shut themselves indoors, out of the sun. The last place where one might want to be is in the campo, watering wilting lettuces.

* * *

"Reader, we bought it."

This must have been the refrain of many people during the buoyant twenty years that bridged the twentieth and twenty-first centuries. A second home had become more commonplace at home or abroad, and having a place in the sun was considered to be an affordable luxury. For us, however, this was not aggressive territorial acquisition but part of a planned retreat. Once we moved here, we would not be going back to England. In any case, the complications and angst of getting Steve's legal work done, the money transferred and ownership finally completed, could not be gone through again.

Jack had appointed a local man, Guy, to act as his legal proxy, so it was with him that we discussed all the detail and agreed on the final price. Of British origin but born in Spain, he was aged about 30 and not particularly extrovert. It seemed difficult to communicate with him, until he admitted that he was not very well and that he was undergoing a series of medical tests in Granada hospital. As he acknowledged later, he was in almost constant stomach pain, very fatigued and on painkillers. This explained a lot. He had been responsible for administering the house letting too, but we could see that this had been difficult because he lived a good hour's drive away and our village was not on his normal route. The place was in such poor repair that he had probably just collected the rent when he could and fixed the odd problem as it arose.

Subsequently, we met many people who were renting sub-standard houses and eking out a living as best they could, but with increasing anxiety. The golden days of cheap freedom were disappearing, government systems and paperwork were becoming computer-enabled and many of them realised with a shock that when they reached pension age, there would be nothing there for them. Living in the Garden of Eden on 5 Euros per day, aged twenty-five, was relatively easy; at sixty-five, finding 20 Euros per day and enough firewood to get one through the night, had become a daunting prospect. In the 1970s and 80s, I had had the chance of living permanently in Provence, but had taken fright at the last moment, not sure how I would survive and support my two children. Looking back, I'm glad that I waited another twenty-odd years before making the leap.

It gradually became clear to us that both Jack and Guy were hoping that Steve would agree to bend the rules in terms of the legally declared house price. It suited them to have it undervalued and for Steve to pay an additional amount in cash after completion of the purchase. This is all very well at the time, but the Spanish authorities are familiar with this ruse and catch up later on, when the owner sells or dies. The property is then re-valued and any discrepancies taken into account for tax purposes, when the original vendor has long since disappeared.

Steve was having none of it and insisted on the full price being declared. At the very last moment, they also tried to change the exchange rate agreed at the outset. As it was, we had not been very organised in our money transfer arrangements, so there was a lot of rushing from bank to bank, drawing out sums of money from different cash machines, but Steve stood firm. Later on, we were doubly glad about this, as they also misled us about outstanding charges on the house. In Spain, it is the property that carries the bills and they are transferred to the new owner. Before buying, it is important to establish that these have all been paid. We, and our *notario*, were assured that there were no outstanding debts, but later on a host of water and community charge bills arrived, back-dated to at least 4 years. As novices, and wanting to start with a clean sheet, we settled all of these and considered them a contribution to the local economy, but Jack and Guy were lucky that we did not sue them for misrepresentation.

* * *

We decided that we had five years to get both properties in a habitable state while we continued to work in the UK, and although mine had a head-start, it did include the essential kitchen and main bathroom. I urged Steve to start planning the layout of the land, for fruit trees and a kitchen garden, as I knew that every year would be a gain as the trees grew, but it was difficult to visualise where things would grow as so much of it was overgrown with brambles, and we had no means of watering anything from afar. In the end, we did not really get started until the final few months of our transition from northern Europe to southern Iberia.

At the time, having bought Jack's house, we were due to return to Suffolk quite quickly, not least so that we could earn some more money to pay Emilio's forthcoming bills. We arranged a major site meeting with him, Martin and, loitering on the fringes at that time, Emilio's brother-in-law and chief peon, Sasha. We listed what needed to be done and agreed on the priorities: the entire roof, which looked as though it might fall in at any time (3-4 thousand Euros, Emilio estimated); a kitchen sink and some stone worktops; new terracotta floor tiles in the large room on Steve's side; and almost all the walls needed to be re-plastered. Then there was the terrace, where we had tried to flood the village. Close inspection revealed unstable timbers, ingress of water and damaged stonework. Eventually it had to be taken down completely and re-built, and now is strong enough to support an extension should we ever need to build one, or a wood oven for baking bread, which is quite likely, and perhaps a vine-covered pergola to shade us from the summer sun.

Just before we left, Emilio and Sasha got going on the roof, priority number one. This measures about 120 square metres and has 5 large, traditional roof lights. These are not the sloping Velux type of skylight, as the roofs are flat, but they have a low, square appearance, topped off with either clear safety glass or a translucent synthetic product. Any roof laying would have to work around their varying sizes and locations. The width of the rooms in these old houses is dictated by the useful span of a chestnut tree trunk, averaging out at about 4 metres. These timbers are laid on, or into, thick stone walls of at least half-a-metre. The resulting structure is very strong and often has its foundations on solid rock too. Most modern Spanish building cannot afford to be made of such valuable timbers or stones, but the locals here renew their roofs in the traditional way quite often, usually in June when it is dry but not too hot. I wish that habit had been in force in our house over the years, but the truth was very different; every time it rained, the inhabitants had simply added another layer of *launa* and carried on as before.

For most village properties, especially those overlooking the narrow streets, building access is via an arrangement of scaffolding, ladders, and hoists. Had that been the case for us, it would have been an even longer and more difficult - and more expensive - job than planned. Luckily, there was a rear access straight onto the roof from a derelict piece of land, and by setting up a temporary bridge for the wheelbarrows; Emilio was able to take material away relatively easily. This also provided somewhere to bring in a dumper truck with materials, or to remove surplus debris. I asked him to keep back all the deficient timbers for winter burning. I have great difficulty walking past any piece of wood that could go into the wood burner and plan to become a gleaner par excellence over the coming years.

We were hoping that Emilio would simply take off the existing *launa*, replace a few timbers and thick slates, then put it all back again on top of a new plastic sheet. As it turned out, the *launa* was much thicker than anyone realised, due to the bad practices mentioned above. He later estimated that they removed a surplus of 8 tons, all of it shovelled into a wheelbarrow, heaved to the dumper and then the whole lot tipped elsewhere (not the local hillside this time) when it was full up. The load on the timbers had been immense and I could imagine a collective breath of relief from the chestnut *vigas* as the weight came off. This was not the case for Emilio. "*Madre mia*," he sighed, sweating profusely, his shoulders sagging, as we said our goodbyes and left them to complete this strenuous task.

Chapter 4

Animal Territory

The house is not just a dwelling for humans. We had, and still have, resident sparrows that nest up under the slates of the little balcony and on top of some of the supporting timbers. Here they raise their squeaking chicks, flying in and out with tasty morsels, and we are simply the janitors, sweeping up the droppings each day. Occasionally there is a disaster and a tiny fledgling body lies spread-eagled on the floor, the remains of its shell beside it. On one sad occasion, we discovered a recent corpse dangling from the nest, attached only by a stretched membrane to the nest hidden above.

These birds are not tame at all and although they perch on the railings or the stronger twigs of my plants, they take off the moment there is any unexpected movement. In early summer they teach the little ones how to fly, encouraging them to go from nest to rail, from rail to the electrical cabling across the street, and thence to someone else's balcony. There is a continuous peeping and squeaking as parent and child express fear, support, and urgency. Down below in the street, scrawny cats lurk in the blue shadows, awaiting any opportunity for a fresh and tasty meal.

We had visiting swallows too for a few years, and Steve spent some happy hours filming one of them as it perched on a shelf indoors to consider its nesting opportunities. He was not very well at the time, having had a bad allergic reaction to a spider bite on his ankle, so the swallow kept him amused as he lay on the bed with his video camera. One day, two other swallows arrived and 'collected' this one from the balcony; it never returned, so perhaps mingling with us and the sparrows was deemed unacceptable, or the house became too civilised for them.

We also had a bat that we named Horace. Poor Horace. Although I was not too pleased to have to sweep up bat droppings on every visit, I knew that as the roof got repaired, odd holes and windows closed off and chimneys put into use, Horace would go elsewhere. We had no idea that this 'elsewhere' might turn out to be the United Kingdom.

Flying back to England, we reached our Suffolk house in the early hours, tired and ready for bed. I took one of the cases upstairs and unpacked our wash-bag and a few bits and pieces. As I hung up my jacket on the back of the bedroom door, I felt something strange catching on my back, rather like a clothes label that has got tangled up. It was just where I couldn't reach, between my shoulder blades, which was rather odd too. "Steve," I called. "Can you come and give me a hand?"

He was already on his way upstairs and could see into the bedroom. "Keep very still," he said, "I think we have a visitor."

At that moment, the bat took off and began zooming around the room, dipping and diving. Then it vanished from sight. Once I got over the initial shock, I felt quite calm.

"Perhaps it's on the curtain rail," I said and jumped up on the bed to get a better look, "How on Earth did it get in?"

It seemed impossible, as all the windows were shut while we were away, and the wood stove downstairs had a sealed chimney plate.

"I think he's come with us from Spain," Steve grinned. "It's Horace."

So there we were, me staggering about on the bed, and Steve peering behind the curtains, neither of us sure whether to laugh or cry. But not a sign of our illegal immigrant.

"We'll just have to go to bed with the window open and leave him to it," we decided.

That's what we did and he must have flitted out into the darkness, as there was still no sign of him in the morning and we never saw him again. We wonder sometimes if he survived the different climate and environment, and whether there are now some Hispano-Anglo bats living in a north Suffolk barn, hunting for flies at dusk along the banks of the Waveney River.

This incident also makes me think of a primitive Norse tale that I heard long ago. It goes, I recollect, like this:

'Somewhere out in the winter darkness stands an ancient timbered hall, full of dozing people, together with their animals and valued possessions. They have been sheltering from a snowstorm, feasting and merry-making in front of a great fire, but are now sated and dreaming. High up, in the darkness of the vaulted roof, is a small aperture, open to the elements. Unseen by the assembled company, a weary bird flies in, out of the storm, and wings its way around the lighted hall, gaining warmth from the fire and taking crumbs from the tables. But its moment of relief and pleasure is short. It is responding to its instincts and cannot rest until it reaches its homeland further south. It makes a final circuit of the room, then ascends to the window, flying out again into the darkness and the storm.'

The metaphor is that this is life, for all creatures. We come out of the storm, we have our moment of warmth, then we return to the darkness.

Here in the Alpujarras we certainly have life and it is always on the move. Depending on the season, we have a variety of snakes (mostly harmless), lizards (and sometimes chameleons), spiders (many varieties), innumerable ants, large blue-black bees, armour-plated horned beetles, and, in the wilder campo, crickets, termites, badgers, foxes and wild boar (*jabeli*). Higher up there are eagles, hawks and occasional vultures. At night, we see glow-worms with their intense, golden-green phosphorescent tails and hear the rustling of rats high in the mulberry trees. The countryside is full of scurrying, flickering activity, most of it untainted by commercial spraying or intensive fertilisation.

The battle with the *jabeli* is continuous, as they cause so much destruction if they get onto someone's land. Powerfully nosing about for grubs and tasty roots, they overturn clods of earth and make deep gouges underneath precious plants, as though someone had been in with a rotavator and gone slightly mad. They love the damp soil near the water-courses, no doubt wallowing about in piggy ecstasy at the end of the long, hot day. Sometimes they travel alone, sometimes in a small group. I have seen a mother and piglet cross our little road in the misty early hours and on one occasion, late at night, we frightened a youngster out on its own by the roadside.

"Where's my knife?" exclaimed Steve, thinking of wild boar stew.

Luckily, it galloped off into the darkness before he could take any action. In fact, these wild animals carry diseases potentially fatal to humans and one should never eat the meat unless it has been checked and certified by a veterinarian.

One damp November day, we met a large male out in the wilds. We had decided to go exploring high up in the Sierras, looking at lightning-struck chestnut trees, ruined *cortijos* and the remains of old waterways. Bumping along a rough track between the fir trees, with a steep hill to our right, I noticed a black tree trunk leaning at an angle to the hillside. It seemed strange but not entirely out of place. Then I looked again, and gently applied the brakes.

"Over there," I whispered, "it's a boar."

The tree trunk had tusks, whiskers, a solid body, and little stubby legs. It looked big enough to overturn our small car. All three of us, humans and animal, remained motionless for a few seconds, and then the beast took off, charging straight across the track in front of us and up the hillside at considerable speed. We were thrilled, yet also highly relieved at its choice of direction.

Although some of our neighbours have brought in hunters and had the *jabeli* shot, most people simply put up fencing and do their best to deter them. Electric tape or wire seems to be a preferred method but we have opted for 2 metre high wire netting plus some of Steve's home-grown solutions. Worrying about evidence of recent activity on the fringes of our land, he went into Baden-Powell mode, donning strong boots and taking his pocket knife, axe and baler twine down into the gulleys where the *jabeli* usually sleep.

"Before you plan to attack your enemy," he philosophised, "find out where he is."

He cut and trimmed branches into sharp stakes and placed them across the well-trodden little paths that only the wild animals or the occasional dog might use. Every day he goes down and inspects them for pieces of hair or skin, or any other signs of movement. To date, nothing has been disturbed. Perhaps we should be hunting for something smaller, a badger or a fox. Perhaps even the Spanish *jabeli* have heard of Boy Scouts...

The biggest destroyers of the man-made environment are the many herds of sheep and goats that roam the hillsides. The *pastores* have agreements with the larger landowners that entitle them to move their livestock around the valleys, feeding off any unfenced grass or young trees. Often they have large herds, led by big rams and encircled by several dogs, although these are usually invisible until the shepherd whistles.

The rams and ewes often wear bells, which yield romantic and evocative sounds as the sun sets and evening shadows creep up the valley, but the hard truth is that these animals are gradually bringing ruin to the terraces and historic landscape of the valley. They will take any shortcut available to them, clambering over and down the stone walls, loosening their tight adherence to the edges of each *bancala*. When the rains come, these gaps between soil and stone become water channels, and the following year a few rocks slip out. More animal movement starts landslides, more stones tumble out and eventually a complete section, perhaps 2 or 3 metres wide, comes crashing down. This makes the through route even easier for the animals, the local farmers choose not to protest and no one repairs the wall. Perhaps the Andalucían *junta* will take steps to limit the roaming rights of these herds before it is too late and ancient Moorish walls are demolished forever.

Twice a year, even bigger flocks pour through our village and along the valley. This is the *transhumancia*, when livestock is taken to higher or lower pastures, depending on the season. Shepherds, horsemen and sheepdogs accompany perhaps three or four hundred animals, travelling for several days to reach their destination. Like a swarm of locusts, they eat everything in their path, leaving behind streets scattered with raisin-sized poo and the heavy odours of lanolin and goat hide. Everyone gets out of the way as they pass through, even our four-legged residents, the cats.

Life in our small *pueblo* would be much diminished if we didn't have these felines. I'm talking about feral street cats that often outnumber the human residents and rarely allow anyone to touch them. There are a few sleek, contented, domesticated creatures that appear outside their own front doors, but the true natives range hungrily through the streets at all hours, watching and waiting for some scrap of nourishment, wailing and wauling as they fight over a dish of prawn shells or the odd chicken bone. Steve has offered to tell their story, not least because he, and previously Lucia, one of our good-hearted neighbours, are the ones who have kept them from total starvation during the colder months.

* * *

The street cats of Panjuila seem to have been here forever, though of course the cast has changed over the years and many have now been forgotten. They have certainly had their lean times in the past, especially during the winters, when they've had to fend for themselves, ignored by most householders. Skinny and miserably patient, it used to be that up to twelve of them would congregate outside our front door from first light; taking any food out for them involved wading through a moving fur carpet to get to their feeding spot.

These days they have life much easier with fairly regular meals, although their mothers, like most caring mother animals, continue to pass on the skills of hunting and scavenging, and all are accomplished thieves. Any window left open or door ajar is seen as an invitation to these silent felons; they'll help themselves to any available food, and be gone again in seconds.

The summer, when the *pueblo* fills up with people coming for the fiestas, is a different story. The visitors enjoy feeding our little friends, and we become a *pueblo* full of contented cats. Their kittens may be more vulnerable however, as little boys run around with fire crackers and little girls yearn to pick them up and cart them about. Sometimes a sack is produced and a pretty one goes off to a new home, struggling and protesting all the way. And not all of those born here survive, having been taken by the fox or through succumbing to a relatively minor ailment. Life in the *campo* can be cruel.

Of course, like humans, the cats all have their own personalities, and while I don't actively seek to give them names, many have earned them. There's The Silent Mew, an attractive, tri-coloured cat with a gentle manner and a cataract in her left eye. At times, you'll look out over the kitchen stable-door and she'll be sitting there looking up sweetly, her mouth moving, but making not a sound. I never knew her from a kitten, so I can't say if something caused her to lose her voice or if she was born like that, but she's a good-looking kitty, very hard to resist, and in different circumstances would have been someone's well-loved family pet.

The cat we call The Good Mother (or more latterly The Foul Spot, for some unknown reason) is just that. She is the most fertile cat we know, having brought forth at least fifteen kittens since we've been here, and is, as I write, pregnant again. A mottled, dark brown and black cat, one couldn't accuse her of being attractive, though clearly some of the toms find her so. She'll usually have her litter in a secret location and later show up at the door looking slim and sleek. This achievement qualifies her for extra rations while she's feeding her young. After a few weeks, she trusts me enough to take me to wherever she has them hidden, and we get them onto solid food.

She's not domesticated by any means, and shuns any kind of physical contact, though she will often accompany me through the *pueblo* like a friendly dog. We know her offspring from different litters, and their relationships to each other, although the fathers can only be guessed at. One of the leading suspects is the chap I call The Paternity Suit, a brutal, tri-coloured tom with a big head, whose colouring of ginger, white and black is quite rare in a male, or so we have been assured by a Japanese film crew who passed through our village in their world-wide search for interesting footage of feral cats. He is not one of ours historically - perhaps he just wandered in like an old gypsy - though now he seems to have made his home here also.

Who else? Well, there's the almost fully-grown Ginger Fella and his three younger sisters (or half-sisters): Pretty Girl, Radar One, and Radar Two. The first needs no explanation - she's just a really attractive cat. The Radars, One and Two, earned their names from the sharpness of their hearing. I have fed them from an early age, and they can hear me coming down the stairs inside the house, even from a good distance. They are always waiting when I get to the door.

These two, who to the casual observer look like twins, have very distinct personalities. Radar Two, the one with a kink in her tail, is growing up to be a cat with an attitude, always looking for any excuse to give the others a sharp dab with her paw, and she doesn't discriminate. She'll go for her sisters, her older brother and even her own mother. Radar One is completely different. She's a run-of-the-mill street cat in most respects, but she does like being made a fuss over. She's the only one who will allow herself to be stroked, and she really enjoys it.

Phoebe's Little Girl is the daughter of a domestic cat who was abandoned here when her owner moved to another village. We don't know what happened to Phoebe, she simply vanished, but her kitten, although quite small at the time, was eventually able to integrate with the others. It was not easy for her, but now she has her place in the feeding programme.

There are many others, not least because no one can get near them to organise some family planning. At one point, The Good Mother, Pretty Girl and both Radars were all showing very rounded shapes, but the

Radars and Pretty Girl were too young to be mothers yet, being no more than kittens themselves, and when they slipped into view over the next few mornings, looking svelte again, we assumed that they had lost them naturally. However, it turned out that Pretty Girl had given birth to three tiny kittens, two of which survived. The weakest of these, a frail little ginger and white thing, had the good fortune to be born just before the summer fiesta when the village was filling up with children. They took it to their hearts, feeding it bread and milk, and it could often be seen being carried around by one or other of them and being fussed over, this time for the better.

The Good Mother brought forth five little ones on this occasion, three of which are still with us and are feeding with the bigger cats, and now she's pregnant again. We are well known locally for being the village of street cats and largely due to the efforts of this one female, it doesn't seem as though that's going to be changing any time soon. However, this little story is evidence of her devotion to the cat population of Panjuila:

The Sad Tale of Gitano's Kitten

A while back, one bright spring morning, Lucia's dog, Gitano, showed up with a present for her. Lucia, who lives on the outskirts of the village, is a woman with a good heart and a kind disposition to animals, and her pets seem to have inherited her compassion. Gitano, a small brown-and-white, wire-haired terrier with a stiff-legged walk and a lively personality, adopted her some years ago, and they can often be seen around the pueblo or taking their evening *paseo* together. The lucky fellow, wandering in from the countryside, has found himself a good home. He comes and goes as he pleases, but at night he has a cushioned bed out on Lucia's terrace.

Now, here he was, arriving on the doorstep for breakfast, with a kitten in his mouth, which he laid at Lucia's feet. She and her husband could not think where it had come from; perhaps the dog had found it out in the campo. The creature was tiny, fitting easily on the palm of one hand, and clearly in need of constant attention if it were to survive. More attention, in fact, than even Lucia could give it.

After some thought, she took the kitten round to The Good Mother who had recently had a litter and was bringing up her babies in a discreet corner of the village, quite near to our house. The cat seemed to accept this addition to her family and Lucia, having done the best she could, went home. As it happened, I had been feeding this newest batch on solid food for a few weeks, so, in fact, The Good Mother's milk had dried up, more or less. She must have found that she was unable to feed it adequately, and while she could have abandoned it, she didn't; her maternal instincts came to the fore and she gave it another chance to live.

Linda was up a stepladder outside the kitchen door, pruning the vine, when she heard a squeaking sound. Looking down, she saw The Good Mother looking up at her in pleading silence, and, close by, a tiny mewing ball of ginger and white fur, its eyes still closed and not yet able to stand. The Good Mother had brought it to her source of food in the hope that we might feed it too. What could we do?

A quick brain-storming session produced the name of a girl, Zula, who lived about fifteen minutes away in the *campo*. She was something of an 'Earth mother' type and if she could not help, she might know somebody who could. The kitten needed feeding as soon as possible. I carried the tiny, weak creature out of the *pueblo* to Zula's *cortijo* and by great good fortune, the girl was at home. Unbeknown to us, her own cat had very recently given birth to three kittens, but had sadly lost one. The new arrival was offered up to her and although much smaller than her own, she took it without hesitation and the kitten started to suckle greedily. We all breathed a sigh of relief. Over the next few weeks, we saw Zula a few times and always asked about the progress of the little one. The reports were good, with the kitten still feeding and growing stronger, but quite unexpectedly, after the third week, Zula had come downstairs one morning to find the kitten dead. She couldn't say why or what had happened to the little fellow, but we were saddened to hear the news.

I sometimes think about the sequence of events in this story and how we all, from Gitano and Lucia, to Zula and her cat in the *campo*, had played our own small part in trying to save the life of a kitten that had nothing to do with any of us. We had done what we could, and no doubt were content with the way we played our parts, but still the kitten had died. The truth is that sometimes, no matter how hard you try, Nature will have her way.

* * *

This area no longer breeds pigs, although there are many ham-curing and drying businesses, especially up towards Trevélez, which is reputed to be the highest inhabited town in Spain. In fact, there are so many hams hanging up to dry, one wonders if in fact countries like Poland and Hungary are supplying them and somewhere in their remote regions there are numerous three-legged pigs! I have been assured that this is not the case and the pigs are all Spanish reared, mostly in Murcia and further east.

Cattle are rarely seen unless one goes walking on the higher Sierras in summer, where upland meadows provide excellent grazing and the cows contentedly suckle their young calves, far from human interference. All the milk in the shops is of the long-life variety and comes from the north. We have heard of one exception, however, which is a tale worth telling. This is the story, as I heard it, of Maya, the most desirable cow in the Alpujarras.

In the early 1970s, when many young people were 'tuning in, turning on and dropping out,' a small group of British friends came from the Atlas mountains in north Africa to live in the Alpujarras. The villages in both these parts of the western Mediterranean are remarkably similar, so this merely represented a boat trip across the sea and a switch of languages from Berber or French to Spanish, rather than a major change in lifestyle. Hashish could still be grown, bought and sold in both locations quite easily and it was possible to live very cheaply whilst contemplating the inner life of the soul. This group were led, it seems, by a charismatic veterinarian called James, whose young wife Mary also co-owned a small dairy farm in southern England. When it suited, perhaps if James was getting too interested in some other woman, she would leave the mountains, taking their two children with her, and spend some time back in Devon.

Not long after settling in the mountains, James realised that it would be helpful to have a cow. Milk was a staple requirement, the group could make butter and cheese, and they both had the skills to look after livestock. He rang Mary in England. "Find a young heifer," he commanded, "preferably a Jersey or a Guernsey. I'll be over in about 3 weeks."

This Mary duly did, without too much trouble, buying a young Jersey heifer from a neighbouring farmer. James returned to England and set about organising the transport of Maya, their bovine Earth mother and goddess, to southern Spain.

First of all, he applied to Spain for permission to import a live cow. This took some time and much bureaucracy, involving a Madrid government office and a sheaf of paperwork, but eventually approval was given. In the meantime, he checked with the British port authorities on ferry transport to Santander. Unfortunately, he was told that livestock could only go by sea as far as Le Havre or Roscoff and from that point on, he would have to continue overland through France with a cattle truck. Not wanting to deal with French bureaucracy, or their somewhat Anglophobic gendarmerie, James decided to try a little deception and ingenuity. One cannot blame him. One domestic cow is not the same as a large commercial herd.

He bought a 3 ton van, complete with tailboard, for a knock-down price, and set about lining it with sound-proofing materials, fresh straw and a spill-resistant water trough. Painted in swirling kaleidoscopic patterns and looking like a mobile pop concert van, he booked a one-way ticket to Santander, gently ushered Maya into her luxurious establishment, packed himself, Mary and the children into the cab and set off for Plymouth.

Initially, all went well. They were among the last to board, whether by chance or design, and quite soon the busy ferry cast off its moorings and set out into the English Channel. Passengers streamed up onto the decks and began to locate their cabins, as this would be a 24 hour crossing. James and his family went to find a comfortable spot to sit and chat, where the children could play without getting lost.

The sea was somewhat turbulent, with a fresh wind blowing in from the Atlantic, and below decks there was a final check by the seamen to make sure all vehicles were fully secured before they reached open water. Maya, shut in her hay-scented boudoir, chose that moment to let out an anxious bellow. She could sense the ship's roll and was not a happy beast. More bellows and moos followed. The seamen, busy checking lashings, paused in astonishment. Had they heard what they thought they heard? The first mate was summoned, followed by the captain. Quickly the order was given, "stand by to go about."

Over the tannoy came an anonymous voice: "Would the owner of vehicle registration HNF 337D, Mr James Allenby, please report to the Purser's office immediately."

James reported as requested and found himself being frog-marched down to his truck and commanded to open the rear access. The tail-gate was partially lowered and the presence of a young, caramel-coloured heifer was revealed, loosely-tethered and rolling her big brown eyes. For the captain, there was no choice in the matter. This was a serious breach of regulations and he had no alternative but to put back to port. For the passengers, there was the mystifying message that, "For technical reasons of a non-threatening nature, the ship will be returning briefly to port. Would the drivers of all cars on B Deck stand by to move their vehicles."

People speculated on what this might imply. Had someone important been left behind? Was there a problem with the engines? Would they be delayed?

In fact, with James having loaded late and his van being so near the ramp, it should have been an easy matter to reverse a dozen vehicles off the ferry, then his. The captain felt confident that he could get this family and their cow back onto dry land, in the care of customs and the local police, and have his ferry under way again in no time at all. Only James knew that this would take longer than expected. His van had no reverse gear. This was why its price had been so temptingly low - or so the story goes.

As the van was too heavy to push it backwards up the ramp, all the vehicles in front would have to be off-loaded first, so he could drive off in a forward gear. It took over an hour to get all the cars off B Deck onto the quayside, drive the truck off, and then put everyone back on again, whilst the captain, furious, paced up and down the bridge. James, his family and Maya were left to answer to the authorities. They were reprimanded by the police and had a report written, then summoned before the local magistrate and issued with a fine, and eventually sent, somewhat defiantly, back to their farm.

Very shortly afterwards, having sent Mary and the children on ahead, James dutifully bought a new ticket for Plymouth to Roscoff and got himself and Maya into France. This stage of the journey went well and the truck, now boasting reverse gear, bowled smoothly along until he reached the Spanish border near Pau. This was before the era of the European Union and open borders, so there were plenty of Guardia Civil to inspect his van and his paperwork. A stocky, dark-haired inspector in an immaculate uniform perused his documents. "You cannot bring livestock into Spain," he announced. "It is forbidden."

"But I have permits," explained James, not very patiently, "Look, they were all stamped and sent through from Madrid."

"They are not correct. You must return this animal to the United Kingdom. Only dead meat can be imported into Spain, in a refrigerated lorry."

James tried several arguments but nothing would prevail. This officer was not going to tamper with the rules as he understood them, even for a mad Englishman with a cow.

"Very well," muttered James, setting off back down the road towards Pau.

Once out of sight, however, he stopped the vehicle, got out his maps and began to make another plan. Waiting for nightfall, he gave Maya some water and checked that she had enough hay. She had become used to this mode of travelling by now and was very comfortable.

James drove eastwards through the first part of the night, into the high Pyrenees, keeping as close as he dared to another, more remote border post. He found a desolate country lane and went even higher, through dense pine trees and rocky gorges until he had left behind all signs of human habitation. As the lane petered out and became a footpath, he swung into a forest clearing and parked the van. He wished it was painted green and brown, rather than pink and purple. Next, he made sure that he had a rucksack with some food, a halter for Maya, his torch and spare batteries, a compass and his map. Leading her out from the vehicle, he realised that the gods were with him. It was a clear night with a moon.

The man and his cow walked all night. They climbed through the forests and paddled across rushing streams. The path worked its way around deep gulleys and enormous, looming rocks. At one stage, they had to cross a large, open meadow where several horses and sheep stared silently at them in the moonlight. Briefly, they paused for their respective midnight feasts: fresh grass and a sandwich.

Then there was a perilous stretch of footpath which frightened both of them, and a final difficult ascent, but as dawn began to lighten the sky, James realised that they were heading downhill, with a small village in the distance. Somewhere, during the night, they had crossed the border into Spain. He began to cast about until he found a discreet spot, where he could tether Maya in safety and solitude.

After a couple of hours sleep, he took his compass bearings and then, leaving Maya with plenty of fresh fodder, gritted his teeth and set off back up the mountain. It was fortunate that he was young, fit, and had good walking boots. Taking the same illicit route back, he walked into France for a late breakfast and by noon he was back with his truck, presenting himself at yet another border post. This time there were no difficulties and he was waved through with a polite "Buenos dias." Finding Maya again took a little time, following narrow country lanes and praying that his compass bearings were accurate, but eventually he spotted her golden hide through the trees. She was lying down just where he had left her, calmly chewing the cud.

So Maya came into Spain. The trip to the Alpujarras went smoothly and everyone in the village welcomed her with delight. She was a fine animal, a pure-bred Jersey. The family put her out to pasture and over the next year looked after her with care as she adapted to the southern climate. James, using his veterinarian skills and contacts, looked about for a suitable bull, and soon she began to produce both calves and delicious milk. Over time, she became a prized addition to the household and was well known in the local farming community.

Many years later, James and Mary made new plans for their own lives, moving to another part of Europe, this time without animals. What were they going to do with Maya? Her breeding days were finished but she was a much-loved creature. Where could she go? A return trip to the UK was out of the question.

One solution lay with the Buddhist monks of O Sel Ling, high above the Poqueira Gorge. They lived a solitary and contemplative existence, as self-sufficient as possible; surely they would welcome a productive creature like Maya? They accepted the offer with pleasure, so James made another, much shorter journey with her, and after seven years down in the valley, Maya lived the rest of her life up on the mountain, growing a thicker and hairier hide against the winter cold, but still giving delicious, creamy milk. It is said that the Dalai Lama, on a brief visit to the monastery, complimented the monks on the wonderful milk provided to him for breakfast each day. When Maya eventually died, she was buried in the grounds of the monastery, with a headstone which can still be seen to this day.

Chapter 5

Old Age Travellers

Our transportation of goods and chattels was much less perilous than that of James, and was done, in the main, without dissimulation. However, it did take two years and a total of four road trips to get all our possessions out here. We're glad that we brought familiar furniture, beds and so on, since much of the stock in the shops here is not to our taste, and we could never replace all the books, kitchen items and family artwork that we own. Overall, the cost of transportation was far less than we might have spent on replacements.

In 2007, I booked a very small commercial enterprise (two men, a van, and a dog) to take the first load overland to their base in Alicante. Despite my concerns as I saw my valued pieces disappear down the road in Norfolk in late August, they duly reappeared outside our house in Panjuila three weeks later, all intact and complete.

We must have caught both the old fuel prices and a team that were about to retire, as the price and the efficiency were worth having. When we looked to do the final trips in 2010, much had changed, not least the costs, so we hunted thoroughly for a viable solution and eventually did the whole business ourselves. Probably, if we had been able to be sufficiently organised, we would have hired a container, put absolutely everything into it in one go and made a single contract for the whole process. But we would have missed out on a lot of fun, only a little misery and a great learning curve. Life is not necessarily meant to be easy.

First, we needed a vehicle. We found a high top transit van on eBay, which had low mileage, a tow-bar and comfortable seating. It had been owned by the Fire Service so it was bright red of course, but it had been regularly serviced and was clean as a whistle under the bonnet. It had a side awning for exhibitions and camping, which proved useful. We tested it with a run to Scotland to deliver some surplus furniture to my son, and then an overnight trip down to the Glastonbury area to a motorbike show. For the latter, we also took a tent and three duvets, as the temperatures were due to plunge that weekend.

A wise move. We put the tent up under the awning, inflated a double airbed, laid our poor quality sleeping bags on one duvet and hauled the other two over us. Well, I did anyway. In the morning there was a layer of ice inside the tent and fresh snow on the ground outside, but we were snug as bugs.

We also bought a 2-bike trailer at auction, as we had three motorbikes to transport alongside the household goods. This was not a flat-bed or box type trailer, but one with two narrow steel runners, side-by-side, with front wheel securing hoops. As each bike was driven onto its runner, the whole trailer tipped first backwards with the weight, then forwards again into a level position. After that, all that was needed was a bit of strapping to secure the bike to its runner.

Steve made adjustments to the trailer, fitting new wheel bearings, ensuring that all lights worked and buying a spare wheel (who wants to be stranded on the hard shoulder of a French motorway in the middle of a Saturday night, with a flat tyre, lopsided trailer and the securing nuts and bolts scattered in the grass verge somewhere in the darkness?).

In the midst of all this scrambling about, we did the Aberdeen run and made a trip with furniture for my son and made another trip to Derbyshire to see my oldest brother. Then one morning Steve, who never admits to any illness or discomfort, muttered something about his vision 'going wonky.' "I've got bits and pieces swimming about," he said.

"It's the optician for you, then," I replied and immediately rang around to find out who could see him quickly.

At first, all seemed well.

"It's nothing," the optician said, "lots of men of your age start to get floaters. But you need some new reading glasses."

The next morning Steve complained again.

"It's as though a grey tide is moving upwards, cutting out my sight," he said.

I decided to break all the rules and email an old friend, the opthalmologist at the local hospital. I described the symptoms, apologised for circumventing the system and waited for a reply. It came back within a couple of hours.

'Get to your doctor straight away. This sounds like a detached retina and you'll need a referral to me or one of my colleagues for an immediate operation.'

The long and the short of it was that the next morning we found ourselves in the eye department of the Norfolk & Norwich hospital, having whizzed up there on the Moto Guzzi. Not a good idea, under the circumstances, to travel by motorbike. They dilated Steve's eyes to confirm the damage, advised him to come back in 2 hours for an operation and told him that someone else would have to drive him home afterwards.

Afterwards? First of all, we needed to get home and switch from bike to car. How does one control an 1100cc sports bike over 15 miles of country road, with both eyes goggling like a Simpsons cartoon character? Personally, as pillion passenger, I closed mine and put my faith in Steve's instinctive skills. Somehow, we made it.

So there we were, with Steve sporting an eye patch, an interesting air bubble keeping his retina in place, and a two week delay in place on our travelling plans. Never mind, it gave us longer to clear out the garden shed and the attic.

Originally, we had planned to get everything out in one trip, with van and trailer, then make our penultimate UK exit on two wheels, taking the last bike and touring France and visiting friends, before we reached Spain. The car could be driven out later. But, as with all well-laid plans, ours went astray fairly quickly. As soon as we began loading up, in fact.

"I don't think we'll get everything in," Steve posited, "we've got too much stuff."

I was determined that nothing should be left behind. "Surely we can go a little bit overweight," I argued, "who's going to check?"

"The French police for starters," he said, "followed by the Spanish ones. If we get that far."

But I had my way and we loaded the van to the gunnels. Tables, chairs, garden pots, jam pans - they all went in, fitting together as beautifully and securely as a Rubik's Cube. However, it was soon apparent that the van was so low on its axle that we might not make it up the hill out of Bungay, never mind the high Sierras of Spain, and that was without the trailer. Something would collapse, probably the entire chassis. Under the circumstances, we did not even bother to go to the local weighbridge. I had to concede defeat, and off came nearly half of the load.

"That looks better," declared He Who Is Always Right. "Now, let's go and load the Moto Guzzi and your little Honda onto the trailer."

Because we had no ramp to accommodate the backward and forward tipping movement of the trailer, we needed to find a low bank or footpath, somewhere free of other traffic, where we could back the trailer up and get a straight run forward with a motorbike. We would need to ensure that the trailer did not tip forward too quickly with the weight but that the bike stayed vertical and in motion. Not too difficult with the lightweight c90, but somewhat challenging with our 280 kilogram Italian beauty.

After driving around for half-an-hour and scrutinising grassy knolls, narrow lanes and the local swimming pool car park, we settled on a quiet lay-by out of town, with a phone box at one end. As it was now 8 p.m. and growing dark, the light from the phone box made a welcome contribution to the task ahead.

We managed a sequence of convoys - van and car to the lay-by, back home with the car, then a motorbike apiece back to the lay-by. Meanwhile, it had begun to rain quite hard, a very cool wind was blowing and someone in a large lorry had arrived and parked up too. We felt like criminals, wearing black beanies on our heads and scurrying about with ropes and ratchet straps, although our position alongside the road was reassuringly public. We put the van and the trailer widthways across the lay-by (sorry, mate asleep in lorry, but you will have to stay put for a while) and wedged the trailer against the bank as firmly as we could. Then Steve made the first of a number of 'runs' at the trailer.

On these occasions, I take a metaphorical deep breath and prepare myself for a sequence of disasters. It's no good expecting instant success and the man must be kept going with words of encouragement, praise and enthusiasm. My supporting role is designated as the One Who Holds Steady (or holds the bike steady) and, of course, can find the missing connector or spanner or piece of wood with a nail in the end of it, as the rain pours down. Steve and I have a wonderfully compatible relationship in such terms and, despite considerable and amusing efforts to destabilise this equilibrium, we manage to get things done without disagreement almost all the time.

On the third attempt, the Guzzi rolled gently onto the trailer bar and stayed there. Straps were positioned and she did not move. Securing the c90 alongside, head-to-toe, was a simple lifting job, although the storage box sitting over the back wheel had to be removed first. All done. We were wet, shivery and tired, but we were ready for the trip out early the next morning.

We had no plans to stay in hotels or even on campsites. This would be as quick a run as we could make it, then straight back for the rest of the furniture and the bigger Honda. We left on the Monday and hoped to be back by Friday. We had money, passports and toothbrushes; I had a change of knickers and a body-warmer. Steve travelled, as usual, in jeans and flip-flops. We had not booked any ferry crossings but made sure we arrived at Dover at an early hour, along with the seagulls and half-a-dozen cars. Despite the tiny number of passengers, we were still charged a premium rate for not booking ahead.

Steve would tell you that I slept through most of France and at least a third of Spain. I can assure the reader that I remember Rouen, Le Mans, and Limoges; that Périgueux was pretty and that hot coffee and a croissant near Bordeaux at six in the morning was very welcome. In Spain for supper, we endured a miserably-small portion of steak and chips in exchange for a lot of Euros, and seemed to spend many weary hours crawling up long hills and then winding our way across the plateaux, through forests of wind turbines. At night, these are a modern wonder, with their small red beacons shining in the darkness like the eyes of mysterious, cyclopean visitors from outer space.

Passing through Madrid at three in the morning was exciting, a city lit up by dynamic neon signs and tall tower blocks, everything on a huge scale and the air redolent of all-night, early summer street life. Modern cities are often at their most exciting after dark. We have wandered with pleasure down the *ramblas* in Barcelona at Christmas time and through London's Canary Wharf when the squares are bursting with New Year revellers. Listening for the sound of horses' hooves in Siena, getting lost in Cordoba, crossing the bridges of Paris and exploring Seville by moonlight are also on the list.

Dawn of the third day found us heading into Andalucía, where the road suddenly changes from a motorway to a two-lane country road, and from fairly straight lines to the winding *desfiladero* of the eastern Sierra de Madrona. By the time we reached Panjuila, all I could think of was being horizontal and in a proper bed. First, however, there was the delicate task of off-loading the bikes and putting them securely into the courtyard, then getting the van as close to the house as possible to take off the furniture. One of our kind friends, Giotti, helped us to carry the bigger items.

Once all this was done and we had had a brief night's sleep, recovering some of our physical sanity, we set off back again towards northern Europe. I doubt if many people in the village even noticed our brief visit.

We returned via the Pyrenees and found ourselves passing through the Tunel de Somport at some unearthly hour, exceedingly tired and desperate to stretch out. We had the trailer in the back of the van by then, and no load, so we were travelling much faster, but this did not make the discomfort any the less.

"We must stop," I urged Steve. "I've got to lie down."

He must have felt the same, so I arranged myself across the front seats and he got into the back, lying on an old bit of carpet. We had no extra coverings and there was still snow at the sides of the road. I wondered how long we would manage to sleep before the cold got to us - vans are not insulated in the same way as cars and we did not even have newspapers to use as blankets. I think barely an hour passed before we set off again.

By the time we reached Calais we were getting short of patience. It was late afternoon, we had driven over 2000 kilometres in two days, and we wanted a quick ferry trip back to Blighty. We went straight to the ticket office. A ferret-like man in a nautical blazer with glistening gold buttons was waiting for us, hunched behind his desk, looking as though his whole career depended on how objectionable he could manage to be. My French is good, but that counted for nothing. We were 'the old enemy' and his job was to demonstrate his power, however brief, over our destiny.

"With no booking," he pronounced, "you can either board the next ferry, for an additional 50 Euros, or wait until 0100 hours for an additional 10 Euros."

We looked at each other. It was only five o´clock in the afternoon, but we had spent a fortune on fuel. Another 50 Euros seemed like a lot of money.

"Tell him we'll go at one in the morning," muttered Steve, reluctantly.

We paid up, took our tickets and went disconsolately back to the van.

"Come on, let's go and find some food."

With hot food inside us and a bit of courage, we decided to drive down to the boarding point and see what was happening. I think Steve already had his sights set on an earlier crossing and knew that he might be able to bluff his way on board. As it turned out, once again there were only a handful of vehicles, mostly trucks. We were guided to a queue and soon found ourselves boarding the ferry without trouble and no additional payment. It seems as though bureaucracy has exceeded its remit in many countries, and is merely there to see how many of its so-called customers can be ripped off. Such bare-faced piracy has to be met with guile and bravado.

Once we were back in East Anglia, a second van trip was needed for the remainder of the furniture, this time with the big Honda VFR 800i on the trailer. I had to admit defeat and let Steve do this one on his own. My paltry excuse was that then he could stretch out in the cab and sleep whenever he needed to. In fact, he made the journey even more quickly - less than 5 days in total - and returned with two excellent vehicles for eBay, in as good a condition as before, plus about 5000 miles on the clock. When we sold them, we made a small profit on the trailer which covered the spare wheel and a new registration plate.

By now, we had almost no furniture in the house and had to sleep on two inflatable mats on the bedroom floor and eat our meals on trays, sitting on a settee which we would leave behind. It would take a further week before we could pack the last items into the car, book a Santander ferry crossing and head down to Portsmouth. Left behind to give to friends and family were some terracotta garden pots, 120 superb Norfolk pamments circa 1880, an old lawnmower and various tools. Also, of course, we were saying a temporary farewell to a handful of people whom we loved a lot, and whom we hoped we would continue to see in the coming years, in Britain or in Spain.

* * *

Because we had to make what might be called 'interior design' decisions at every visit, it was important to have a clear vision and stick to it. Ours was governed by three main principles, familiar to most Spaniards: *bueno, bonito, y barrato.* Well-made, attractive and cheap. We could rely on Emilio for the first element, but sometimes we had very little time to combine the second two. We knew that we wanted to retain all the original chestnut timbers in the ceilings, over the doorways and above staircases, off-set by simple, white walls. There were no new openings to put in except the kitchen window. But refinements crept in. Did we want smooth plastered walls with squared-off corners, or rough rendering and an 'adobe' feel to the rooms? Would the old floors, made from river-sand with a primitive, cement surface that was as smooth as polished stone, cope with everyday wear and tear? In addition, most of these floors sloped a little, but did a level floor really matter? What kind of lighting should we go for and, importantly for me, what type of wall tiles should go in the bathroom and what colour did I want (Steve kindly stepped away from this delicate area, to preserve domestic harmony).

The Lakeland farmhouse of my childhood, with its slate-cooled dairy and shady, straw-bedded cow byres, had always had stone walls rendered over and painted with a white lime-wash, but not skimmed or straightened in any way. This seemed a good option down in the *cuadras,* the old stables, while the main rooms were to be skimmed to an approximation of a fino finish but without squaring off the corners, as there were many delightful curves and ledges that gave the house its personality. These should not be lost.

We decided that the same principle applied to the floors. A gentle slope across the big *salón* could be accommodated and if some tables needed a wedge of wood to stabilise them, we did not mind. As we began to settle in and make these decisions, many people wandered in and gave advice. Harry from Devon thought the old, polished cement flooring was part of the house's heritage and should be preserved no matter what condition it was in. Emilio had more modern ideas and was concerned for us about the dust and the maintenance. Someone mentioned laminated wood, another spoke of the winter and under-floor heating. In the end, we compromised and gave ourselves as much reasonable variety as we could. We chose absolutely plain 30 centimetre terracotta tiles for the main rooms, the cheapest we could get from our excellent, local builders' merchant. The second bedroom had decent, smaller, reddish tiles already laid so those could stay. The small balcony that I first fell in love with, overlooking the street, has retained its lovely, shiny, polished surface and the terrace has rough-shaped slates of the same neutral grey. The floor of the cosy 'snug' for winter use is still undecided and has a hotchpotch of cement, red tiles and many blemishes. A plentiful supply of rugs will see us through until we make up our minds.

The terracotta tiles, despite their cheap price, have been a mixed blessing. No two are the same so they have had a worn-in look from the start, but we made the fatal error of not sealing them before any other work was done, and much later on, when the builders had finished, Steve spent days and days on his knees, cleaning off patches of cement, paint, varnish, and gesso. Once he was satisfied, he sealed them with a matt product mixed with white spirit or *aquarasse*. This needs renewing every few months to prevent fresh spillages and other marks from penetrating the clay. He is also the person in charge of floor mopping and does a much better job of it than I ever could. His mis-spent youth in the Merchant Navy, swabbing the decks, has taught him that you need to put down a lot of water in order to take up all the muck. It's no good hoping that a damp mop will do more than push the dirt from one side of the room to the other.

"Stand aside, woman," is the usual command. "Men are here."

I am delighted. Washing-up, yes; ironing, yes; sweeping and hoovering, yes; dusting, if I must. Floor-mopping, toaster-fixing, tyre inflating, and carrying heavy boxes are willingly abandoned to male hands. I may be a feminist, but in the interests of balance and fair play, I am very happy to relinquish such tasks.

The bathroom, only 9 square metres, has the same terracotta tiles on the floor, but I wanted an intimate, jewel-like feel to the place and it had to be warm in winter. A bathroom is a haven of comfort and relaxation, not to be despised or neglected. I can remember (who cannot?), icy and lonely student digs with a three-quarter, sit-up bath and damp, streaming walls, followed by shared accommodation where the tidemark had to be removed before you could run the bath water. Also, sometime in the seventies, an impoverished French hotel which had a gloomy bathroom the size of a small bungalow, with a bare light bulb hanging from the ceiling, the bath in one corner, the loo in another and a grand bidet holding centre stage.

If one is going to look at wall tiles, or *azulejos*, in southern Spain, the starting point has to be the Alhambra in Granada. One of the wonders of the modern world, this astonishing sequence of defensive buildings and gardens, palaces and fountains, is a miracle of Islamic architecture. Abandoned for many centuries by the Christians, after they drove out the Moors in the 1400s, its rescue was initiated in part by the American, Washington Irving, who lived there in the 1820s. Careful repairs and restoration continue to this day. Many of its courtyards and palace rooms have tiled walls, patterned in diamond, star and tree shapes, or decorated with interweaving linear patterns similar to Celtic designs. The colours range from pale turquoise to yellow ochre, cerulean blue to dark brown or black. Some of the domed ceilings drip with successions of hand-made ceramic stalactites in white and gold, representing the starry heavens. It is a place of great beauty and in our tiny bathroom I wanted to capture something of this magic.

By good fortune, it turned out that a woman in our area, named Fatima, was making ceramic tiles that reproduced the Alhambra shapes and colours as accurately as possible. Her studio was not too far away and one could commission a design or pattern exactly as one wished. We made several visits, pondering over our options, comparing different colour schemes and tile sizes. I knew that although there were many attractive colours, I could not leave out eau-de-nil green or deep turquoise, and we both loved her pale creams and subtle browns. I also felt that a simple diamond pattern would be best in such a small room, framed within a narrow banding. We added dark green to the palette, for contrast and strength.

My brother Simon, a sculptor, provided us with a green bronze relief to go on the wall, Venus with Pomegranate, and the towels are white or green depending on the laundry situation. The heating comes from a thermostatically-controlled, electric, stainless steel towel rail. We were told never to go for painted or cheaper metal, however pretty. If you want dry towels and winter warmth, spend a bit more and get the real thing. Together with the tiles, which both Emilio and our friend José painstakingly put on the walls (the former with precision, the latter with rather too much creativity, probably due to an excess of 'the herb'), this room proved to be something of a financial indulgence on my part, but I have no regrets and enjoy it every day.

Electricity was a difficult area and decisions had to be made quickly so that Roque, our electrician and plumber at the time, could get his work done before final plastering. Often he and Emilio would clash over the timing of their work. Just when a wall had been skilfully and carefully patched up, rendered and plastered, Roque would come swinging along with hammer and steel, to chase in his cabling. Great holes appeared for sockets and switches, while Emilio ground his teeth and tore at his hair. As a result, when Roque needed access to the house, Emilio somehow managed to be elsewhere and had the keys with him, or was working on that precise section himself and could not move aside. We had left them to it and were fortunate, I am sure, not to hear the acrimony. Spaniards tend to talk at shouting level anyway, so the sound of two angry caballeros letting rip might have been too much for us.

Roque is an interesting character. He arrived on the scene about 7 years ago, a tousle-haired (later, a skinhead style), quite good-looking man in his late twenties, with reasonable English and a working knowledge of electricity. He seemed to have the same approach to life as a fourteen year-old and took our jokes and himself very seriously, but he was certainly a hard worker.

Some evenings, we would meet him, his mate Salva and another man, Gabriel, going out on the town.

"Oh dear," I would say, "here's trouble. Watch out girls!"

They liked that and adopted a swagger as they left the village. Often some slim, dark-haired beauty would appear for a while with Roque, passing through the plaza in tight jeans and a cut-off top, which I am sure the older men, clustered outside the bar, must have appreciated. Whether he himself understood his good fortune, we were less sure of; at that time, only the teenage part of him seemed to be in control, physically and emotionally. Yet in entrepreneurial terms, he had an older head on his shoulders.

One day we were told that he had bought the old *molino*, originally a wood mill, situated a good 15 minutes walk out of the village along a footpath, and was living there. This seemed incredible. The *molino* consisted of a roofless, ruined house on the inner side of the path and a dangerously-teetering, ruined remnant of the mill-wheel and its housing on the other. Up behind the house was a gaunt rock-face, buttressed by exquisite stone walling and pocked with a few natural caves, probably once used for storage or goat shelters. Fifty vertiginous metres below the mill-wheel rushed a narrow stream, littered with collapsed timbers and shrouded by dense undergrowth. This was not a place to stumble upon in the dark, or casually explore in daylight, nor was it a project to be tackled by anything less than a team of experienced engineers. Although he may have paid only *centimos* for it, Roque had taken on a challenge of epic proportions.

Over the years, we have watched both him and his mill develop. He moved into it in its derelict state and began by roofing in the main house. This gave him some protection from the weather and he started to fit it out with 'liberated' furniture from the rubbish dump. We gave him an old water heater that we were replacing, which went straight into his wheelbarrow and off down the path. I think we passed on a double butler's sink and a surplus bath, too. Often, he could be seen on his ancient motorbike, balancing all sorts of items fore and aft as he puttered along home. Occasionally, drunkenly, he has been known to fall off into the *barranco*, but always re-appears in great good humour the next day.

On one occasion, we were amazed to see an upside-down armchair and a pair of human legs hurrying up the village street. It was Roque, combining a fitness jog with the acquisition of a comfortable seat. Another time, together with 4 or 5 other young men, he managed to drag many timbers up from the stream below and make safe the mill-wheel housing, cantilevered out over the drop.

He is not just a fitness freak, however. We have found him building a delicate edging of small stones along his footpath, in the Moorish style, and have tested his 'invisible' stone fountain, gushing from solid rock. We have also found him stuffing huge slabs of bread into his mouth, in desperation, having worked all day and eaten nothing.

There is always something new to see at the mill. I think he has been given sensible advice when needed, but often it is his own ingenuity and will-power that takes the work forward. He is a man of irrepressible energy with a strong creative streak, growing roses and tomatoes on any rocky outcrop with enough soil for them to take root. What an addition to our village family. When the burden of responsibility for local knowledge and upkeep of services, such as the location of the drains or who owns which parcel of land, passes to his generation, he will be an important asset. However, there is just that missing adult element to worry about...

Chapter 6

Fiesta Time

In the early days, our visits always seemed to be too early or too late for the village fiestas, and we would arrive when plans were incomplete or the decorations were coming down and everyone was exhausted from too many late nights. Our balcony was frequently used for tying up bunting, and we might find spent fireworks on the roof, but we had not had the chance to join in. Perhaps, as occasional strangers, this was a good thing, but as our language skills progressed and we got closer to becoming residents, we wanted to participate fully.

Our luck changed for an unlikely, but welcome, reason. One of our neighbours, Antonio, had had a kidney transplant and wanted to give thanks for a return to better health. He had spent many years travelling to and from Granada for dialysis, leaving the village in an ambulance early in the morning and getting back late in the afternoon, at least twice a week. At last this was at an end. His cheerful face, which had been yellow with jaundice, returned to its normal colour, and he was able to spend even more time in his garden, growing beautiful flowers and improbably large vegetables.

The village never advertises its fiestas, relying on word-of-mouth almost all of the time, so we knew nothing until we walked through the plaza at six on a Sunday evening to find a very large, empty paella pan balanced on some dying embers and people sitting about looking well-fed and somewhat inebriated. We were offered a sweet cake by Antonio's wife.

"It's the feast of San Antonio," she explained, "and my husband is celebrating his new kidney. What a pity you missed the *arroz*, the rice, but please stay for the rest of the party."

The ice was broken. Everyone made us welcome as we stumbled out thanks and congratulations in our fledgling Spanish. We were grubby and dressed in our working clothes, straight from the kitchen garden, but no one seemed to mind. In this village, some of the ladies retain their dressing gowns until midday, their slippers until the evening and rarely wear jeans, whilst the older men never bare their legs and a clean shirt on market day is de rigeur. Foreigners can do as they please.

Soon afterwards, we managed to be around when another saint's day occurred and a rabbit stew was served up, with mountains of sliced potatoes cooked in large, flat pans awash with olive oil and heated from below by butane gas burners. There was enough for second helpings of everything, and we all enjoyed the stew's strong flavours of meat, onions, garlic and carrots. It had been cooked by Trini, the bouncy and hospitable wife of 'the man who never smiled', and was brought into the plaza in large, glazed stew pans known as *cazuelas*.

Although Andalucían cooking in restaurants is often limited to fried food and staples such as rice, potatoes or couscous, and this stew was a typical meal, the women are always buying fresh vegetables in bulk on the market, so they must be cooking or eating something different at home. Perhaps they are making pickles and sauces, or gazpacho, that wonderful chilled tomato soup; perhaps a huge salad is served for lunch, to eat with the daily supply of long, crusty loaves that turn rock-hard overnight.

Moderation is not a familiar word in this part of Spain and pride is taken in buying vast quantities to feed the family. This may go back to the years after the civil war, when Andalucía in particular suffered terrible poverty and hardship. Many adult men went off to find employment in Germany, rebuilding itself after World War II, and they sent money home when they could; the women did their best to eke this out and keep children and elderly parents alive. Nowadays, thanks to membership of the European Union and legitimate social aid, families do not need to starve, so buying in bulk is as good an indication of affordable consumption as any.

In this instance, at the end of our simple meal, eaten off our knees, we were quite surprised to be asked for 8 Euros (about £6) each. Meat is expensive here, even rabbit, but we wondered if we were being charged an inflated price as *extranjeros*. In fact, I don't think this was considered a large sum by our neighbours, but we knew of family-run restaurants where we could eat a 3 course meal for that amount. However, we did not demur and paid our dues.

Someone who was more seriously disconcerted at the price was Joleen, a woman trying to live off her craftwork and struggling to make ends meet. She too was in the beginner's class with her Spanish and working hard to integrate into village life.

"I can't afford 8 Euros," she said to us, bluntly but too late, having eaten her plate of stew already.

We could not afford to subsidise her and she must have felt robbed as she wandered off to get her purse. At the time, we felt that we needed to be on our guard against a local assumption that we were rich and there to be fleeced, but so much generosity emerged over the next couple of years that we soon realised that this was not the case.

* * *

The next party was the big one in August, the Fiesta en Honor a la

Virgen de la Gracia. Preparations had begun several weeks earlier, when the church walls were stripped of vegetation and re-painted, the streets cleaned and various grassy areas trimmed back. Because I swept the little streets to the front and back of our house every week, I hoped that the council men were pleasantly surprised at the lack of litter for them to pick up.

As the weekend grew nearer, many families began to arrive, rattling along our few, tiny streets with hefty suitcases and wheelbarrows laden with food, trailing small children and gangly teenagers behind them. Houses that had been closed for months had their doors and windows thrown open and bedding hung over balconies to air. The car park filled up, the vehicles squeezed together as tightly as possible, something alien to Spanish drivers, and friendly voices echoed around the plaza.

These were the children and grandchildren - and great grandchildren - of people who had been born here during the early part of the twentieth century, when poverty was normal and almost everyone lived a harsh, cramped existence. Rural Victorian England might well be a good parallel: no sanitation, little private ownership of property, strong moral codes and social rules, children put to work young. Pigs were killed in the backstreets and conserving food for the winter was essential.

There were other newcomers, however, not just us. Our nearest neighbours have no long-standing roots here, but have acquired a village house as an investment and holiday home. They all hail from Granada, a family of two retired parents, four sons, their wives and a host of grandchildren. They don't all come at once, even though they have dormitory-type sleeping arrangements for the children and could squeeze everyone in if necessary. On this occasion it was the eldest son Carlos and his wife Raquel who had decided to join in with the festivities. Arriving late in the evening with their two small daughters, Claudia and Rihanna, they made several trips from car to house and flung open their windows with exuberance. Carlos is a fitness fiend and strode back and forth, bringing the bedding, toys, boxes of food and a crate of beer. Usually, he's in his blue, green and white Lycra cycling gear, one hand steering his bicycle, but this time he was in the usual jeans and T-shirt. On one pass, he noticed Steve's motorbikes through the courtyard doorway and went in to have a look. "I have a trails bike," he said, "for off-road riding, but mostly I prefer my bicycle."

This was an understatement. It turned out that he and his brothers could achieve astonishingly rapid times in getting to the village from Lanjarón, down on the plains, taking only slightly longer than a car, and most of that uphill. We are often amazed at the tenacity and endurance of Spanish cyclists, vigorously pedalling up the steepest inclines, sometimes with a mobile phone pressed to one ear at the same time.

"Shall we have sausages for supper?" we imagined them to be saying, or "I should be home about seven o'clock," just like their contemporaries on the evening train into the suburbs of south London.

Later on, we witnessed several mountain-bike races, when often more than 100 muscular and svelte cyclists hurtled up rocky, pot-holed roads towards Mulhacén, gaining altitude at an impressive rate. Groups came from Sevilla, Alicante and Granada to participate, women as well as men, with the rewards of free paella and a certificate at the end of it. Maybe some prize money too. Tonight however, Steve was happy to talk wheels of any sort, and the two men ended up sauntering into the plaza and the bar, to continue with this most vital discussion.

Fairly early the next morning, I was busy painting the back wall of our house, by the kitchen door, when Claudia and Rihanna came to investigate and have a chat. Claudia in Spanish is pronounced 'Cloudiah' and we would often hear her mother calling loudly for her, "Cloudiah, Cloudiah!"

"Hola," I said to them, "What are your names? How old are you?"

Claudia was spokesperson and the only one of the two whom I could understand. At five, she spoke clearly and simply, whereas her three year old sister let fly with a volley of excited words which I found incomprehensible. Claudia used her arms in the expressive way that Mediterranean children have, shrugging her shoulders and shaping her hands, whilst Rihanna scrabbled in the dust looking for ants and anything else of interest. They both wore colourful shorts, T-shirts and sandals, with beaded braids in their hair and the ubiquitous stud earrings. After a while, they began to create a small shop in the soft dirt, so I gave them a little plastic saffron box to fill up and 'sell' to one another. Raquel briefly appeared to make sure that they were not being a nuisance.

"You must understand that this lady comes from England, so you have to speak to her slowly," she told Claudia.

The little girl nodded gravely. Already she had a few English words and seemed to understand the linguistic difficulties that we were encountering. Later on, during the fiesta, we saw both children in fancy dress, looking enchanting as, respectively, a small pink princess and an even smaller, pale green fairy with wings.

Although our fiesta started officially on the Friday evening, we had already made plans to go to another village for what we hoped would be a Blues night, with several bands. We went out on the Suzuki motorbike, knowing that it would be easier to park, and found ourselves in a tree-lined square, right beside the church, with only a handful of people scattered around. We had yet to learn that if the programme or poster says 9p.m., Alpujarran time means 'we'll start about an hour later than advertised' and 'don't bother to turn up until midnight if you want to dance.'

So we were there in time to watch the various acts go through their warm-up routines and for the sound equipment to be tested. Familiar territory for Steve, after his days as a roadie. We got chatting to the female lead singer for the main set, who was from Granada but spoke English with a perfect Scottish accent. It turned out that her husband was Scots and she taught English in a secondary school during the day. One would never have guessed, given that she looked strikingly Spanish in a tight, black silk dress and a quantity of gold necklaces, her hair pulled back in an immaculate chignon.

"What do your students make of your extra-curricular work?" I asked.

"They seem to think it's quite exciting," she smiled, "but they are only twelve year- olds."

I asked her about her route into both teaching and singing. She said that she had found languages and music very easy at a young age and had followed her instincts in choosing these as both her formal and informal careers. She could certainly sing, probably too well for the type of songs her band had chosen, but at least the acoustics functioned properly, pretty much for the only time that evening.

Her set gave way to some heavy punk music á la Sex Pistols, which brought the dancers onto the floor, maniacally leaping about, but by 3 a.m. we were heading for home and bed. It's interesting that these days this type of aggressive, loud thumping and yelling appeals to the laid-back, hashish-smoking cool dudes, who would have been chilling out to Dylan, Procol Harem or Led Zeppelin, back in the day. None of this evening's songs were ones you could hum the next day or sing along with in the bath.

We heard later that this music played on all night and into the morning until, at 8a.m., the local ladies had had enough. They came to the square in numbers, hurling fresh eggs at the DJ and demanding that the raucous noise stop. It seems that although everyone wants to have a good time and there is a lot of tolerance for local youth enjoying themselves, the limits have to be observed. If not, beware!

For us, the day began in earnest about an hour after this. Still in my nightie, sipping tea, I had just suggested a cooked breakfast, when the banging of a drum and the clarion call of a trumpet brought us to our feet. A full brass band was beginning to strike up.

"Quickly," Steve said, "Let's get out there."

We pulled on some clothes - luckily I chose a respectable dress rather than the usual vest top and shorts - and scrambled out of the kitchen door into our small *calle*. Coming down the slope, fitting tightly into the narrow street, was a band of ten or twelve young men and women, playing all sorts of wind instruments, together with cymbals and drums. They were dressed in black trousers and pale blue shirts, and knew their pieces by heart. Hastily, I moved Carlos' wheelbarrow out of their way. Raquel put her head out of a window above, somewhat bleary-eyed but laughing. The children danced about with excitement. Steve, video camera in hand, tried to capture the moment, then we marched behind the band down into the plaza, where a fiesta breakfast had been prepared - warm, sweetish sponge cakes, and some interesting bottles of alcohol. Luis, Carlos' father, beckoned us over and poured us a tot which combined neat anis with brandy. This was *sol y sombra*, sun and shade. Strong stuff and usually taken in the bars at six o'clock on a winter's morning, by men heading off to work. Clearly, this was going to be a long day.

Gradually the throng swelled until the plaza was full. We had no idea so many people had arrived overnight. The band sat down under the tree, in the shade, and worked their way through a number of tunes, often pausing to chat to each other in any musical interlude that did not include their particular instrument. The cymbalist had few occasions to clash his discs so he managed a gregarious conversation with his colleague on the kettle drum. The girls playing the clarinets and oboes did less well in the chatting stakes. After an hour or two, and an additional circuit of the village streets, the band departed to a round of applause, and we all went off, stage right, to our respective homes.

"What next?" we wondered.

We did not have long to wait. At midday precisely, the band was heard once more, and we all rushed out towards our little church. It was procession time. Toddlers, young children, teenagers, men, women, and the elderly made their way along the well-swept street. Most people had gone home to change and were now in their best clothes, the men in navy-blue or dark-grey trousers with clean, well-pressed shirts and the women in flowered frocks or simple two-piece outfits. Some of the teenage girls, as decorative and glowing as summer flowers, teetered along in high heels and tight dresses, with their little sisters in frilly skirts and sandals. Except for some of the onlookers who happened to be passing through, there was not a pair of shorts in sight.

One of the senior ladies, Juanita, beckoned us inside the church. 'Come and look at the flowers,' she insisted.

The simple, pale turquoise interior and altar were neatly bedecked with bouquets of white carnations. A single bouquet of pale pink flowers caught my eye and I wondered why it was the only coloured one. Facing the altar stood a wooden frame with a platform on top and positioned on it, ready to go, the statue of the Virgen de la Gracia carrying her Child. She looked delicate and well-carved, with an elaborate crown and a flowing red and gold robe under a blue cloak. We had just sat down on one of the benches to take it all in, when Juanita caught at my arm. I had trouble understanding her rapid speech and local accent.

"You have to contribute to the fiesta," she seemed to be saying. "It's half-price for children and the elderly, but for you it's 100 Euros."

I gasped in surprise. About £80 for both of us! That couldn't be right. "Are you sure?" I struggled to say, "50 Euros each?"

She was adamant.

"There are the flowers to pay for," she indicated, "as well as the music, and you get churros with hot chocolate tomorrow night. And you have two houses."

This did not make complete sense to us, but fortunately events swept us up before Steve could get his wallet out. It was time for the Mass, so we slipped away. This part of the celebrations was not for us but, nonetheless, we felt somewhat disappointed at the conjunction of the spiritual with the mercenary at that particular moment. The Spanish are a very pragmatic people.

We sat in the shade of a large tree with some Glaswegian friends and waited for the Mass to finish. In due course, people began to come out and wind their way down the slope from the church, once more with the band going strong and the Virgen held perilously high on her wooden catafalque, resting on the shoulders of four strong men. She was bedecked with the bouquets of flowers, the pink one forming the centrepiece at her feet; the virginal significance of this was apparent now.

Walking at the front of the catafalque came a woman and a child of eleven or twelve, the latter carrying a tall, lightweight cross; behind them was the priest in his flowing, cream robes. We joined the crowd following behind and made our way to the square, waiting patiently at strategic corners where great care had to be taken to ensure that Our Lady did not get dashed to the ground by a low-hanging electricity cable or someone's washing line. An elderly woman, Trini's mother, leaned out of a small window and threw down rice, blowing kisses of joy to the crowd below.

As we entered the plaza, Steve stayed back with his camera, but Jesús from the bar touched my shoulder and indicated a good place to stand. I watched as the local women formed a semi-circle and sang a tentative yet tuneful song of praise, lighting long sparklers which they held down towards the ground.

Salve a la Virgen de Gracia - Adulation to the Virgin of Grace

Dios te salve Reina y Madre (God save you Queen & Mother)
Virgen pura de Sión (Pure virgin of Sion)
El señor está contigo (Jesus is with you and)
Y con nosotros tu amor. (Your love is with us.)

Siendo la esperanza nuestra (Being our hope,)
Te pedimos con fervor (We fervently ask you)
Que después de este destierro (That after this exile)
Nos muestres al Salvador. (You will show us the Saviour.)

Madre de Misericordia (Mother of Mercy)
Amparo del pecador (Refuge from sin)
Vuelve a nosotros tus ojos (Turn your eyes to us)
De refulgente esplendor. (In shining splendour.)

Cobíjanos Virgen Santa (Shelter us Sainted Virgin)

Con tu manto protector (With your protective cloak)

Para que podamos verte (So that we can see you)

En la presencia de Dios. (In the presence of God.)

Viva la Virgen María (Long live the Virgin Maria)

Que al pobre da su jornal (To whom the poor give their daily wage)

Viva la Reina del Cielo (Long live the Queen of the Sky)

Que protege esta hermandad. (Who protects this community.)

Ruega Madre por tus hijos (Plead Mother for your children)

Que te piden con fervor (Who beg you with fervour)

Y también por este pueblo (Also for this village)

Échanos tu bendición. (Give us your blessing.)

¡Viva la Virgen de Gracia! (Long live the Virgin of Grace!)

I had not thought too hard about the feminine characteristics of Catholicism before, but here was a welcome manifestation of female religious belief and involvement in a generally masculine, and often misogynistic, faith.

The band struck up once more and we were treated to a fresh round of drinks. I managed to locate Raquel and had a hasty conversation with her in French, a useful common language which the locals might not understand, about the requested payment. "What are you giving?" I asked.

"50 Euros for each household," she replied, pulling a face. "We don't believe in the religious bit, and it's a lot of money, but we are three families so 150 Euros seems about right."

This eased my mind a little, but I still thought 100 Euros was too much and when next I saw our treasurer, Juanita, I pressed a 50 euro note into her hand, saying, "We are retired, that's all we can give. I would like to see the accounts as well, sometime, so I know where the money goes."

These days we do get to see what other people are giving, but there's still no sign of a full set of accounts.

As the *Virgen* was transported back to the church, we decided to go back to the house and have a late lunch. Who knew when we would eat again that day? As we turned the corner we saw, standing beneath our balcony and gazing up at the flowers, a swarthy man in his fifties, dressed in a dark suit, white shirt and red tie. I felt slightly uneasy about him, as he seemed to be loitering there with a purpose and I was not sure why. As we reached him, a blonde woman appeared, coming in the opposite direction, plump and a bit breathless, her frilly white blouse heaving with the effort. They were both very smartly dressed for our little village, even on fiesta day.

"Hola," we said politely, preparing to go past them and through the front door.

"Hola," he replied, then, "do you speak English? Are you German?"

We clarified our nationality, wondering where the conversation was going. His English was quite good.

"I used to live in your house," he said. "This was my family home when I was a boy. I am Jesús Rodriquez."

This was a surprise, since several members of the original family still lived in the village but had expressed little interest in the house or what we were doing to renovate it, nor mentioned Jesús Rodriquez. He, on the other hand, was clearly deeply affected. He pointed upwards.

"My bedroom was here," he gestured towards one end of the house, "and my mother, she slept here," indicating a window overlooking the street. "She grew many flowers, the balcony was always full of them."

His eyes had filled with tears. I reached over and patted his shoulder, as his companion said, "He's never been here at fiesta time before or seen the old house looking like this."

She had a good, solid, North Country English accent that I felt I recognised.

"Where are you from?" I asked.

"We live in Penrith," she explained, "in the Lake District. We're getting married there in two week's time."

I knew that voice now. This was a proper Cumbrian (once Westmorland) lass. These two people came from my part of the world, where I grew up, and yet here we were, standing in a village 2000 miles away, which had been part of his childhood. How extraordinary.

"You must come in and have a look round," we said.

90

As we worked our way around the house, Jesús Rodriquez exclaimed over many things and told us a great deal about the way of life here in the 1960s and 70s. In his tiny bedroom, his mother had done her sewing, hung up drying vegetables and kept a small cupboard of spices. His father would go out onto the shared terrace to work on pieces of wood, repair implements, or smoke his pipe.

In the stables below they had kept, in different corners, some chickens, a pig, mules, a donkey and a cow. There were concrete feeding troughs and ancient hollowed-out stones for water with, not far away, a human toilet against one wall and animal channels in the floor elsewhere. In the little street outside the kitchen they had held the annual *matanza* or pig killing, with the dead animal hung up from a length of timber to catch the blood for black pudding *morcilla* sausages. Nowadays, this practice of killing animals within village boundaries is forbidden.

The little barn at the back, which we call the *granero*, and which was falling into serious disrepair, had changed little since his childhood. It had been used for more mules and horses down below and for grain drying and storage up above. In fact, the animals, their foodstuffs and the harvest all benefited from more space than the humans, yet we sensed that the confined, close-quarter living of his family had been one of warmth and affection. They were not totally impoverished, but life was hard. He told us how, at a young age, he was sent by his mother on the donkey to the neighbouring villages, to sell bread and eggs, and of his pride when he came back with an empty sack and money in his pocket. He also described a mysterious event from his earliest years.

"I must have been about 4 or 5 years old," he said, "and my grandmother was living with us. She was old, feeble and bed-ridden, but always had a good word to say to me. One morning, very early, my sister came and got me up, dressing me in my best clothes. 'Granny has died in the night,' she said.

"'I know,' I replied, quite calmly, 'she came in the night and sat on the end of my bed. She told me to be a good boy, and that one day I would leave the village and travel to far-away places.'"

The family had been astonished at this fantastical occurrence. Granny certainly could not have made her way to his bedroom in the middle of the night and very few village boys went further than Granada at that time. Yet much later on, aged 16, Jesús left the village and travelled to Mallorca for work. Marriage, divorce, and many years of wandering took him to England and Penrith, where he met Karen, his fiancée, and together they opened their Spanish themed restaurant. Granny's prophesying had been correct.

We were very moved by this surprise visit and all the coincidences. We showed him an old wooden spoon that had been found in the wall by Emilio, thinking that he might recognise it and that we could give it to him as a gift.

"Oh, it probably came from the coast," he said, dismissively, "as a souvenir, a toy."

Hastily, I put it away again!

We all went back to the plaza and the festivities, but we knew that somehow a broken link had been repaired and old memories laid to rest. Two years later, on a visit to the UK, I had reason to pass through Penrith and thought I would call in and see them. It was a chilly February afternoon and I had not notified them that I was coming, yet as I crossed Market Street, I saw Karen with some shopping.

"Hola señora!" I shouted at the top of my voice. It almost stopped the traffic. She stared across at me in amazement, then realised who I was and greeted me with enthusiasm.

"I must call Jesús, he's at his allotment."

A short time later, an unusually small, green van came into sight, laden with wood, plants, vegetables and tools. I was transported back to Spain in my mind. This child of the Alpujarras had found a niche in the Lake District and I was surprised that his vehicle was not a donkey and cart. In his bar, I took a photo of him standing proudly in front of a picture of King Juan Carlos. That photo, now, is pinned up in our own bar, here in the village, maintaining the connection.

* * *

The fiesta continued into the early hours. There were plenty of fireworks going off, like cannon-shot, most of them ignited with a cigarette butt by the *hombre de fuegos artificiales*, as I called him. Intriguingly, anything connected with fire is strictly controlled and water laid on nearby, as no one wants to risk a fire spreading across the hillside, and indeed one could argue that a stray spark could ignite anywhere and be out of control in seconds, but at the same time the Spanish are delightfully insouciant about all matters pertaining to health

and safety. The cigarette butt probably got chucked into the bushes after it had done its job and one assumed that the hombre still had all his fingers intact.

Fancy-dress also played an important part. As Japanese geisha girls clustered together and two young men paraded in nappies, a troop of Roman soldiers charged through the square, swords and shields at the ready. The chief centurion produced a collection of wind-up toy bulls and proceeded to organise a miniature bullfight. Then some teenagers arrived in motorcycle leathers and denims, while the younger children paraded as cats, witches, a long-nosed Pinocchio, and various types of cowboys. We even had a large black-and-white cow prancing about, who might have been old Andreas and his son, but no one could be sure.

Packets of sweets were awarded to the best entrants and yet more thrown into the crowd for the children to fight over. Steve had helped me to wrap myself in a striped, Egyptian-style tasselled robe with a pale-yellow dish-dash on my head, a green jewel hanging on my forehead. I salaam-ed everyone with enthusiasm and got a few acknowledgements in return.

As night fell and a female singing duo, positioned above us on a wooden stage, got into their stride, I danced a paso doble with a moustachioed gentleman with a paunch, and watched as a handful of locals executed a few neat steps. Many of the women sat looking on, and, as usual, one wished for a little more effort from the men. Steve was cornered by several 'gals' and managed an embarrassed jig before retreating to his chair and his camera. After midnight, I saw Roque and his girlfriend Miranda hastening across the square with several dogs and a wheelbarrow. Knowing them, they probably had a much more exciting party to get to, somewhere down in the valley. Miranda was a young, flower-like girl with a ready smile and a tiny physique, yet she was often at Roque's side, doing her best to share in the work on the mill. We hoped that he was taking good care of her, living so far from modern conveniences and modern entertainments.

We managed to get to bed before dawn, unlike many others, and we could hear the shrieking singers until at least six in the morning. We were told later that one of them, having drunk almost as much as the assembled villagers, had managed to fall off the stage, but was soon picked up, dusted down, and re-installed, microphone in hand.

This had only got us to Sunday. At nine o'clock, those who wished to, went to another Mass. The rest of us piled into the square for children's games and more anis. Carlos won the table tennis tournament, Steve brought one of his motorbikes into the square for the little boys to admire, and the rest of us chatted together in the sunshine. Other, secret activities were taking place in Antonio's house on the outskirts of the village.

At midday, the band re-appeared, the brass section struck up again and we scurried along the backstreets to the assembly point. Another procession got going and we followed the band around the village a second time. More cannon-fire accompanied us. I was not sure at what point the religious and the sacrilegious had become intertwined, but we were certainly more pagan than Christian by now.

The rest of that day passed in a blur of yet more music and attempts to drink only moderate amounts of the local *costa* (homemade) wine. Plus quite successful attempts to practice our Spanish, which got better with every glass. Perhaps we all went off for a siesta during the afternoon, but then, as dusk fell, the final ritual occurred, as it does every year, with the ceremonial burning of el Zorro, the fox.

A superb papier-maché, life-size fox, painted a suitable reddish-brown and stuffed with sparklers, bangers, and small fireworks, was carried into the square on a wooden stretcher. His nether regions consisted of a rather large pepino cucumber cunningly suspended with black cotton, and two generous plum tomatoes... an impressive beast indeed. He was placed on the ground in the centre of the plaza and a primitive chanting began, berating him and his female equivalent for stealing chickens, eggs and other precious village objects. '*Puta*' was shouted quite often, the Spanish for whore.

As the chanting ceased, Antonio stepped forward and lit the resin-varnished beast. Zorro burst into flame, crackling and sizzling, the exploding fireworks adding to this theatrical moment. Despite the earlier celebration of the *Virgen*, this was a much more primitive cultural event and I could easily imagine that it had been going on for hundreds of years, long before the arrival of Moors or Christians. Chickens and eggs were valuable possessions, the fox a curse on everyone's livelihood. Purging the village of such an aggressor would have been seen by all as vital to survival. Now, we were collective witnesses to this sacrificial moment, all of us, even the youngest children, cheering as the creature finally collapsed into a burning heap. After the fire went out, hot chocolate and churros (a type of long, sugar-coated doughnut) were served, then most of us retreated homewards. Others partied on into the dawn, this time without the drunken singers.

As the last weeks of August passed, families began to pack up again, locking their holiday homes and disappearing back to Granada or Barcelona or Almeria. A few grandchildren stayed behind for a while with their grandparents, to be entertained in the evenings with a variety of films, projected onto a white sheet pinned up in the plaza. Screening began promptly at midnight, when it was cooler and everyone either brought a chair or simply sat on the stone seating near the fountain. We had a natural amphitheatre. The biggest success was Chicken Run, with 12 or thirteen small faces upturned to the screen in riveted silence. Free packets of sunflower seeds were handed out; the bar did a good trade with the adults, mainly the men, in beer and wine; everyone shuddered, gasped and laughed in unison. The heights of sophisticated entertainment had been reached, in a remote mountain village far from places like Hollywood or Cannes.

* * *

Other village fiestas turned up other opportunities. My search for someone, anyone, who might be interested in Argentinian tango dancing, finally paid off. It seemed that a couple of visiting Germans, who had relatives in the area, were giving demonstrations of their tango dancing skills in the tiny villages of Fondales and Capillera, so one evening I abandoned Steve and hurried down to Plaza Gerald Brenan, where the tiny square had been lit by a couple of lamps and a simple speaker system set up.

Red-headed Renate waited patiently in her leather-soled high heels and short, tight, white dress, whilst Boris on violin, a Brazilian vocalist with her caxixi-style maracas and an Argentinian with a bandodeon, began their warm-up session.

The audience was perched on walls, doorsteps, rockeries and, for the lucky few, chairs. I found a white-washed wall to sit on beneath a fig tree, with my dancing shoes in my bag just in case a *milonga* was announced and we all got a chance to tango round the little plaza. I was conscious that this was yet another precious moment, bringing together a simplicity of surroundings, the unique proximity of live music and dance, and, as added texture, the warmth of the southern summer night. Soon, with very basic equipment and no formality or elaboration, we were given an hour or two of riveting spectacle - song, dance and energetic music.

I think that the only person to suffer during the evening was a slim, glamorous woman seated on a low-level rockery near me, her long, dark hair and sequinned skirt attracting not just human attention but also that of many tiny and vicious ants. She told me later that they had got into her clothes, her shoes and even her hair, biting as they went. As soon as the dancing ended, she headed for home and the shower, at top speed. Many months afterwards, we began to get to know her and her South American husband and their semi-wild, grey horses; yet another intriguing pair of expatriates.

After the Fondales exhibition performance, we heard that Boris and Renate were offering to do a tango demonstration to be filmed for YouTube, but had not selected a location. I suggested the plaza in our own village. It was a natural 'theatre in the round', had a fairly level surface for dancing, a bar, a romantic fountain, and an opportunity for them to showcase their skills to the locals. They agreed, so with 24 hours to go, a lot of hurried activity took place to ensure that we were prepared and the villagers knew what was planned. Our friend Fran printed off posters and stuck them to walls, trees, and doorways in the nearest villages, Steve set about acquiring marinated olives to make focaccia, an Italian tapas that we could offer round, whilst I located our CD player and reviewed my limited wardrobe. I might get to dance this time! Hunting out a tight, midi-length, leopard skin printed shift dress which had always constrained my walking ability, I grabbed a pair of scissors and chopped off 12 inches. By teatime, I had a sexy, knee-length little dress with a slit at the back.

At 8p.m., we began to assemble in the square and finalise the details. Where should we plug in the music system? An ancient and questionable electricity meter, hanging askew on someone's front wall, was suggested and Fran, taking his life in his hands, plugged it in. It seemed to work. Jesús opened up the bar, looking sceptical. One or two people trickled in and sat down. The children raced through, chasing hysterical cats. Boris, Renate, and another dancer from Uruguay appeared, together with the video publicist, who selected the best spot for his tripod and camera. Steve checked the oven and his focaccia. It was very quiet. Would this all be a waste of time and effort?

We had reckoned without Alpujarran time and how people behave during the warmest months. By 9 p.m., when it was getting slightly cooler, the square began to fill up. Out came chairs, older residents, more children, visitors from Pitres and Orgiva, even a stray dog or two. Francesca and José arrived, bringing with them Carla, the glamorous, but seemingly frivolous, Australian. The presence of José bridged the divide between the 'off-comers' and the 'locals'. If he was there, one sensed that a united effort was being made. The dancing demonstration began, slow and sensuous; a full moon rose above a balconied house, a drift of perfume scented the air; light shone from the open door of the bar. Had we all died and gone to heaven?

Tango is the product of African and Latin American bordello pastimes, when women smouldered and simmered, men swooped and seduced. What emerged was the notion of a dance that contained a secret, silent dialogue combined with languid rhythms, which then evolved into a sequence of elaborate steps with erotic undertones. The couple are physically very close from the waist upwards, often dancing cheek to cheek, forming an inverted 'v' shape. It is the opposite of the North European 'waltz' configuration.

The woman might have her eyes shut throughout, sensing direction but lost in the music. She generally moves backwards or sideways. Her partner, moving forwards, will ensure that there are no obstacles in their way, that she looks and feels beautiful and maintains her balance easily. Together they work towards some kind of dreamy ecstasy. It is sex without shedding any clothes, stimulated only by the music and the dialogue of their bodies. He proposes a movement and she accepts or declines. Neither partner is the leader, both must give and receive, perhaps even battle, to reach tango nirvana.

Tonight all of this was played out for an audience of perhaps 30 people, many of them simple rural folk whose dancing preference is for the paso doble. But they clapped and cheered, enjoying the spectacle and Renate's fine legs, and ate every scrap of focaccia afterwards. If they found the dancing a bit risqué, they didn't say so. José decided that he too would learn this dance, much to Francesca's amazement, and some of us began to plan the next event: should we go for a flamenco sevillana or a type of Irish ceiligh? Or more tango? Boldly, I solicited a dance from Boris and managed a very simple sequence of tango steps without disgracing myself. Not everyone has to be an expert to gain pleasure.

Chapter 7

A Village Wedding

Down on the land, meanwhile, we had been very busy. Emilio had fenced the vulnerable parts of it for us, to keep out the goats, sheep and wild boar, and we had a water source in the form of a large black pipe or *tubo*, about 10cm in diameter, that had been put in very recently, just after we bought the place. This started life about half a kilometre away, in one of the *barrancos* with its fast-flowing water, and had been laid along the old *acequia* route to make sure that as much water as possible reached the kitchen gardens lower down the valley and made its way, eventually, to a large reservoir and the golf courses of Málaga.

We were deeply upset to lose the sight and sound of running water, one of the main attractions in the Alpujarras, and reckoned that much ambulatory tourism would be lost thanks to this notion of progress. From the cultivation point of view, there was little difference. We needed as much water as we could get or our plants would not survive the scorching summer sun, and whether it came in a channel or a tube made no odds.

As we began to examine the soil in early June, we realised that much of it was richer and deeper than we expected. Steve had spent 5 weeks the previous summer attacking the deep banks of brambles and weeds, and their decay over many years had rotted down into the ground alongside the mulberries and figs. If we could just get the weed roots dug out and the soil turned, we might be able to grow a few vegetables before the season passed. Many brambles had re-grown, so this was not going to be an easy task. Despite wearing gloves and overalls, we were ripped to shreds by these tenacious and vicious plants. They must be amongst the most successful species on the planet - cut them to the ground and they grow again, stronger than before; dig out their roots and you may have to go down 3 feet before you give up; spray with weed killer and there will always be some that survive. Even the lightweight, dead branches manage to rear up and tear your ankle at the slightest opportunity. If you have no hatred in your heart when you begin to battle against brambles, you will develop it quite easily within a few days.

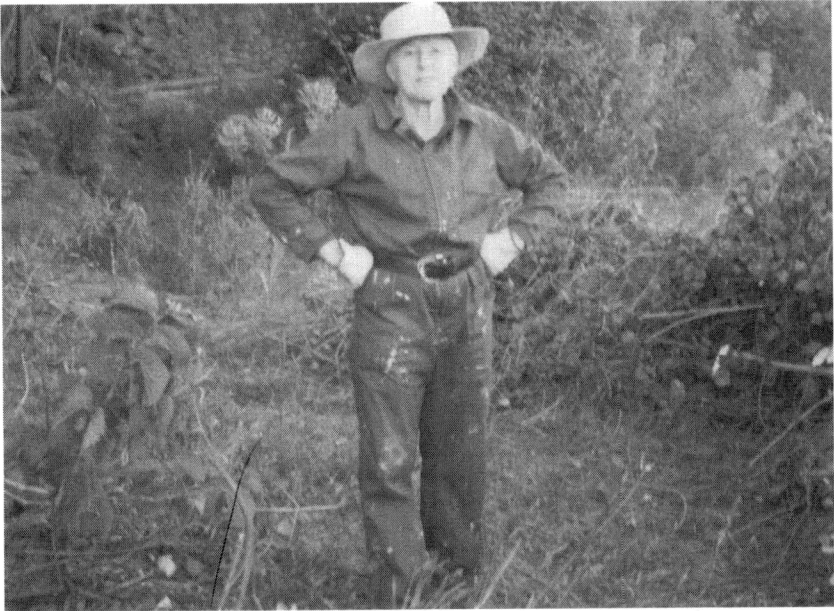

However, we were determined to create some growing spaces and simply dug, heaved, raked and removed as much as we could of these terrible *zazamoras*. Then we bought trays of small plugs on the market and put them in, mostly guessing, such was our ignorance, which were peppers and which were aubergines and where they might fare better. Tomato plants we could recognise, and onions of course. Sweet corn 'nuts' would go in straight out of the packet. We were not sure which plants would prefer a bit of shade, under the mulberry tree, and which could cope with full sunshine and the intense summer heat. They would all need plenty of water in the early stages.

That spring, I had been given some free, indigenous trees by an Andalucían environmental authority, which Emilio had heeled-in for us near to the *acequia* and around which he had dug a short water channel. This planted stretch followed a slight curve, which Steve immediately named 'the fertile crescent', and we thought it best to follow his lead. The locals know what they are doing in respect of sun, water and planting. It's in their blood and handed on from parent to child, and we knew that if we grew the same plants as them and used the same methods, we would achieve results. Despite the early summer warmth and infrequent watering in our absence, these baby trees were looking reasonably healthy. Two or three white poplars (*alamos blancos*) seemed to have failed, their leaves burnt and falling off, but the rest looked fine.

"I'll prune these poor things back," I said, "though I think they've had it."

We carefully took up and replanted some of the stronger looking saplings, wild olives, pomegranates and cypresses in other parts of the land, but they would require substantial watering-in. It was time for the putative engineer and landscape architect to show his skills. "We'll create an irrigation system," he announced, loving the challenge.

Fortunately, the land falls away from the *acequia*, so any channels we dug would allow a slow trickle and sometimes a swiftly-flowing narrow stream, to pass through the barren patches to any outlying young tree. We dug these channels by hand, pulling out weeds and twigs and the odd handful of ants or termites. Gauntlet-style gloves are essential out here, preferably leather ones. The ground varies immensely, from stony shale lying millimetres below the surface, to the good, rich soil we were so pleased to discover under the brambles, so around each tree we created a miniature stone circle and moat, to hold the water while it soaked downwards. As the water flowed, so we walked along the length of our channels, hoe in hand, clearing out floating debris or allowing a further trickle to get beyond one tree to the next.

The other essential part of this system, which the locals also use to excellent effect, is the blocking and unblocking of main arteries with stone slates or large flattish rocks. As soon as one tree or planted patch has had enough water, you simply close off the route and divert the water elsewhere. It made sense to work the water along the topside of a square-ish patch of ground, perhaps containing the tomatoes and then channel it down the sides or through the middle, and subsequently off towards the sweet corn section, or to our young trees.

When we were planting the sweet corn, we had a difference of opinion about how to water the 60 or so plants. I had a vision of a rectangle with a diagonal channel running across it, thus achieving 5 water courses and keeping the middle plants damp.

"It won't work," said Steve with infinite patience. "Once the plants are fully grown, you won't be able to get to the middle to weed or to keep the channel clear. Much better to cut a course vertically or horizontally, straight through the centre."

I couldn't see much difference between the two options and I think we both realised that in order to maintain horticultural peace, one of us would have to be in charge and the other would have to obey orders. I am not very good at the 'obey' bit, but since I have control of the decorative plants on the terrace and in the courtyard, and it was, after all, his land, I couldn't hold out for too much. As we often do, we took a few hours out to maintain our stubborn positions, and then settled for the 'straight lines' option. In fact, once the plants began to shoot, our excitement was so great that any old shape of ground or watering system would have been acceptable. Although the seed packet recommended putting three kernels into each hole, I opted for two in each, but almost all of them came up. We would have a glut. It was clear that the next year we would be able to put only one kernel in each hole, cover more territory and have a considerable crop.

During that early summer, I re-visited the pruned and once-dying *alamos blancos*. "They're alive!" I called to Steve. "They're shooting again from the base."

The short, bare stems had put forth new life and fresh, green leaves with silvery undersides were developing nicely. This was one of the many surprises this land had in store for us; two or three years later we had a surprise for it, in the shape of The Beast, our terrifying orange rotavator.

Watering our land at the appointed time on a Friday afternoon was insufficient in those early days. We had no means of saving the precious liquid except in a couple of buckets and a watering can, and we were using these daily, as well as the irrigation system. We began to snatch the odd ten minutes here and there, on other days of the week, turning on the water pipe and quickly running water around our plants. But nothing happens in the countryside without someone noticing, and word soon got about that we were acting outside the rules. The man responsible for the disposition of water caught up with Steve at our fiesta.

"You can't do this," he said, not aggressively but very firmly. "You must stick to Fridays. Other people below you in the valley are not getting all of their water."

We decided to try another tack, and began to slip down to the land after dark, sometimes as late as midnight, when no one else would be working on their *huertos*. We also tried siphoning off a small amount with a very narrow pipe, a constant low-level trickle that could run continuously. This worked when there was plenty of pressure in the main pipe and water hurtling through, but if drought took hold and the water decreased in volume, it failed also. One way or another, we were cheating, but we were desperate to see our first vegetables succeed.

In the main, our plan paid off, with the exception of the peas (too late), the fennel (ignorance) and the parsley (more ignorance). By early August, we were eating our own lettuces and rocket; two weeks later we added long green peppers to the salad; by the month end, our first mature aubergine had arrived along with glistening onions and large, red tomatoes. The magic of a ripe, dark-purple aubergine appearing in the vegetable patch never fails to excite us. This is a special moment. From pale yellow flower-head to rich, plump jewel takes only a few weeks and the joy of eating one's own crisply grilled or fried egg plant is a culinary delight, not easily surpassed.

More latterly, we have added beetroot, garlic, various squashes, raspberries and herbs to our kitchen garden selection. Celeriac is still under review and the parsnips failed utterly but must be attempted again. Potatoes are too much trouble and a cheap option at the market, so unless we decide to go for some very specialist ones, or for sweet potatoes, we probably won't bother with them.

Country living has always had its stories and characters. As a child in the Lake District, I heard many versions, some true, some apocryphal, of the clash between farmers and city folk. One such tale featured our neighbour, Bill, who was out one day, tending to his hedges and dry-stone walls, making sure that there were no gaps for the sheep to get out. A smartly-dressed man stopped in his car and wound down the window (nothing was electric in 1955), "I say, Bill," he called, in an upper-class accent, "how far to Ambleside?"

"How did tha' know me name were Bill?" asked our somewhat

taciturn neighbour.

"Oh, I just guessed," replied the driver cheerfully.

"Well," replied he, "tha' can bloody guess tha' way to Ambleside then."

Further south, towards Kendal, and 20 years later, we had a small neighbourhood shop that also functioned as a garage, tobacconist, and post office. It was run by a strange, pint-sized man called Bert, whose spectacles must have been several millimetres thick and whose wife had left him years before, running off with the dustman. Bert kept his stock in the ground-floor rooms and alongside the stairs of his small cottage and there was little that you could not obtain. Gumboots, rolls of baler twine, gobstopper sweets, loo paper and tins of baked beans were all available, also gun cartridges, penknives and walking maps. But woe betide anyone in a hurry or who chose to be rude. Bert would simply refuse to serve them. "Tha' can bugger off," he would say angrily. "Just bugger off."

Sometimes he got depressed and would hit the bottle. If you went in on one of his bad days, he would remain slumped in the back sitting-room, whisky in hand, and call out, "Help yerself, lass. Leave money on't counter."

Bert's shop and double petrol pump (diesel or petrol, nothing more complicated) has long-since disappeared, the cottage renovated and given a Georgian front-door with a brass knocker. It is probably someone's holiday home now. But we are sure that another Bert exists out here in Spain and we will stumble across him eventually.

* * *

One Sunday afternoon we were invited to the *cortijo* of José and Francesca, tucked away up the valley and only accessible on foot. A *cortijo* is often a fairly small, single-storey building with an acre or two of land, as opposed to a *finca* which is larger, has land and perhaps animals too. José had bought this place for a tiny price from a local shepherd, way back in the 1980s, when it was almost a ruin and surrounded by shale and weeds. Slowly, bit by bit, he re-built the stonework and cleared the land. From other parts of the countryside, he collected tiny clumps of grass, some cuttings and saplings of indigenous trees, then added to them a variety of home-grown seeds. Everything was re-planted.

The one great bonus is the continuous presence of water - a small stream that runs through his land free of charge - so he has been able to divert this to every plant or cluster of vegetation. When he needs a new water channel, he simply gets out the mattock and hacks a narrow pathway through the soil. Now, he has many fully-grown trees including a quince (*membrillo*), a walnut (*nogal*) and a fig (*higuera*), some chestnuts (*castaños*) and two cherry trees (*cerezos*); his tomatoes are globes of wonder, occasionally achieving an individual weight of half a kilo, and all grown from his own, preserved seeds. He has plenty of fallen wood too, so a regular supply of fuel for his hefty wood burner-cum-cooker is easily come by.

He and Francesca have acquired a *khaima*, a genuine Berber or Bedouin tent of luxurious proportions, made from dark sheep's wool and canvas, with thick guy ropes of twisted wool and hemp. It can sleep 8 or 10 people without trouble and is often cooler at night than being in the *cortijo*. We were invited to sit inside it and partake of wine, salted jamón, French paté from Francesca's home village and a delicious tomato and onion salad, dressed with herbs. The usual simple fare that one can eat every day without complaint.

"We have heard about a theft from your house in the village," I said, being keen to know more. Local crime is almost non-existent.

"Yes," replied José, morosely, "someone decided to remove my personal cannabis plant from right outside the kitchen window. Scoundrel. I'll pare his fingernails for him when I catch up with him!"

We were astonished. For one thing, this was a substantial plant, probably a metre high, but tucked away very discreetly on a small terrace and out of view from the nearest street. For another, José was surely far too well-liked in the village for anyone to steal from him, although I thought he might have a dangerous temper if roused. Woe betide the culprit; fingernails might be the smallest items to get damaged if there was a confrontation.

"Who would do such a thing?" we asked.

"Oh, it happens a lot," replied Francesca. "Stealing other people's cannabis is a commonplace, almost expected. I just mind the idea of someone creeping about in the night, near our house. The windows were open, probably the door unlocked too."

"Surely it would be pretty heavy and there would be a high chance of bumping into someone in the village, at any hour," Steve pointed out. "A bit awkward, trying to explain why you're staggering through the square carrying a plant that size, at three in the morning."

"The pot was only plastic and the soil quite dry," she responded, "so it wouldn't have been much trouble. But it must have been someone who has come to the house and seen it, not a chance theft."

We all agreed that this was likely, so that narrowed the options significantly. José said that he had been talking to as many people as he could, to gauge their reactions.

"I think I have a fair idea of who it is," he said, "but it's difficult. He's a man of low intelligence who might have taken it on behalf of someone else, because they told him to. He looked guilty as sin when I asked him about it."

"What will have happened to it?" I asked. "Will it have been taken to sell on or what?"

Not having been a cannabis user for over 35 years, I had no idea about its present day usage and particularly not for living plants.

"By now it will be in someone's drying room," he responded, somewhat grimly, "and then sold on in small quantities in Granada. My winter supply will fetch somebody a lot of money."

I think Steve would have been very happy to help José in his quest to find the culprit, just as he would have been pleased to hunt down a wild boar. Stealing could not be condoned and it meant that we would all need to be more safety-conscious. Locking one's door to pop out for some bread or visit a neighbour, might become essential. However, José thought that he had done enough research for the time being and could manage this on his own. Also, cannabis stealing seemed to be regarded as a form of opportunism that was actually quite funny, given that it was illegal in the first place, so no one was going to take it too seriously.

The High Alpujarras definitely appeal to expatriates with an independent, stubborn streak who are able to think for themselves and don't wish to run with the herd. This does not make them better as human beings or more likeable, but they are often more distinctive, even eccentric. The region has a history of rebelliousness which has not diminished much with time. However, there is space for everyone and it seems to be implicitly recognised that 'neighbours is neighbours, when friends are far away', an old English saying that arose from the winters of great hardship when everyone in a community had to pull together to survive.

We had some intimation from José of what the coming winter would be like in the village, as we sat in his Berber tent that hot August afternoon.

"There's probably only one house occupied in every street," he explained. "People hardly ever see each other, or only by chance, and often they are huddled indoors by the fire, reading or fixing things. I like to go out early in the morning, when it's still very cold, and see the smoke from the chimneys going up into the misty air, but with no sound at all. It's very tranquil, very private. I feel as though the whole place belongs just to me."

I had visions of Steve and José stumbling around in the dawn light, perhaps in the snow, and, like a French farce, missing each other by seconds at the intersections of our little streets. José would be puffing on his first roll-up of the day and huddled into a hooded jacket or long coat; Steve would be more stalwart and still in his flip-flops but wearing a leather waistcoat or a sweatshirt as a concession to the temperature. I had no doubt that both Francesca and I would still be in our respective beds, waiting for the sun to provide extra warmth.

My seductive bedtime outfit in mid-winter, before we had any heating, consisted of merino wool base layers, a winceyette nightgown, socks, fingerless mittens, and a Peruvian bobble hat with earflaps. This, plus two hot-water bottles, two duvets, and Steve's body warmth, just about managed to sustain me for the first hour or two, then I started throwing off the layers. Unfortunately, at about 4a.m., I would cool off again and have to huddle closer to Steve or force myself to wake up enough to pile the clothes back on. A tricky arrangement.

The other challenge is how, before breakfast, to strip right down, have a wash, get some underwear on and then base layers again, without losing too much heat. As a child on our Lakeland farm, I had this same problem and the only solution was to drag one's clothes under the blankets and get dressed there, half-asleep. Now, fifty years later, I am doing almost the same thing.

José expanded on his theme. "You have to have an occupation to survive the winter," he said. "Working on the land helps, but most people need to be painting pictures or throwing pots or knitting sweaters. I make leather items like belts and bags that I can sell in the summer markets."

"I want to repair the stone walls," I said. "It's good for keeping you warm and active, and there's no shortage of material out here. We have a lot of hill-walking to do as well."

I didn't mention writing and proofreading as a further occupation. Or horse-riding. Or visiting hospitals.

Steve was happy to contemplate whole days spent down on the land, but I wondered if he might not turn his hand to carpentry or motorcycle maintenance. Something practical and useful. Certainly our own motorbikes would keep him occupied, but there wasn't a repair shop for 40 kilometres so I reckoned he could help other people too. In Chapter 11, he tells his side of this story, the prequel to Spain, about how he became a 'born-again' biker, bought four in the space of one year and lost his heart to a Moto Guzzi.

* * *

One day in early September, we were lucky enough to be present for a village wedding. Not only was it to be held in our church, but both the bride and the groom were born here and are second cousins. This was the first truly local marriage for over twenty-five years and it meant that almost the whole population, who either arrived for the big weekend or were already living here, was related. Festivities started slowly on the Wednesday, with a few people trickling in, dragging suitcases and greeting one another affectionately. All day Thursday the numbers grew, shutters banged open on houses that had been closed for years and the bar ran from 8a.m. through to the early hours of Friday, then soon opened up again for alcoholic 'elevenses.'

By great good luck on that first evening, as we all milled about in the streets, an Eastern European women's choir came along to sing an impromptu concert in our little plaza, which quite naturally evolved into a celebratory pre-nuptial event. They were giving a big concert in a nearby town the following evening, but I had heard that they needed somewhere to practice the night before.

"Why don't you come to Panjuila?" I asked their organiser. "We have a lot of people in the village for a wedding, who would enjoy hearing them and perhaps they could sing something extra for Montserrat and Antonio?"

So there we were, in the plaza as dusk fell, drinks in hand, listening to some delightful harmony singing, unaccompanied but utterly musical. The women were completely absorbed in the sounds they were making and had obviously sung together many times. There were no costumes or matching blouses, just happy people making good music. As a finale, the choir circled the happy couple, who had been lured out of their house, and sang them a Hungarian love song, fluttering their hands in the air to summon up the spirits of harmony and wedded bliss. The youngsters stood in the middle, guiltily hiding their cigarettes behind their backs, not understanding a word but getting the general meaning. As usual, dogs ran in and out of the square, the men continued to play cards in the bar and the occasional stranger passed, mystified, through this hectic little throng, but it was a unique moment.

"What does it mean, what are they saying?" asked Trini, in a whisper, obviously thinking it was an English song.

"I have no idea," I responded, "I don't speak Hungarian!"

More folk arrived the following day, and in the early evening we could hear much female chattering coming from a street nearby (do men 'chat' in quite the same way, I wonder?). Going out to investigate, we came upon a noisy group of women, with the bride, all catching up on each other's lives. The *charla* moved on into the square, which quickly filled up with our regular neighbours as well as the in-laws, more cousins, friends from Madrid, youngsters and oldies. José, the bridegroom Antonio and several other men strode in, having gone to trim the grasses around the church and generally tidy things up. They carried hooks, loppers and rakes. More hurrahs and holas followed as people recognised each other.

Montserrat moved gracefully from group to group, dressed without any fuss in jeans and a striped top, her hair tied back casually. Clearly this was an informal, combined hen and stag night, with all generations involved. Mixed in with it was the usual Spanish chaos - a dumper truck passed through carrying large stones, so everyone had to leap out of the way, sweeping up chairs and children; Roque arrived on his motorbike, without a helmet, loaded up with a 40kg bag of peat, a box of groceries, and several hoops of plastic tubing; a horseman trotted by, waving but not stopping.

Trini brought me some fresh bay leaf branches for drying and putting in our winter stews. I teased her about her husband, Juan, "When we talk to him about his plants or his garden, he smiles, but the rest of the time he is very serious."

"Si," she responded buoyantly, "*es un hombre muy serioso.*"

In fact, we felt that he was an admirable man, not rushing into friendships or familiarity, but with his priorities in the right balance and well able to take a joke. While the women's choir were singing, I went into the bar and told him and his three fellow card players that four male voices were needed immediately. A visible shudder ran through them and all denied being able to sing, but I think Juan got the picture straight away, merely grimacing, then smiling, but saying nothing.

Saturday dawned, a peerless Alpujarran morning of clear skies, light breezes and birdsong. We had breakfast outside on our private terrace, then Steve went to check on village activities whilst I reviewed my wardrobe options. He came back to report that someone was down in the square, hosing it clean; the women were busy in the church, decorating the pews and altar with yellow roses and white carnations; the chauffeured black BMW was being similarly decorated, ready to take the happy couple off to the reception later on. By 10a.m., the final details were being completed - I checked that all the geraniums and pelargoniums on the balcony were dead-headed and looking their best, and took out a simple, floral dress from the wardrobe, together with a pair of really elegant, high-heeled Italian sandals and my grandmother's pearl necklace.

We knew that Montse would pass our house on her way to the church and I began to wonder about some music for her. Steve would probably have suggested Pink Floyd or Led Zeppelin, but I had other ideas. "Let's move the music centre to the balcony," I suggested. "I have some lovely Handel that would be ideal for this."

We put the CD player down behind the flowers and faced the speakers out onto the street, and after a second cup of coffee, took ourselves to the square and watched as people began to assemble. Luis and his wife Marie arrived from Granada with their sons, wives and grandchildren and a quantity of bags, bursting with fruit and vegetables. Luis presented us with a huge, pink-hued tomato from his garden - a love tomato he joked, nudging Steve - and insisted on buying us a beer. Various young men, looking like mafiosi in their smartly-cut suits and dark glasses, wandered in with girlfriends dressed in very short skirts and lots of eye make-up. The older women, usually seen in pinafores or apron-dresses, appeared in smart outfits of chiffon or silk, also with high-heels and lipstick. A temporary drinks bar was being put up beside the fountain to ease the pressure on the little bar-room we used normally. Claudia and Rihanna ran excitedly around, making sure that that they were not missing out on anything.

"Have you got a dress to wear for the wedding?" I asked Claudia.

"Maybe, I don't know," she shrugged. It was not on her list of priorities at the age of five.

Suddenly there was commotion outside the bride's house and we could hear the church bell pealing. Time to get to battle stations. Steve collected up his spare video camera and positioned himself at the street corner, while I checked the CD player for volume. He could give me a signal and the sound of *Let the Bright Seraphim* should ring out just as Montse and her entourage came into view.

I could hear calls of admiration for her - "*Qué guapa! Qué bonita!*" and then there she was, all white lace and ruffles, with a bouquet of dark red roses, accompanied by her father, dapper in his suit and matching dark red tie. A true flamenco bride, she wore the strapless, tiered dress with slim elegance, her long, dark hair piled up and caught by a diamanté tiara at the back, which also held her mantilla-style veil in place. Two little girls preceded her, in white frocks decorated with dark pink roundels, carrying small silk cushions with tassels.

As she passed beneath our balcony she looked up and waved, appreciating the musical accompaniment to her procession. Most of the village followed on, us included. The handrail up to the white church had been festooned with dark green ivy and beyond it we could see the valley stretching away into a misty blue haze. A few tourists lingered, having stumbled unawares on a very special occasion.

As we reached the church doors, I saw six or seven women slip in ahead of us, dressed in either red or yellow flamenco costumes. Also, a man carrying a guitar case. What part would they play, I wondered? Once again, different cultures and beliefs evidenced themselves. The service began with a dramatic and traditional canto from these same musicians, positioned up on the mezzanine floor above our heads. Antonio and his best man stood waiting, and listening, at the altar, as Montse and her father trod down the aisle, watched by all eyes. The priest waited patiently for his turn, standing in front of the Madonna and Child, the same *Virgen* who had processed through the streets such a short time before.

Reluctantly it seemed, the 'artistes' yielded to the formalities of a Catholic wedding and fell silent. In a simple ceremony, in Spanish that even we could understand, the young couple sitting on their white satin stools were blessed, married and received the sacrament. Vows and gold rings, placed on the little cushions, were exchanged, prayers were interspersed by more flamenco singing and at the conclusion everyone shook hands on a deal well done, shouting "*Olé, olé!*"

Slowly people filed outside, but we were not done yet. The musicians came down from the mezzanine floor and clustered in the entrance, breaking into song once again, calling "*Quiereme, quiereme*" (love me, want me) as a reminder to the bride and groom of their promises of fidelity. The guitar strings thrummed, the castanets clicked and the brightly-coloured skirts twirled. Finally, as Montse and Tonio emerged, rice and dark red flower petals were scattered over their heads and on the ground. Many kisses were exchanged, many hands clapped and a sense of real joy pervaded the little area outside the church.

There was more to come, an impromptu arrangement that took everyone by surprise. As the pair made their way slowly down to the village street we could see a dark-brown donkey waiting patiently, draped with an embroidered rug and saddle. The owner, Chico, held its bridle and looked suitably attired in straw hat, cotton dungarees and a casual shirt. The bride was carefully lifted into place, her dress spread over the donkey's hindquarters, the bridegroom took his place alongside and off they sauntered to the main square. What could top that?

More flamenco of course! As we reached the plaza, the singers broke into song again whilst the mother and father of the bride performed a slow fandango. Then a single dancer treated us to a few moments of pure Spain, all red and black silk as she flashed and twirled, arms raised above her head, fingers twining and clicking. She was followed by Montse, who demonstrated that she too knew how to dance flamenco. Picking up the hem of her wedding dress and showing off her strapped shoes, she too paced, whirled, flaunted and beguiled us with her beauty.

"We are so lucky," I whispered to Trini, standing next to me, "to be here on this day, at this moment. *Qué suerte.*"

She nodded, "My husband and I were married here thirty years ago," she said. "It feels like yesterday."

Someone touched me on the arm. It was our neighbour, Sebastián. He indicated that I should follow and we made our way to the bar where he bought drinks for several of us, including Steve, who was still filming as much as he could of this event. My mind went back to the previous fiesta and Juanita, who had demanded so much money from us. I think this neighbour was trying to make amends for that in the best way he knew, but none of it mattered now. We were a community, brought together by a very unique event and as a community we would go forward together.

After an hour or so, the bridal party prepared to leave for a formal reception and lunch at a nearby hotel. I darted back to the house and progressed Handel's music to the *Arrival of the Queen of Sheba*. I could see departing guests being photographed beneath our flower-filled balcony and as the happy couple appeared I pressed the 'play' button. The fanfare sounded, the bride waved and smiled once more, and stopped to pose with her husband for photographs beneath the hanging baskets of geraniums and fuchsias. Manolo, her uncle from Granada, who loves classical music, beamed with delight. It was a splendid moment. Then the procession passed on and I went back inside to kick off my shoes and have a glass of water.

We had a few hours' respite while the reception took place, then the evening's celebrations began. These did not live up to the daylight successes - the local lads with responsibility for the music system arrived in a tangle of cables, speakers and CDs and took hours to sort it all out. The Andalucíans are immaculately tidy in their *huertos* and gardens, but modern conveniences such as electricity, motor engines and computers often bemuse them. When these boys finally gave us music it was of poor quality and didn't encourage much dancing. The sun had gone and soon it began to get chilly, so the older ladies had to fetch shawls and cardigans; the bride had almost lost her voice after too much chat and speeches, and I noticed that Sebastián looked drawn and tired.

Churros and hot chocolate made a welcome appearance about midnight, but with them came a number of uninvited guests and a different kind of music. Now, we had an amateur DJ in army fatigues and waist chains, his much-tattooed mates stomping about and a loud, persistent techno-sound. Skinny women with henna-ed hair, layered skirts, Doc Marten boots and long cardigans drifted past. The 21st century had arrived.

It felt as though our village was merely providing a venue for this New Age group to congregate, in complete ignorance of the fairy-tale wedding that had preceded it. The reasons why we were there were lost and the sense of a unique celebration was dispelled. Many of us headed for our beds. We made sure the house was securely locked and I shut out as much of the din as I could. Around about three in the morning someone got so fed up that they must have sneaked up to the electricity supply and pulled the plug. All sound ceased. The village slept at last.

Throughout these celebrations, just as he had done for the fiesta, Steve wandered around with his two small cameras, photographing and filming the oblivious crowd: children and the dogs; the local men so smart in their well-pressed shirts and straw hats; some private moments of joy and all the other minutiae of the day. Slowly, he was building up his own library of short videos, set to music of his choosing. Usually he gave a copy to someone else to enjoy, and in this instance, of course, it was to Montserrat and Antonio. They came round with some friends and were overjoyed to be given two small cameos, one that covered the preparations for the wedding and the visit by the choir, with the soundtrack of *It's Raining Men* by The Weather Girls, and another one that focussed on their big day, set to the romantic singing of *I Love You* by Simon and Garfunkel. When they had seen them, all agreed that one could pay a lot of money to a professional and not get such an intimate and personal record of the weekend. Another couple who came with them signed Steve up for their own wedding, scheduled for two years hence. Our lives were expanding. Not only could he become the village baker and motorbike mechanic, here was an opportunity to be its visual historian as well.

Interestingly, after the wedding, all our neighbours began to treat us as part of the village family in a noticeable way. The men looked up from their card game the next time Steve went in the bar, and asked him about himself, was he from Scotland? What had he done for a living? How were the vegetables coming on? The women were similarly forthcoming to me, with recipes for preserving tomatoes and questions about my children. Perhaps they had realised that we were a permanent fixture and wanted to contribute to the life of the village, and that we were not there to make use of their piece of paradise in a selfish way. Or maybe they had got used to our faces and were happy to have us around. Even Juanita and her husband became more open and, much later on, were the first to rally round when my health began to deteriorate. Whatever the reason, we were delighted, and with our language skills improving, we felt that this was a state of affairs that could only get better.

* * *

Soon after, we made a 5 day motorcycle visit to the east coast, stopping with friends in Javea, near Valencia, and then travelling up as far as Barcelona to see Steve's brother and his wife, who were celebrating their 20th wedding anniversary with a short holiday.

It was a bit of a culture shock to go from our little hill enclave to the hotspots and highlife of such large and busy places. Javea is a biggish fishing port and holiday resort, with many British expatriates living there, and though it's not a high-rise holiday city like Benidorm, it is well-endowed with smart villas, expensive restaurants and chic dress shops. Barcelona is, of course, Spain's second largest city and has a glamour and style all of its own. It is the capital of Catalunya, which regards itself as an independent region with its own language; to the Catalans, Madrid is an irritating irrelevance.

The highlight of our visit, travelling on our Honda VFR 800i, was an evening spent in the historic seaside town of Altafulla, south of Barcelona, which happened to coincide with their Fiesta de Diabolos. There are many extraordinary fiestas in this part of Spain, involving giant-sized dolls and insects, but this was our first 'devil' event.

One moment we were sitting chatting with our friends Heather and Dominic in their garden, and the next minute we were alerted by a loud drum roll coming from the town centre.

"We'd better get out there and see what's going on," said Heather, sweeping up their daughter Anabel, aged 6 and grabbing her shoulder bag.

We followed suit and walked swiftly to the central plaza, a stone-built rectangle of honey-coloured arches, steps, flagstones and mediaeval administrative buildings. In one corner is the impressive stone sculpture of the Tower of the Acrobats carved by a famous son of the town, Martí Royo (1949-1997). The routes leading away from the plaza are a rabbit warren of jasmine and ivy-shrouded steps, tunnels, cobbled streets and stone doorways. Up above is the old church, and the castellated walls of a monastery.

Tonight, a host of people were gathering, all flowing into the square, including many adolescents with scarves tied round their faces and caps on their heads. Was this some type of costume, we wondered? Then we noticed a group of youngish men and women dressed in baggy, brown canvas trousers and capes, with hooded caps topped by red horns. They wore thick gloves and trainers and were sharing out quantities of plainly-wrapped fireworks. One or two of them had more elaborate, monk-like robes and carried long poles with candelabras and rounded wheels of fireworks stuck on the ends. The loud and impressive drumming came from a group of eight or ten people in black T-shirts and jeans, each with his or her own set of drums hanging from straps on their shoulders, that they were hitting with solid wooden drumsticks. It sounded like a call to arms, or to a beheading. What were we there to witness?

As these mysterious 'devils' formed a group and the drums banged harder, the more knowledgeable members of the crowd began to retreat up the side-streets and steps. They knew what was to come. We hesitated, curious, and delayed too long. A white flare of sparkling flame and a whoosh of rockets set the whole thing in motion. The devils ran at us with determination and with fire, hot sparks tingling on our bare arms and legs. Everyone shrieked and ran away, hiding behind pillars or each other. Then a somewhat chaotic procession formed, led by the devils and their cowled masters, followed by the drummers and then the crowd of spectators. We scoured the town, clearing all before us. Individual devils would run full pelt up a narrow, ascending street, rockets firing, scattering every living thing in front of them, with not a cat, dog, human or any other creature spared. From time to time we entered a square, the crowd were emboldened and clustered closer, only to be scattered again by wickedly-laughing demons.

At last the town was cleansed and we returned to the main square, but we were not done yet. Larger fireworks, the size of cake tins and encased in coloured paper were set down on the flagstones. The great candelabras were replenished, new sparklers lit, the drumming intensified. The youngsters gathered in small groups, each group assigned its own fiendish leader. What followed was a mad, dervish-like frenzy of rushing feet and crouching bodies as each group went swooping around the square, trailing light and flame, pursued by hot sparks. Sometimes an individual boy would be harassed all the way across the plaza, sometimes a group would turn back on the crowd and we would press ourselves into the stonework in mock terror, mingled with a very real and primitive fear.

Finally, the whole host of children and devils formed a spiral of chasing feet, swirling first clockwise, then anti-clockwise, faster and faster as the drumbeats gathered pace. We were all part of some pagan, fiendish celebration worthy of Dante himself. The crescendo reached its peak and, with a final shouting and shrieking, a mighty flourish of sound and a cacophony of rocket fire, the event was over. Cheers and clapping echoed around the plaza. We had witnessed a memorable and extraordinary occasion. We were exhausted.

Chapter 8

Medical Matters

Out of our village on the western side and down a meandering footpath, we have a small parcel of land with two outstanding features: an enormous yet ageing sweet-chestnut tree, still in full production, and nearby, its deceased partner, with just a few live shoots at the base. A third one had been unilaterally felled by a neighbour about 6 years previously, just as Steve took ownership. Cutting down live chestnut trees is illegal here, as they form a significant part of the historic natural park and its indigenous vegetation, but it is difficult to find anyone who will actually take action through the courts. Besides, one cannot glue a tree back together again. Ninette, who objected to having a decaying giant between her bedroom window and an exquisite view of the valley, had simply picked up a chainsaw (or arranged for someone else to pick one up), given a Gallic shrug and chopped it down. We adopted the English stiff upper lip, made sure she knew that we knew it was her, but let it pass. What cowards. Our Spanish friends might have done quite a lot of shouting.

Each time that we came out from the UK, we went down to this half-acre and mooched around beneath the remaining two trees, pondering on their usefulness. Often the wild boar had circled too, leaving great gouges in the soil and churning up the decaying chestnuts.

119

These fruit were rather small and it did occur to us that some healthy pruning might give us a better crop. Chestnut flour is a local speciality and my favourite chocolate cake would be a failure without the unique taste and texture of the mashed nuts.

Both trees were over 15 metres (50 feet) high and presented us with significant challenges. The living tree needed its top canopy trimmed and some big lower branches taken out. The dead one needed to be felled to ground level, somehow missing the village electricity supply, Ninette's swimming pool (did we care?), a wild cherry tree and, naturally, any puny humans who happened to be underneath. The land is only accessible on foot and too far from the road to use any kind of wheeled machinery. On one side, between us and Ninette, is a narrow *barranco*, usually without water but full of huge boulders and smooth-sided gulleys, and on the other a public right-of-way down to the next village.

"How on earth are we going to do this?" I asked Steve one sunny October morning, as we both stood looking upwards, getting cricks in our necks.

The dead tree, on the edge of the *barranco*, was the really tricky customer. It leant slightly uphill towards Ninette's swimming pool and had one sinuous, but hefty branch elegantly disposed over the top of the electricity cable. The base of the tree had some reasonably strong off-shoots, but after that the trunk became shiny and smooth with no toe-holds, branches or other useful points of contact. There were several short and broken-off stumps at a higher level that needed to be avoided in case they were rotten, and the drop was straight down onto bare rock and brambles almost all the way round.

"With a lot of looking at and thinking about," he responded, "and not too much action just yet." I knew then that carpentry (measure twice, cut once) would suit him perfectly. Four years and a horse stable later, I have been proved correct.

In fact, part of his 'looking at' consisted in buying some 20cm (6 inch) nails, gathering up lengths of rope and a climbing harness from his days as a roadie, and making an initial assault on the monster. Well, on the first 12 metres at any rate. With me acting as belay down below, he climbed carefully up the first few metres, then started banging in the nails to give himself footholds on the smooth trunk. Climbing vertical surfaces without a top rope, at the age of 60, is not as exciting as doing it at 15 or 16, but he only discovered this at the 6 metre stage and by then it was too late. He had to get to the main branches and secure himself. I could hardly bear to watch.

What he discovered once he got to the natural v-shaped safety of some major branches, was that the electricity cable was definitely in the way and that the problem did not improve with elevation. There were, in fact, two branches that would have to be removed before the main tree was felled.

"Coming down!" he shouted.

Almost as soon as he reached the ground and we began to investigate other options, we managed to disturb a wasps' nest in a piece of fallen timber. A swarm of angry yellow and black creatures emerged from the bark and made straight for us. Spanish wasps are definitely more potent than English ones. We both got stung and mine resulted in a visit to the local Centro de Urgencias a few hours later with a hand that looked like a baseball glove. Over time, my reaction to these wasp stings has got worse, the last one resulting in minor anaphylactic shock. Time for an Epipen, no doubt.

Further research on the chestnut trees was postponed, although we had no shortage of offers to help us achieve our goal. Emilio had three chainsaws of different sizes that he could lend us, José came over from his *cortijo* and give his opinion, Giotti could bring an axe, some wedges, and simply lop it down. I decided that this was going to be men's work and that when they were all assembled, keen as small boys on an apple-stealing expedition, I would quietly slip away. As it turned out, slipping away proved to be easier than expected, at least for a while.

* * *

Although we had established our toehold in Paradise and everything was proceeding nicely, we hit something of a wall at the end of that first summer. I was notified by the National Health Service in England that my bi-annual, routine breast scan had revealed 'an inconsistency' and that I should attend my local hospital for a second screening. Given that we were still technically resident in the UK, this was only a logistical matter, and I flew back at a convenient date, whilst the tree felling was still under discussion. I had had a fibrous area in my right breast for many years and felt confident that, finally, this had been picked up by a more sophisticated type of scanner and would not represent a problem.

I was wrong. Like so many women before me, my scan evolved into a consultant appointment, which was extended into the taking of a biopsy and some lymphatic node samples. Just before I returned to Spain, I was summoned to the hospital again.

A male doctor from the cancer team, accompanied by the breast cancer nurse, was friendly enough but did not smile. "Your results are not good," he said firmly. "You have a tumour of about 4cm that is malignant. The node samples are inconclusive, but we think you will need a mastectomy of your right breast."

I have always tended to respond positively to unpleasant events or bad news. That does not mean that I have not understood the implications, but just as one might throw up a hand to ward off a blow, it is my way of protecting myself from immediate attack.

"My partner and I have talked about such an eventuality, as one does," I said, "and if one breast is coming off, then so is the other one. I dislike asymmetry, so just turn me into a boy."

I think they were taken aback by such a calm yet confrontational style and I don't blame them. I had jumped straight to a very drastic solution, into the fast lane, which is not the direction that clinicians like to take. Theirs is a process of elimination, starting with the obvious and only proceeding to a more complex diagnosis or solution when they are sure that there is no alternative. Generally, this is the best method, but it can also be the slowest.

Breast surgery nowadays is quite sophisticated, especially with so much cosmetic work being done, and much effort is made to keep women feeling feminine, self-confident and attractive. The breast cancer nurses are trained to offer tailored support and advice on 'life after cancer' although they seem to assume that losing a breast always results in a serious identity crisis. I quickly gleaned that most women choose, or are encouraged, to have reconstructions or implants, using their own skin whenever possible. Prostheses (fake breasts or fillers) are commonly recommended.

I did not think that I wanted the fuss and bother of either. Reconstructive surgery would take up more time and weaken my back muscles; I hated the idea of artificial material being inserted into my body or under my skin; except for the loss of my nipples, I thought I would manage better with a flat chest or, for special occasions, a pair of modest 'falsies'. Looking online at the range of 'breast enhancers' and 'chicken fillets' may not be inspiring, but it is certainly enlightening.

Cancer might as well be called the 'unknown destination' or the 'invisible horizon'. Once you start on this path, you have no idea where you will end up and over what timescale. The clinicians don't know either. Although nowadays they have some well-researched scientific understanding of this deadly disease, they continue to move in a medical fog, searching for clues, familiar markers and indicators, when in fact each person is unique and each human body follows a different direction. Much depends on genetic disposition, early detection, pinpointed treatment and, at some point, natural physiological temperament. That first diagnosis may be seen as a death sentence or just another incident in life. For some people, the cancer is too far advanced to be operable or even treatable; the dice is already thrown. The patient can never get enough information, although the ostrich approach is very tempting.

A week later and a second discussion with the surgeon herself took me back into the middle lane of my personal highway. She would try what is called a 'wide local excision' which would remove the tumour but leave most of the breast and the nipple. Some nodes would also be removed to see if there was a risk of the cancer having spread elsewhere in my body.

I liked this woman a lot. She did not look at a screen or her paperwork but actually felt the tumour and gauged its density, as well as feeling with her fingertips for the nodes in my armpit. Once you have had the odd operation or given birth, and certainly having gone through cervical smear tests and breast scans, you lose most inhibitions about your body. It did not bother me at all to sit there, stripped to the waist, while she considered the problem. Trust is an important feature of all medical interactions and I knew that I could rely on her good judgement and, as was later proven, her careful handiwork.

Unfortunately I did not consider the fact that a surgeon will always veer towards a surgical solution, when there might be a medical treatment available instead. I didn't see an oncologist and no one suggested any preliminary therapy; perhaps the tumour was too large by then, anyway.

When I went for my first operation I had a sense of optimism. I felt physically well and thought that my body would be capable of rejecting any invasive changes to the cells. What had occurred was just a bit of bad luck. They would cut out the tumour, give me some radiotherapy perhaps and then I would have the all clear to go back to Spain.

As it turned out, I was too hopeful. There are always delays built into the British health system, probably all such systems, and it was not until

10 days after my operation that I went to see the consultant again. Bandaged, and with a very tender right armpit, I found that some other physician had been delegated to give me the next set of bad news, which he handled very quickly.

"We have removed the tumour as well as 10 nodes from under your armpit. Of these, 8 tested negative for cancer," he said, not looking me in the eye. "These lymphatic nodes circulate cancer-bearing cells round the body, so we have more work to do."

The nurse corrected him, "13 out of 18 were negative," she said, pointing at the paperwork.

I should have asked to see the papers myself, but the numbers were less significant than the word 'negative'. While they removed some stitches (using a very sharp little blade which made my poor, wounded breast tremble), I contemplated the potential next steps. These were confirmed by my consultant when she arrived on the scene.

"It's a shame, but we will have to proceed to a mastectomy. We will also do a CT scan to see if the cancer has spread elsewhere."

"I still want both breasts removed," I said. "My life is too busy and too energetic to be limited by prostheses and imbalance. It's a shame because you've done such a good job so far and it's all wasted."

She did not seem too bothered by this and we fixed up some dates for the scan and the surgery. The train was moving on, with me aboard, but I could not see the station or the platform it would take me to.

I went back to Spain for a short time, then together Steve and I caught another flight back to the UK. Autumn was moving into winter, the house in Suffolk was in the process of being sold and contained a few sticks of furniture, nothing more. We bought an old black-and-white TV set and an inflatable mattress and camped out as best we could. The only convenience was that Steve also had a medical reason to be there. Although the detached retina had repaired nicely, he needed a check-up and possibly a cataract operation.

By total mischance we were attending different hospitals, 25 miles apart, but the appointments always seemed to be on the same day. Our travelling arrangements were interesting to say the least. Mostly Steve went by bus whilst luckily for me, the local Community Drivers service was available, so for my next few trips, at a cost of about £10 a time, I was chauffeured back and forth by a terrific ex-helicopter pilot named Henry, who had recently been employed flying personnel and equipment in and out of the Kandahar region.

An heroic, yet modest man, tall and rubicund, always dressed in corduroy trousers, he had been retired (involuntarily) due to his age and was having some interesting experiences whilst job hunting. On one occasion he applied to be a van driver with a local delivery company. He reached the interview stage.

"Have you had any multi-drop experience?" asked the manager.

"Not really," replied Henry, thinking that it might be presumptuous to say 'only with helicopters.'

What a pity he kept quiet, as he didn't get the job. In reality, he belonged in *Country Life*, out hunting and shooting somewhere, not rushing around the country in a white van. His wife, wearing a sensible, pleated navy skirt and Guernsey sweater, taught adult literacy and numeracy in the local prison. Two people doing their bit for those less fortunate than themselves, who sounded posh, but who had kind hearts and a host of black Labradors.

Eventually, a date was fixed for my double mastectomy - on my birthday as it happened. Was this to be a celebratory event, I wondered, or an indication of the future, losing non-essential parts of myself as the years went by?

Winter had come early and it was snowing hard that morning, but Henry was full of confidence, "Don't you worry m'dear," he announced, his Barbour jacket and deerstalker hat keeping off the worst of the white stuff. "We'll soon have you there."

He had run the engine of his old Peugeot Estate to warm up the car for me, and as we negotiated our way over the dozen miles to the hospital, we eased our way past snow-drifts, stationary buses and even a struggling tractor. This was all routine stuff for an old-school helicopter pilot. When we got to the hospital entrance, I took my little suitcase and waved him goodbye. I felt somewhat apprehensive as I took the lift to the 3rd floor.

The hospital put me into a private room at first. All other ward beds were taken. At first, I was quite pleased - my own bathroom, a TV, peace and quiet. After 15 minutes I felt less sure. I could hear the distant clatter of trolleys and doors, the sound of voices in the corridor, a buzz of activity. I felt very alone and thought that almost any kind of company would do. When a nurse appeared, I was delighted to hear her say, "We're putting you in Ward C, come with me."

This was a ward with 8 women-only beds and mine was at the far end, next to the window. Wonderful. I could see the snow falling softly outside, whilst we were cosily ensconced in the type of insulating warmth that only hospitals can provide. A crumpled tissue lay under the bed, the covers were in a heap, presumably from the previous incumbent, but this was better than the pristine isolation of a private room.

My neighbours were in for various operations - hysterectomy, eye surgery, bowel cancer, and breast reconstruction. One lady had already had two operations for reconstruction and both had resulted in serious infection.

"I can't stand another anaesthetic," she groaned. "If this fails I shall put up with what I've got, it can't be any worse."

I got changed into a nightgown and awaited the final process of being marked up by the surgeon with indelible ink, having my blood pressure checked yet again and a brief conversation with the anaesthetist.

"I'm always sick after a general anaesthetic," I told him, "always."

"We'll try to avoid that," he smiled. "You haven't eaten or drunk anything since last night, have you?"

"Not a thing," I assured him, truthfully.

Of course, I was sick, but only bile and maybe morphine. By the time I re-surfaced, the whole thing was done and all I wanted to do was go on sleeping. Time passed in a haze. I felt no pain, but did not care to look downwards. A drip was attached to each breast area, thin plastic tubes leading to half-litre bottles which lay on the sheets at either side. I didn't want to look at them either. Steve appeared, gave me a kiss and disappeared again. Nurses passed and re-passed, night came and went.

In the morning, I felt full of beans and ready for my breakfast. The surgeon appeared, with acolytes. "How are you?" she asked. "Can we have a look?"

"I feel fine," I said. Sitting up in bed, I lifted my gown to show them the wounds and minimal bandaging. I felt no shame; the morphine was still in my system, clearly.

"You can go home later today," she said. "You'll do better there."

I knew the score. These days no hospital wants a bed occupied for any longer than necessary. The conveyor belt brings in many, many people and as soon as you are dealt with, it's time to push you gently off, back into the real world. It seems incredible that only 20 years ago I might have had to stay for 10 or 12 days. Nowadays, unless there are complications, you are discharged within 36 hours. I didn't dare tell her of the primitive conditions that applied to 'home' just then.

At the appointed hour, with some difficulty, I got myself dressed, requested hospital transport home and was installed on the sofa again by tea-time, armed with boxes of painkillers. Psychologically, one is no longer a vulnerable patient and the healing process has started, in the mind and consequently in the body. Of course it would take weeks for the twin semi-circles of my wounds to close up fully, and still longer for internal bruising, fluids and nerve endings to recover, but the deed was done and I felt able to rebuild my suspended life. As it turned out, this was not the end of the matter at all, but I did not know it at the time.

A couple of weeks later, the hospital asked me back for my CT scan. This was in itself no big affair. Exquisitely attired in boots, knickers, and hospital gown, still sporting bandages and scars, I sipped on an orange-flavoured drink, was injected with an intravenous iodine dye and passed several times under the white plastic dome that took the images. A remote American voice told me first to 'hold my breath' and then to 'breathe.' It was all over in a few minutes. I sneezed a couple of times, which gave the clinician a moment's anxiety, as he said it sometimes presaged an adverse reaction, but I seemed to be fine and soon left the building. My problems started about 4 hours later.

Sitting reading in a big leather armchair, I began to heat up and felt itchy under my chin and on my right side where I had had the lumpectomy. I could see that my tummy was turning pink and slightly swollen. By the time we reached the house of our friends Pennie and Charles for supper, I was looking decidedly sunburnt and feeling quite warm. This did not prevent me from sipping some wine and eating Charles' delicious risotto and Pennie's excellent apple crumble.

Fatal. My insides soon began to protest and as we moved out of the dining room to have coffee, I only just made it to the loo. Kneeling on someone else's bathroom floor with your head in their toilet belongs to one's misspent youth, not retirement. Clumsily, I staggered back to the sitting room.

"I'm so sorry," I mumbled, "I must lie down," and slumped onto the sofa.

Lying there, alternating between shivering and sweating, I listened to the conversations in the room, but I really wasn't able to concentrate. I had to make yet another rush for the loo half-an-hour later. Despite protestations and an offer of the guestroom upstairs, we headed off home and, although we should have called a doctor immediately, I just went straight to bed and hoped to sleep it off.

The next day saw a small improvement but I spent the day lying on the sofa and feeling fragile. Even the following day I was still red and swollen, especially around my eyes and lips.

"My little pink blowfish," Steve joyfully announced.

It seemed that one of us still had a sense of humour, but I was not much amused. Thanks to the internet, I discovered that this was a fairly rare allergic reaction to intravenous iodine. Why had no one told me of this possibility before I left the hospital? Was there no preliminary testing that could have been done? Steve insisted that I went to our local GP, who took the matter very seriously and prescribed some steroid cream and an emollient. Little did I know that a leaflet, explaining possible side-effects, had been sent to me some days earlier and forwarded by the Post Office to Spain.

Despite this complication, we needed to know the outcome of the scan. We battled to the hospital in the teeth of an icy north-easterly wind and waited patiently as the consultant finished an administrative meeting and got back to the breast cancer clinic. As soon as we went into her little room she put our minds at rest.

"The CT scan was clear," was her forthright statement.

For a tiny moment it didn't sink in, then I realised what this meant. The cancer had been limited to my right breast and had not strayed elsewhere. This was good, good news. I had passed a few sleepless nights, hot and prickly, wondering how I might respond to being told I had other affected organs and perhaps only a few months to live, but now I had been handed a reprieve. My imminent demise was postponed and, *ojala* (God willing), I could expect some years yet. There was no saying that cancer would not return one day, but for now the horizon gleamed with sunlight.

"That's fantastic," I squeaked, "thank you so much."

Although I had tried not to be pessimistic, I had wondered, in those long midnight stretches, who would be worse off if I died within a short time frame, Steve or myself. What a ludicrous statement that seems, but I knew that were our situations to be reversed, I would be so deeply bereft that I would probably turn my face to the wall and give up on the world.

Before we returned to Spain, Steve had his cataract surgery done and we finalised the sale of his Suffolk home. We had been lucky to have a base camp during this extended stay, especially as all the time that we were there, we were proceeding towards an exchange of contracts and legal completion, which, once concluded, would mean that we would be homeless.

It was fortunate that we had some heating as it was so wintry, and a functioning kitchen, but goodness knows what the district nurses made of our Spartan surroundings when they came to change my bandages and check the drips. We had a respectable bathroom and were able to keep ourselves clean, but they must have wondered what was going on. Perhaps they just thought we were poor, starving pensioners with barely a spoon and fork between us. Perhaps that was a more than familiar setting to them.

Other callers included the house buyer, a rather eccentric spinster who dropped in at all hours; her builder, who made grimacing faces behind her back as she led him around and explained some of her novel renovation ideas; two local authority Conservation Officers whom she had called in to examine the chimney breast (it was a Grade II listed building after all); and someone to measure up for curtains. I just lay on the settee, sometimes asleep, while they wandered around.

As it was, we set off back to Spain on a Thursday and the house sale completed on the Friday. We had squeaked through a rapidly closing door, and could not return. Life is not like Narnia and some growing up had happened in the interim.

Because of his eye operation, Steve was told not to fly for 3 weeks, so we had reviewed our options and decided to travel by train, sea ferry, and then a hire car for the final leg. These turned out to be good choices and meant we could fill at least one suitcase with DVDs and videos for winter nights in the Spanish mountains, and another with all my medication, books, and clothes, and, best of all, not worry about the weight. We left the UK just as serious winter storms arrived, but the sea voyage from Portsmouth to Santander, however brief, provided the best night's sleep I had had for some time - a quiet spell down the Atlantic coast and through the Bay of Biscay yielded the gentle rocking of a maritime cradle. My skin had finished shedding its sunburnt layer and my scars were beginning to heal nicely. No matter that Britain was experiencing its first sharp frosts and snows of a harsh winter. We were fleeing south to a warmer climate for rest and recuperation. Or so we thought.

* * *

We arrived in southern Spain in the middle of a torrential downpour. As we drove south from Madrid the skies in front of us grew blacker and the rain heavier. The winding mountain road into Andalucía shone silver and liquid in the car headlights, and we cursed the many drivers who had their fog lamps on. Unsurprisingly, the one element missing that night was ... fog.

"Why?" howled Steve, as we overtook yet another dawdling motorist whose rear lights blinded and dazzled us. "Why?"

Finally, we were on our lonely route into the high hills. Small rocks and stones littered the road; narrow streams of mud slid gently down steep embankments; an occasional toad gleamed white as it hopped away. We turned down to the village with considerable relief, knowing that we were now within walking distance of our own front door.

Our friend Carla had left some lights on for us and a welcoming note. She referred to 'a bit of water coming in near the chimney' in the sitting room, but this did not prepare us for the shock of a spreading pool of brown liquid that was rapidly advancing towards the rugs on the floor, and a pale green washing-up bowl on the hearth that was already almost full. Rainwater was running along the underside of the white plaster chimney breast and dripping methodically into it. The wall behind was patched with moist, brown stains. Hastily, I gathered up two jam pans from the store room, set them also under the drips and laid newspaper over the wet floor. We had never had water getting in here before, so where was it coming from?

A quick glance by torchlight confirmed the source. Emilio was working on the old *granero* at the back and had removed the last of its collapsing roof. His protective tarpaulin had blown away in the storm and the rear wall of the house, usually not exposed, was receiving the full force of the rain. It was affecting the lower floors too. A visit down into the old stable below, the *cuadra*, revealed pools of water gathering on the uneven flagged floor and more ominous dripping coming from the end wall, which was made of stone and had probably been the back wall of the house for several hundred years. We had boxes of clothes and household paraphernalia in that section and I could see tidemarks of wet cardboard that filled me with dread. But it was two in the morning and we were very tired.

"Let's leave all this and get to bed," I suggested. "There's nothing we can do at this hour."

So we shut the bedroom door, drank a quick cup of Rooibos tea and snuggled down. The rain hammered on the skylights. We had been away for almost 7 weeks.

It took a hot summer, another winter and part of the following year before we resolved the effect of so much water ingress on the chimney breast. In the end, most of it had to be rebuilt and reinforced, but since some of the brickwork turned out to be paper-thin, this would have been necessary anyway. Clouds may have silver linings, but rain often produces 'dry' facts, and the rain in Spain falls, mostly, in the mountains.

* * *

I was unprepared for the drop in temperature at night once we were settled in again. Partly this was due to our weeks of indolence in England, some of it in a constant hospital temperature. Partly also thanks to the complete lack of heating in our absence. We had forgotten that the secret is to isolate the rooms most in use and keep them heated at all times - kitchen, bathroom, bedroom, and sitting room. Stairwells and window openings require thick curtains, draught-excluders and, ideally, double-glazing. At this time, we had none of these, so during daylight hours we needed layers of warm clothes and plenty of exercise to keep ourselves comfortable.

At night, despite warm pyjamas and bed-socks, there is a moment at about 4a.m. when a penetrating and deadly chill settles over one's bed and any body parts that are sticking out. It is as though the thick walls are releasing their stony breath into the darkness of the house. Steve's longstanding habit, acquired at sea, is to get up at this hour, take a dressing gown and a rug, and settle himself with his Spanish books or a DVD in front of the dying wood-burner. He is usually asleep again within the hour. I, on the other hand, gradually bunch myself into a chilly foetal position, reluctant to wake up fully and locate more bed coverings. Where has my human hot-water bottle gone? I gather the duvet and covers closely about me, cut out all draughts and go into hibernation mode; if I am very lucky he might come back to bed with some hot tea at about seven o'clock and we can doze again in intimate warmth, but it is a big effort to leave the bed for breakfast and the advancing day.

The December rain had brought a significant drop in temperature and on our first morning back, I made sure that I had an electric fire to warm me as I got dressed. On went the usual underwear (but no bra anymore, with nothing to fill it), merino wool leggings and a long-sleeved vest, followed by warm socks. Then jeans, a sweater, then another sweater or waistcoat and, finally, thickly-soled climbing boots. What else could I put on if January brought further falls in temperature? Perhaps I would become inured to the cold over time and be able to shed these layers. It seemed eons ago that we had drooped with the heat and even a sheet or a cotton dress had been too much.

More detailed explorations of the water situation revealed that Emilio was progressing well with the *granero* conversion at the back of the house, but, as we realised the night before, it had no roof on yet. Where the water had poured in there was also a 10 by 3 metre hole in the ground, full of mud, collapsed timbers and fallen stones from the roof and walls. Hastily, I sent him a text while Steve began moving boxes and furniture out of the flood zone.

Luckily, the rain had stopped and we were able to do some mopping up, but we did have other priorities. The hire car had to be returned to Granada airport that evening, our own car was out of service with a dead distributor cap, and we had very little food. It was a Sunday too, which was not helpful.

Thankfully, Carla had left us with milk, fruit, and a loaf of bread. The Granada solution was to break out the VFR motorbike and convoy to the airport, then ride back together on it. This would require some courage on my part as my poor, wounded body shivered reluctantly at the idea of the exposure on two wheels to storm-lashed roads. But there was no alternative, so I put my motorcycle clothing on the back seat of the car and followed Steve back along last night's mountain roads. A small consolation was turning on the car heater system and basking in its warmth while I had the chance.

We were fortunate with our timing. The heavy clouds lifted for a while and as we rounded the bend and gazed towards Capileira, the arc of a clearly-defined rainbow reached across the Poquiera gorge. I smiled and saw Steve raise a pointing arm. The mountains were welcoming us home with a biblical gesture of blessing.

Coming back, two-up, we found ourselves hurtling down the motorway between opposing weather patterns. On our left, the Sierra Nevada peaks rose up into deep, blue-black rain clouds slashed with more gleaming rainbows; on our right, towards the sea, lay flat washes of cobalt sky, bright with sunlight. We were heading straight down between the two, towards shining, white wind turbines which clustered on hilltops or were strung out across the valley. The scale of the landscape here gives them a distinction and grace that is often not present in other regions. We prayed that we would get the better of the two weather fronts until we reached home. We had our 'wets' on over our leathers but did not fancy shingle-strewn high roads streaming with water. As it turned out, we were fortunate and kept the sun and fairly dry roads with us until safely parked up in the courtyard.

Over the next few days we were greeted enthusiastically by those of our neighbours who lived in the village all year. They thought we had gone off for a holiday! I was honest with them about the real reason - they would surely notice my flat chest - and we all agreed that there was more to life than one's boobs. *Cáncer de mama* is the Spanish phrase for breast cancer, and now we would have to make do with Steve's manly ones rather than my sorry scars. In the countryside, injury or death seems to be accepted as part of nature's great scheme and even deformity contributes to the pattern. I was simply a tree that had had some severe, but necessary, pruning and little more was said.

Besides, Christmas was coming within a week and everyone had shopping to do, food to cook and extra mouths to feed. The local shops were taking orders for lamb and turkey, the bars steamed with coffee and damp clothing, and small groups of young people could be seen stomping along the roads. There was little overt commerciality, just an air of relaxation and holiday spirit. Emilio and his team worked right up to Christmas Eve, by now putting on the layers for the roof - timbers, slates, insulated plastic sheeting and the *launa* (stone granules). We were not sure whether or not there should be a 'topping-out' ceremony, but were relieved to think that future rainstorms would find their way elsewhere and not into our basement or sitting room.

In Andalucía, as in much of Spain, it is the Old Night (*Noche Vieja*) and the New Year (*Año Nuevo*) that receives the most attention in December, plus the celebration and procession of the Three Kings (*Los Tres Reyes*) on January 5th. Apart from some interesting cooking smells that permeated through the streets on the 25th, the village was quiet right up to mid-afternoon of the 31st December, when a rush of traffic filled our modest parking area once again. The 'visitors' had arrived, carrying boxes of food, small children and a weekend's bedding.

Darkness was falling as some fairy lights were hastily strung across the plaza and on our balcony we switched on a small fibre-optic Christmas tree, together with garlands of golden bells made from wire mesh. It was a rather inauspicious evening with low cloud and light rain, but as we set off towards Giotti's house we were pleasantly conscious of being in an enclosed and remote place, far from the world and all the usual razzamatazz.

Music, light and chatter flowed from beneath the old wooden doorways as we hastened up the street; inside there would be much familial eating and drinking until the midnight hour was achieved. We carried a basket of chorizo-filled bread balls, like little doughnuts, a couple of bottles of decent wine and a boxed game of poker, complete with cards, chips and a green baize cloth. This turned out to be a wise choice, as we were the first to arrive and poor Giotti, worried that no one would come, settled down happily enough for an hour or two of childish gambling. We stopped as the clock struck twelve, to eat the obligatory 12 grapes, one for each midnight chime, which would bring us good luck in the coming year.

Of course people did appear, at first a trickle of *estranjeros* like us, but by 1a.m. the equivalent of first-footing had started and some of our Spanish neighbours began to arrive. The front door stayed open as young men drifted in, the smell of marijuana drifted out and the girls danced to 70s blues music. Giotti performed a marvellous karaoke to Sinatra's *New York, New York* with Laura managing the obligatory 'Ginger Rogers' dance routine clad in her jeans and hiking boots. We all gave them a round of loud applause at the end. No one else was as brave, but I seem to remember doing the Uma Thurman routine from Pulp Fiction with someone, and watching one acquaintance pour vodka down his throat like a parched desert wanderer who had discovered an oasis. I think most of us were safely tucked up in our beds by four in the morning.

The following evening we went to Emilio's house for supper and to make better acquaintance with his wife Olga, their two little boys and Olga's older son. Also her mother, originally from Volgograd. Emilio had indicated that '7 to 7:30' would be a good time to arrive, but somehow we assumed he kept to Alpujarran time, which usually meant a significant degree of flexibility. We were still having baths and getting changed at 7p.m. when my mobile rang:

"Where are you?" asked Emilio. "Are you lost?"

"Ten minutes," I replied gaily, "we're just leaving."

My hair was still wet when we arrived outside his house and parked the car. I could see him peering out of a window, then Olga doing the same from the kitchen. We were definitely late, but they made us very welcome. Olga's mother turned out to speak less Spanish than we did, but her teenage son Platón, or Plato, whom we knew from the building work, had quite good English, and the younger two were either very quiet (Andreas) or hurtling about (Iván el Terrible).

We sat down at a low table, covered with a variety of tapas: grilled aubergines, slices of dried ham from Trevélez, Japanese sushi, dates stuffed with walnuts and slices of fresh orange and kiwi. We were unsure how greedy to be. Perhaps this was it? Fortunately, we left enough space for a large platter of roast pork, accompanied by a delicious Russian salad and, later on, some interesting meringues and little cakes. All of this we washed down with an excellent red wine and a small dram of brandy.

"So, Steve," asked Emilio, "why Spain and why just here?"

"I've had enough of England," he replied. "It's not the same country that I grew up in. People are too greedy, the politicians are too corrupt, there's a camera on every street corner and everyone spends their time shopping."

Emilio nodded and laughed, "We know about corrupt politicians. Spain is much worse in that department, I'm sure. We have a lot of problems right here, with money spent that isn't accounted for and families filling their pockets at the expense of everyone else."

Little did we know then that he himself would be running for election within a year, as part of the Independence and Partido Popular coalition, to oust the Socialist PSOE. Nor did we know that the community bank balance was already in the red with a large deficit accumulating. But we did start to go to a number of community information meetings, to try and understand what the issues were and how local government functioned. Unfortunately, the language barrier often held us back, but we did the best we could. In fact, when the coalition did get control, Emilio and his fellow councillors spent a lot of their own money travelling back and forth to Granada, trying to sort out the financial mess that they had inherited. Legal proceedings to recover vanished *dinero* were commenced and are still underway as I write.

Tonight, the children ate swiftly and disappeared to play video games; they were as polite as they needed to be and did not pester their parents for attention. One sensed that they were a secure and happy family, with a loose set of rules, yet no one taking any nonsense. Very easy. The house was not particularly interesting or lavish, but it had plenty of Olga's paintings on the walls and was wonderfully warm for such a chilly winter's night. Olga and I agreed that once spring arrived, we should meet in the local café-bar and exchange conversations in

Spanish and English, to our mutual benefit. A new year had arrived and we were all making good resolutions - a sure recipe for failure!

We saw the family again a few days later when the Cabalgata de Los Reyes occurred. This was a simple march around the town by all the children and their parents, following 3 colourful mini tractors and their trailers, each one carrying a King wearing a bright robe and feathered turban. One of these was made up as a Moor of course. A brass band kept up as best it could, ducking the torrent of sweets that were thrown into the crowd. Emilio had sensibly brought a plastic bag for Iván's collection which we scurried about trying to fill with him, whilst Andreas raced to keep up with the procession. The finale took place in the town hall auditorium, where the children received their gifts from the Kings and their parents took digital photographs and videos. We crept out after a while and made our way home.

Chapter 9

Eccentrics

One of our first priorities after the festivities was to get some fruit trees planted on the land. We had mulberries and figs around the perimeter and a single pear tree, but we wanted to complete our *huerto* with olives and almonds, and have the benefit of more shade too as they grew bigger. So we went to see our favourite *jardinero* in Orgiva one wet morning and selected 13 saplings - 5 olives, 5 almonds, 1 nectarine, 1 cherry and 1 walnut. Señor Perez is a delightful barrel of a man, knowledgeable and honest. If the plant won't survive at our altitude, he will say so. On this visit, as the rain got heavier, he rushed to get us an umbrella but then stood beside us, getting soaked himself, without a care. When we went into his so-called office to pay, we discovered a log fire surrounded by cats and dogs, kittens and puppies, all piled up together in the cosy warmth and occupying every wonky chair and battered cushion in the place.

Getting the trees into the ground involved some serious hole digging, particularly for the olives. These were four years old and about two metres high. Opinions vary on the best method for planting olives, including dropping the saplings into holes a metre deep and a metre in diameter and covering up much of the stems. Our pot-grown varieties seemed too mature for such radical treatment so we followed normal planting procedure including staking them against wind-rock and putting down some fertiliser. Steve dug them into the sloping and drier part of the land (but not as arid as the almond patch) while I put the nectarine tree in as sheltered a spot as possible and surrounded it with a 'duvet' of dried leaves and twigs. In digging trial holes, we discovered a small area of land that quickly evolved from shale to claggy, grey clay about 40cm down. I wondered if we had stumbled upon a natural site for our *alberca* or water hole. Most farmers have some sort of large water container for those dry spells when the water does not run in the *acequias,* nor the rains fall from the sky.

Indeed, what we needed right now was some good old precipitation to prove the point. We were rewarded in late January with a plentiful downpour, of which several inches settled in the bottom of one of the holes and lingered there for weeks. Immediately I set about enlarging it, bringing up spadefuls of oleaginous lumps that gladdened my heart. Some lurking hippopotamus in my soul rejoiced at the sight of so much mud. I couldn't wait to complete the hole, bring down a capacious mixing bucket and start to line the *alberca* by hand. The secret, of course, was not to dig too wide or too deep and breach the impermeable clay barrier. I asked Steve if we could construct some kind of narrow-gauge boring tool that would not create as much havoc as a spade.

"You'd need a Land Rover, a 4 ton derrick and considerable skill," he remarked, "and a means of getting it all down there - a gigantic crane perhaps."

I could see his point, but was pleased to have planted the seed of an idea in his mind. Who could tell what cunning device he might not come up with? In the meantime, I was quite prepared to do a spell of slow and painstaking hand-digging and hope that the clay seam was extensive.

By mid-February, we were overjoyed to find some tiny almond blossoms on one or two of our young trees, and optimistic buds on the nectarine and the cherry. On the downside, the walnut had a sombre air and no shoots of any kind, and one of the olives was shedding leaves on a daily basis. However, plants out here seem to find ways to survive, even growing up from beneath the soil, so we would wait some time before removing anything on a permanent basis. The presence of many healthy garlic shoots, a brightly carmine-tinted ladybird and some tiny lilac flowers amongst the grasses reassured us that spring was not far away, despite the fact that the mountain tops were white with snow and night-time temperatures were about 3 degrees Celsius. The warmth of the daytime sun compensates all life forms for the chilly evening air.

One method of keeping warm, which we were to experience many times over each winter, was to gather wood from down on our land and then haul it up to the house by hand. Steve would disappear down the steep and scrubby perimeter, find a fallen poplar or chestnut tree, start up the chainsaw and cut metre-long sections of about 30cm in diameter. He would bring them up the steepest section, drop them in the grass and go back for more, whilst I began the ant-like process of getting them further up the path to strategic resting points. Piece by piece, log by log, this weighty yet essential timber would advance in stages to the village, then to our house and, finally, the wood-store. A few words cannot describe adequately the remorselessness of ferrying heavy logs up a stone-littered path, whilst muscles and mind are begging for a rest. Each time I went up, I swore that this would be the last load of the day; each time I went down, enjoying the view and the fine weather, I thought, *perhaps just one more*, and thus the job got done. We should have hired a donkey or a mule, or better still, an elephant.

On one of the last journeys of the day, when we were both struggling up the hill in the fading afternoon light, our Belgian friend Eric, who lives mainly in the Pyrenees, appeared on his off-road Montesa, booted and goggled for some strenuous fun. He stopped right in the middle of the path. I thought that at any moment he would leap off, abandon the bike and help us to haul wood. No such luck. He chatted about our predicament and watched me stagger on past, but was not inclined to help. He is probably in his forties, so he may have felt it was too exhausting for him, or poor training for off-road biking, or better left to the over-sixties. As it was, I felt like the little dung-beetle we had watched the previous summer, rolling its sphere of muck up the hill, hoping that nothing would block its progress. However, unlike the beetle, which froze in terror at the reverberation of our footfall, I did not feel inclined to stop for long.

"I must get on," I said, "or I will seize up."

"Are you cold?" Eric asked with surprise.

"No," I grimaced, "just making sure the moving parts keep going."

We were glad of our labours when the snow arrived. Within the space of one week we transited from twenty degrees of warmth to an afternoon of sudden chill and continuous white-out. From icy droplets to small fluffy berries of *nieve*, we watched the grey streets pearling over and the oleander branches bending under a new weight. Every twig and leaf of the delicate birch tree by the fountain was picked out in white floss, while the glistening water continued to spout and little sparrows fluttered darkly through the branches.

Steve quickly went down to the land to gather some even bigger pieces of wood, the workmen packed up so that they could get up the hill and safely home, and I stood in the plaza alongside Jesús, the barman. He had definitely been celebrating the change in weather with some suitably fortifying liquid.

"I've seen this every year for forty years," he said, staggering slightly, "and it's always just as wonderful."

"I love it too," I replied, "*es muy bonita, la nieve.*"

Just then a small, hooded figure ran across the top of the square and gathered some snow in his hands. It was Tao.

"Come on," I shouted, spreading my arms and legs to give him a target. "How good a shot are you?"

In answer, he sent a snowball whizzing straight at me. I had to turn a shoulder to avoid being smacked in the face. Jesús and I both cheered loudly, while Tao ran off in a sudden crisis of pleasure and panic. He couldn't know that I had had two sons and was well-accustomed to a good snowball fight, which they would always win.

Four more creatures passed by soon afterwards, just as the flakes began to fall in dense flurries. A small ivory-coloured mule plodded through, led by the Frenchman Josión, with two riders on board: Anna and her baby daughter Carin. Anna was wrapped in a long, dark-red shawl, sheltering herself and the baby from the winter wilds. As they passed silently through the plaza, the religious symbolism was all too apparent. Minutes later, her partner Zak appeared.

"Have you seen a woman on a donkey?" he asked, somewhat breathlessly.

"They went that way," we pointed.

They had disappeared along the track that led out of the village and into the far reaches of the valley. They must have been heading towards Josión's *cortijo* or to the mill. Zak hurried after them and I felt as though we had been transported into a crime fiction by Dorothy L. Sayers. Some footprints in the snow would lead us to a body at any moment.

In fact, Zak was involved with a crime, about six months later, when three thieves passed in broad daylight through the square carrying a stolen TV set, some gold jewellery and a stash of marijuana. It was a 'revenge' theft, by people outside our area, and drug related, but Zak unwittingly accosted them. He was carting yet more firewood into the plaza for a fiesta bonfire, and casually asked them, "Can you help me carry this wood?"

They ignored him and rushed past, leaping into a van and heading off towards the main valley road. Zak was bemused by this attitude, so untypical of our *pueblo*, but carried on hauling timber. It wasn't until later that he realised to whom he had been speaking. When the whole business went to a police trial, Anna began to worry.

"The police have used this sighting to identify them," she explained, "and for some reason they've described Zak as a tall, bearded Englishman, so now the thieves know who denounced them. They could decide to return one day and punish him - or his family. That's what *gitanos* do around here."

I thought about this for a moment. "Well, Steve is a tall, bearded Englishman too," I told her, "so I wouldn't worry. He's just as likely to be confronted by an angry Spaniard with a sharp knife as Zak is!"

Of course, everything was forgotten quite quickly. The TV and jewellery were retrieved and a sentence imposed, but the drugs were never found. Either they were handed over to a third party somewhere en route to Granada, or they're still lying in a roadside ditch, wrapped in plastic and waiting for an ex-con to come back and collect them.

* * *

A far more mundane and less criminal activity that took up much of our time, was changing our various vehicles from British to Spanish registration. In theory, this has to be completed within 6 months of becoming residents of Spain. The whole process is called *matriculación* and is often delegated by expatriates to an agent, or *gestor*, for a considerable fee. We had 4 motorbikes and a car, which would cost us quite a lot no matter how we went about it.

On the advice of a fellow biker, we started out by contacting Manolo from Granada, who, it seemed, would scrutinise our papers and the vehicles in order to ensure compliance with Spanish requirements, and who would then introduce us to the ITV process (the MOT in Britain). Once we had an ITV for each one, we would undertake the taxation and registration processes ourselves, learning how the system worked as well as saving a bit of money.

Though a pleasant man, Manolo turned out to be less than useful and as expensive as a *gestor*. Both the Moto Guzzi and the car failed the ITV test, for mainly administrative reasons. In both instances, the numbers on the chassis and on the DVLA registration paper did not match. We had to go through the slow and painful business of writing to Swansea for new papers, as well as the Moto Guzzi factory in Mugello, Italy. Also, although Steve never rides the Guzzi at night, its headlamps were designed for left-hand drive and were deemed non-compliant. We had already bought second-hand headlamps for the car for 40 Euros, but could not locate left-hand Guzzi lights from Spain or Britain on the internet or in any other outlet. At the time of writing, it is still in mothballs.

The other vehicles were awarded their ITV, valid for one year for the car and two years for each bike. Those successes were followed by the more challenging steps of going to Granada and the Tráfico office. With only addresses to guide us, we made use of satellite navigation and found our way through the city to the suburbs of Pulianas and a modern, yellow-painted, two-storey building. Inside were several different queues at a number of glass-fronted desks, just like the British Post Office system. We had no idea which queue to join, and simply picked the shortest one.

Quite soon, we found ourselves in front of a young man with a brightly-printed T-shirt , a long black pigtail and an engaging smile. He spoke a little English. As soon as he realised what we wanted, he passed us a form and a list of instructions, circling the relevant parts with a red pen. It was clear that we needed to visit another couple of offices first - the regional tax office (for import taxation or *Impuesto*) and our own local *Ayuntamiento* for road tax. I remembered buying bread in Moscow in the late 1960s and using a similar system: one queue waiting for a price ticket, another queue to pay it and another one to actually receive a small loaf of black rye bread. The difference here was that some of the necessary offices were 60 kilometres apart.

We left the place without a clue as to where the *Impuesto* building was, but managed to get directions from a driving instructor across the road. However unlikely it seemed as a location, we found ourselves entering the ground floor of a block of residential flats and standing in front of an armed and uniformed guard with his own airport-style security system. We piled our motorcycle helmets and rucksack onto the conveyor belt, along with a mobile phone, laptop and small change, then walked through the scanner. Everything was in order. We collected yet another ticket and joined the small group of people waiting to be seen, steeling ourselves for what we thought would be a confusion of languages and bureaucracy.

Not a bit of it. Our number came up and we found ourselves in front of a friendly woman who, as soon as she realised our nationality, summoned her manager. He was a youngish man, dressed casually in a striped rugby top, who, it transpired, was studying English at the Granada Language College and was delighted to have some practice. The forms were quickly filled in and the tax calculated for our twenty-year old Ford.

"990 Euros to pay," he said, scribbling the figures on a piece of scrap paper. It seemed that the car was valued at 7,500 Euros and that was the basis for his figure, something over 10 per cent of the value.

Our jaws dropped. We had paid a mere £500 for the car two years earlier! Our horror must have been apparent. He looked again at his paperwork. We all looked at it.

"*¡Soy un idiota!* I'm an idiot!" he exclaimed. "I've based it on the price of a new car. For yours, which is over ten years old, its value is only 750 Euros and the tax is 99 Euros."

What a relief. We dashed off to the nearest bank, paid the tax and dashed back again. It was three minutes past two in the afternoon and everyone had gone off for lunch very punctually, but out of kindness our man and the guard were waiting for us to return. Quickly the papers were finalised.

"There you are," he said, "I hope you enjoy your life in Andalucía."

This was typical of the whole process. Honesty and helpfulness, embellished with a laid-back and pragmatic approach. The same attitude applied to paying the local road tax at our Ayuntamiento and the final rubber-stamping back at Tráfico. It's true that it was bureaucratic and time-consuming, but also well worth doing ourselves. Finally, papers in hand, we were able to buy new number plates and Steve fixed them on.

Insurance was expensive, but essential. In Spain, it is the car that is insured, not the driver, which is helpful when friends come to visit and want to borrow the car, but motorbikes have to be covered individually. We have never shirked this obligation and must look thoroughly bemused when some people explain, with pride, that they 'don't bother with insurance.'

Now, with Spanish plates, we were indistinguishable from other drivers on the roads, but, like them, we thought that we were far more likely to be pulled over by the Guardia Civil. Where they might ignore foreign vehicles, we thought that they would not hesitate to stop local people with local bank accounts who could pay on-the-spot fines. This is only partially true. There is a lucrative business in detaining foreigners who exceed the speed limit, don't bother to put their headlights on when entering tunnels, have allowed their tax or ITV to expire or who simply don't have their driving licence to hand.

Some people just have bad luck. Our friend Carla, from Hong Kong, used her extensive charms to borrow several cars in the space of a few weeks from different owners, but then managed to overturn one of them, have two punctures in successive days with another and suffer a failed distributor head with the fourth. This persuaded her to buy her own vehicle, get it fully legal and go to Spanish language classes too, for a while. Standing wailing by the side of the road is sufficient to bring most gallant Spaniards to a halt, but the situation is not helped if neither side can communicate thereafter.

Carla's presence in the mountains and her habit of lurching from one drama to another, kept us all enthralled for many months. It was impossible to dislike her, yet most people were astonished by the tabloid events that followed her endless quest for company. Company of any sort and at any price, or so it seemed.

She had an aura of glamour which was enhanced by a model girl's physique, slicked-back auburn hair, and a habit of flirting outrageously with everyone, no matter what their gender, age or reaction. In fact, she was almost sixty but took good care of her skin, her fitness, and the limits of her pecuniary assets. There was a great deal of personal discipline lurking beneath her girlish exterior and she paid much attention to her appearance. Her diary was full of social events, parties, lunches, and outings. As her income diminished, these activities were sometimes replaced by short-term jobs, but nonetheless she made strenuous efforts to fill her days and nights to capacity. She hated to be alone.

One could be unkind and say that she made comprehensive assessments of individuals and then played a game to gain their approval and make use of them to her own advantage. Alternatively, one could suspect her of naiveté, believing that nobody could deny anything to her inner, perhaps still juvenile self, or one could accuse her of having too big an ego, which placed her and her affairs at the centre of all interest. Or of living like a goldfish, going round and round in her own tedious social bowl, denying herself any intellectual challenges.

All this was a disguise that hid an immense vulnerability. Gradually we realised that she was terrified of making a fool of herself or of being alone; of driving at night or of having to buy, and use, a computer; of getting to a party and knowing no one; of not being noticed. Somewhere in her past were cruel parents and lost lovers, neglectful husbands and abandoned children. Now there was just her and 'the Mountain,' and as our friend Goldie observed, 'the Mountain will find you out.'

Another personality who provided occasional gossip was a strange, bony little man who, over a period of forty or fifty years had gained a reputation as an 'eminence' on all things Andalucían. What had started as an ambitious intellectual carapace, no doubt of impressive structure, became a self-endowed and shock-resistant shell which did not bear much close scrutiny. We can call him the Crab, and briefly observe him scuttling silently about the pueblos, note-book in hand; or we can make the long journey to his lair, carrying an intellectual tit-bit for him.

In that situation there is a degree of certainty as to the result, as he is ever-ready either to verbally attack his visitor, subtly but viciously, or he prepares to run, metaphorically-speaking, for the shelter of the nearest large rock (usually a glass of whisky). Carrying about him an air of diffidence, his ego nonetheless craves superiority over everyone else on all topics that might be deemed to be academic or intellectual. His hovering attention lasts as long as it takes to identify a weakness, a tasty morsel of mental or emotional vulnerability, then he will go in for the kill.

It is impossible to tell what satisfaction he gets from this type of humiliation and those who have met his type before, simply avoid giving him an opportunity to use his claw. To her credit, Carla has been one of these, telling him that she was too stupid to read books and therefore not worthy of his attention. Steve refuses to be drawn into competitive debate with him and the local people have learned to tolerate his presence and get on with their lives, as they are, it seems, mere ignorant peasants and therefore beneath his interest. The rest of us either have developed strategies of avoidance or tacitly agreed to carry on prolonged arguments about history, language, archaeology, architecture and, sometimes, the village drainage system. No doubt even Amazonian tribes have such human crustaceans in their communities and endure them in similar fashion. He will probably outlive us all, malevolence often giving people more stimulus in their lives than any other emotion.

We have other eccentrics living nearby and the Alpujarra certainly has its share of egoists, who do not seem able to maintain any kind of normal relationship, or even a sensible conversation, for very long. If they are not talking about themselves, they have little to say. A spirit of enquiry, or even curiosity, about the rest of the world is noticeably lacking - but they provide us boring, normal folk with a bit of gossip.

In this strange group we could include the Secret Squirrel, who has declared publicly that he holds top secret material on his computer; the Trespasser, who appears on holiday from time to time and feels entitled to enter other people's homes uninvited, to 'see what they have done to the place'; the Horrible Horace, who thinks that as an ex-politician he has a privileged right to being 'great friends' with total strangers; the Creature, who wanders, drunkenly and unpleasantly, from village to village; and, last but not least, the Awful Antonia who probably once belonged in the Home Counties, selecting fashions for her benighted customers, but who happens to have ended up forcing herself on innocent bystanders in the quiet bars of Capileira or Lanjarón.

Not all of our Spanish neighbours are so special either. One day, I happened to stroll out towards the village car park with a bag of rubbish for the *basura*. There, spade in hand, was one of our local second home owners, filling up two buckets with our building sand. She greeted me pleasantly enough and I decided that, well, we could spare a small quantity and perhaps she didn't know it was ours. We knew that she and her husband were doing some building work on their house, so perhaps they had run out of their own supply.

A couple of days later, I set off for the shops and came upon the husband and his friend in the same place, this time filling a wheelbarrow.

"Hola," they smiled, shovelling diligently.

"Hola," I replied. "This is our sand, you know."

"Is it?"

They seemed astonished, but I detected an air of guilt. They certainly knew it wasn't there by accident. As I drove off, I could see them in the rear view mirror, wheeling their ill-gotten gains back into the *pueblo*. I considered the options and decided that another Spaniard was the solution; the next market-day I saw Emilio and explained the problem.

"It's our sand, and we don't mind them having the odd bucketful, but regular quantities - well, they should ask, for one thing, and offer to pay for it, for another."

That same afternoon, Emilio appeared in the square, talking heatedly with the local bar owner. The Sand-thief, as we dubbed him then and forever more, was nowhere to be seen. However, word must have got passed back, as our sand remained untouched for the rest of the summer and we were the only humans who made use of it. The cats, of course, continued as before, regarding it as one of their preferred toilet facilities.

A few people are, as anywhere, genuinely affected by mental health problems and their needs are much more profound. Getting the right attention and treatment is sometimes difficult; there are lots of counsellors, gurus and alternative therapists in the area, but their skills fail when confronted by true psychosis and they probably do more harm than good. If the benighted person has no legal right to mental healthcare services in Spain and they have allowed that right to expire in the UK, they are well and truly stuffed, but it seems out here that finally a sense of humanity overcomes all and the local health system does its best to support them. A white-garbed health assistant will come to take someone for a daily walk, make sure they are eating properly or chat with them in the shade of a protective poplar tree. Sometimes a visit to the doctor will be arranged, to check that prescribed medication is being taken.

Many people come to the Alpujarras to 'find themselves', usually hoping that a mixture of meditation, organic food and marijuana will bring enlightenment and happiness. When the quest fails in Spain, they might move on to India or South America or, eventually, the harsher realities of a suburban flat and a job in Bristol. Some of them, of course, are Spanish and will eventually grow up and become part of their country's identity and purpose, which may be a saving grace for them - a country in economic despair has little space for dreamers or druids.

The most stable people seem to be those born and bred in the area and doing ordinary jobs - builders, lawyers, shopkeepers, café owners and teachers. Although the expatriate community and tourism brings them some additional facilities, nonetheless these mountain folk are busy earning a living and bringing up a family. They have married other local people, often their cousins, and keep to traditional pastimes, albeit mixed in with modern conveniences such as the Internet, TV and cheap clothing made in China or India.

Straddling the two distinct groups of locals and foreigners are the artisans and artists, who may be Spanish or Argentinian, German or Swedish, busy making jewellery, guitars or hand-printed silk scarves. Often they mix more thoroughly with the indigenous folk of the Alpujarras than anyone else, especially when the chief point of contact is an art exhibition, musical performance or fiesta event. Some may say that there remains an intellectual divide, yet when the hot August days come, and the old men gather under a huge tree outside the medical centre and the young women chat, fanning themselves, in the hairdresser's, then as Laurie Lee said, '...the pure sources of feeling... are still preserved by the paradoxes of poverty, illiteracy, bad roads and the great silences of the mountains and the sea.'

* * *

I saw another social mix come together in an unlikely way when I returned to the UK for my brother Tim's funeral. This was soon after my cancer surgery, when I really didn't want to go anywhere, but this was a family matter, not to be ignored. Steve drove me to Málaga one cool January morning, where I caught a flight to Liverpool, then picked up a hire car to drive up to the Lake District. I was heading back to old stomping grounds, where I had lived on and off for twenty years, from the age of three, and where my parents had farmed during the 1950s and 60s.

Tim had lived almost all of his adult life in Lancaster, just south of the Lakes, in a small 'two up, two down' terraced house that backed onto the canal that ran through the centre of town. Once upon a time, this canal had been at the heart of the industrial life of the town, with barges travelling, fully-laden, up from Glasson Dock, Morecambe Bay and the Irish Sea and returning, empty, for another load of cotton or sugar. During Tim's time there, the old tow-path saw a few men cycling their way to factory jobs early in the morning, or young mothers pushing prams after lunch; summer cruisers were able to get part of the way along and elegant swans, noisy ducks and, occasionally, water rats also made their way up and down.

Lonely and often wretched, Tim had fought his own battle with mental health in this place and watched the town change from a sooty, impoverished, 70s backwater to a cleaner, modernised - yet in his view, aesthetically impoverished - university town. Sadly for him, he died just before one of its biggest Victorian buildings, Lancaster Castle, ceased to be a loathed and reviled prison and became a museum.

Whenever I visited him, we would walk around the town, calling in at the covered market, later revamped as a mall, to buy fish, tea, bread and, always, cigarettes and tobacco. The shopkeepers knew him well and tolerated his eccentricities.

"Mornin' Tim," they would smile, "how 'yer keepin' today?"

"Got my sister with me today," he would respond, putting his purchases into a thick, oily, plastic carrier bag. "Come to see the working classes. Come to see how the rest of us manage, rotting away up here in the north."

Probably I smiled tolerantly and just said hello. There was little point in intervening. In the town, Tim saw himself as a working class man, despite a public school education and academic honours; it was part of his disguise. Sometimes, with another hat on and safely ensconced in his armchair, he would adopt a right-wing, military officer's approach and become deliberately snobbish. At other times he was just an ageing hippy, listening to old LP's by Cream, rolling a joint and watching the joss-stick burn its way down to the ashtray. Religion, politics, and art had all been abandoned long since. He was an older brother with whom I had spent much of my childhood and I loved him, but it was difficult to do more than humour him, clean his kitchen and bathroom, and try to persuade him to give up smoking, the addictive demon that would get him in the end.

Now, on a cold and bare winter's day, I drove to the crematorium, a couple of miles outside town, having organised a wreath, spoken to my eldest brother Simon and found a short poem by T. S. Eliot that I thought contained some hint of Tim's struggles and that I might be able to deliver without breaking down:

<u>USK</u>

Do not suddenly break the branch, or
Hope to find
The white hart behind the white well.
Glance aside, not for lance, do not spell
Old enchantments. Let them sleep.
'Gently dip, but not too deep',
Lift your eyes
Where the roads dip and where the roads rise
Seek only there
Where the grey light meets the green air
The hermit's chapel, the pilgrim's prayer.

[The Waste Land and other poems, Faber and Faber, 1940]

As I locked the car, I spotted Simon and his family standing on the gravel. They had all turned up, journeying from Bristol and Derbyshire. My own sons had offered to come too, from Scotland and East Anglia, but I had advised them not to make a special trip. They had seen Tim rarely and this would be a small, brief affair. Waving to the others, I hurried over. Bigger groups of people were assembling in other corners of the car park, so I assumed that ours was not the only cremation that day; we might have no more than our allocated one hour slot.

As we began to file into the cremation hall, I realised that I had miscalculated. Some of the larger groups were walking in too. In fact, all of them. I recognised a few faces from the past, but plenty of people were strangers. Where I had expected half-a-dozen, we were at least sixty. Two or three youngish men in leather jackets, one with biker tattoos, settled themselves into a pew; they were soon joined by a fourth, older man with a plump, pink face. A group of twenty-something girls sat down near the back. Plump women from the market appeared, followed by a nurse wrapped in her blue jacket and a tall man in a black suit. Who were these folk?

It was not until after the cremation, when we assembled in a local hotel for a glass of wine and some sandwiches, that matters became clearer. The tall man came over and shook my hand. "I'm so glad you read that particular poem, it was spot on for Tim," he beamed. It turned out that he had been one of Tim's psychiatric nurses.

"Hey'up," came another voice, from one of the three young men. "That were a good do."

I began to chat to this trio. Where did they fit into the picture? It gradually dawned on me that these were drinking buddies, chaps who met up with Tim on a Saturday night in the local pub.

"How did you hear that Tim had died?" I asked.

"Oh, Jim's sister lives in't same street, across the way. Once we knew, it were just a matter of getting 'ere."

"Aye and thanks to Bob," gesturing towards the older man, "we made it."

It turned out that none of them had any transport so they had set off to walk to the crematorium. Bob, a local butcher driving past in his delivery van, had spotted them and called out, "Whur are you lot off to then, in yer fancy jackets?"

"Tim's dead," they told him. "Yer know, old Tim. Wu're goin' to crematorium."

"'Op in then," he had said, "I'll come too. I liked Tim."

Many people had liked Tim. He was a vital part of the street he lived in, part of the local community, part of the fabric of Lancaster. The town that he had spent much time hating, whose traffic systems he detested and whose architecture he despised, whose mental health 'bins' had locked him up and spat him out again but whose care system had continued to support him; the town that he often resented - in the end its people had turned out in numbers to give him a good send-off.

Before I left Lancaster, unlikely ever to return, I drove down to Glasson Dock, where he and I had come on many occasions, to eat fish and chips and wander around the old basin with its green-slimed lock gates and neglected fishing smacks. I revisited the marina, with its clinking masts and quacking water hens, and the concrete, tangled corner that looked out over the bay. The tide was out and the brown mud sucked and gurgled; sea gulls hovered above, questing for tit-bits. Far away to the north were the white-sieved Langdale Pikes, the fell tops of our childhood, set against a pale blue sky. I looked with Tim's eyes and enjoyed that iconic view, a brief glance back at the past, when childhood and innocence protected all of us from the harsher realities of our adult lives.

Chapter 10

Winter Warming and Summer Dancing

Every year the dark month of January is enlivened by a festival known locally as the Chisco. Sometimes it coincides with a saint's day, San Anton, but usually it refers to the mediaeval tradition of burning heathens. Centuries ago, most villages and towns took the opportunity to light bonfires, cook pork and then test the religious persuasion of their neighbours. If you wouldn't eat the pork, you were likely to join the bundles of broom and branches of fresh olive leaves, as well as bigger pieces of timber, and be burned alive. This ritual is a bit less bloodthirsty nowadays. No one asks about your religious beliefs and with luck you might end up winning something in the raffle instead: a fattened pig or a computer or a box of over-sweetened chocolates.

We went to Torviscon on a bright, cold evening, with snow in the hollows and stars in the sky. On the way, we startled a wild mountain goat at the roadside, its head crowned with magnificent 'pitchfork' horns. It was just about to cross over, so I politely dipped the headlights and came to a halt. Elegantly, it wandered across the tarmac, stepped up a small incline and disappeared into the darkness. Later, we spotted a couple of cream-coloured foxes in hunting mode, their eyes glinting, intent on some prey that we could not see.

Torviscon, a small town hiding in the 'v' of a steep-sided ravine, below the Contraviesa hills, is criss-crossed by narrow streets, or *ramblas*, that slowly wend their way uphill. Out of breath and only half-way up, the visitor is amazed at this slalom of tiny poured-concrete roads and the skeins of electrical wiring that are draped across them, not much above head height. Tonight, once the town had achieved full burning mode, one guessed that it was only luck and some degree of Spanish commonsense that prevented serious damage to the cables and the consequences of electrocuted humans.

We started at the top with supper in a friend's house, then worked our way down, from bonfire to bonfire. Each barrio or quarter had its own focal point of leaping flame, sometimes at a junction of lanes, sometimes in a small plaza. One or two people with pitchforks kept an eye on proceedings in each location, and ensured that the fires burned well. Bundles of cut broom were stacked ready for use, as well as bigger pieces of chestnut or poplar. We watched with fascination as an old man pulled on a piece of rope beside the edge of a terrace and heaved up his own individual bundle of olive branches, then commanded his teenage grandson to throw it on the fire. A prayer for a good farming year went with it perhaps.

The local band was also working its way round to each fire, mostly youngsters in jeans and jackets, playing the cornet with one hand and texting a mate with the other. They were escorted by men in black T-shirts who acted as organisers and raffle-ticket sellers, and a swarm of younger children wearing huge, globe-shaped, painted and decorated masks. We came upon a trio of older girls who lined up for a brief, modern-day can-can, dressed in tight leather jeans and high heels. They quickly collapsed into screams of laughter and the band moved on.

Finally, we found ourselves down at the main square, beside an even bigger bonfire, eating churros, which are essentially sugared doughnut coils, dipped into hot chocolate. There was no point in speculating about the calorific content, this was party food. We could see the flames leaping up against the white houses, multi-coloured rockets exploding over our heads and drifts of smoke stretching away down the ravine. Even as we drove away, well past midnight, it looked as though the celebrations - and the bonfires - would carry on for some time.

The next evening our little village also held a *chisco*, but on a much smaller scale. Lack of preparation meant that although we all brought wood for burning and the bar was open, there was unlikely to be any food and certainly not a band. But miracles do happen up here in the hills, and by about 9 o'clock we had a drummer, a guitarist, a flute player and a fiddle-player seated by the fireside, while a few of us scoured our cupboards and fridges for sustenance. Maria from Argentina produced bread, guacamole, and aubergines in olive oil, and I managed a bowl of herb-flavoured black olives, some spicy grilled sausages and a few *hamburguesas*. The drummer turned out to be a vegetarian, so I rushed back to the house and put together a cheese and *membrillo* (quince jelly) sandwich for him. I think we drank, at various stages, caramel-flavoured vodka, good red wine and very strong, not quite as good, local *costa* wine. This led to some wild dancing of the Highland Fling and the energetic leaping of the flames by our tattooed friend Devine. Several languages were shared around, mostly Spanish, French, and English, but after a while we all understood each other perfectly. The cold of the January night was driven away by fire, flame and good-humour.

* * *

Spring arrived in stages throughout February, bringing either pink or white blossom to every almond tree, and a variety of small, starry flowers half-hidden in the lush grass. Fresh green leaves began to appear on the poplars and we started to pack away our winter clothes. There were days when it rained heavily, water pouring down the little streets and dripping off the roofs, but we were glad to have it. Summer droughts would follow all too soon.

Much has been written about the gorgeous almond blossom of Andalucía, but not enough perhaps about the contrast of the roughened and charcoal-dark trunks of the trees themselves set against the bare landscape in which they flaunt themselves. Gazing across the valleys one can see each unique tree growing aslant its hillside home, often in an angular Y-shape and topped off by the delicate drifts of pale flowers. Persephone has reached her earth-bound home and yearns to dance, but the dark fingers of Hades still hold her down. I am reminded of the fairy-tale images by Edmund Dulac of the Buried Moon, struggling to escape from the swamp.

We waited also for the yellow broom to burst into flower, bringing with it that delicious perfume which permeates the fields and even the motorways. Orange tree blossom has the same impact in the cities, its heavy sweetness almost unbearable. One bright day, I went with Marianne to Granada, where we picked, surreptitiously, some Seville oranges from the trees in the Generalife gardens, to make our marmalade. We drank coffee and strolled arm-in-arm through the broad streets in our long coats and black leather boots, two older ladies enjoying a moment of elegance in an enchanting city. All the trees in the avenues and parks were ready to burst into leaf. The season seemed to have paused and we looked at Nature renewing herself.

Later, in high summer, Steve and I would look back and wish that we had stopped to stare for even longer at the freshness and promise of the Alpujarran spring - clear skies, glittering water, snow on the mountain peaks and jewel-like fruit in the valleys.

In March, a group of us went to dance tango in Granada. The plaza in front of the great doors of the cathedral, laid with smooth, marble slabs and surrounded by cafés and tall houses, was the perfect setting for an afternoon of sensual dancing and exhibition pieces. Young women in short, flouncy skirts or harem trousers circled in the arms of their admirers, stepping with complex deliberation and flirtatious hip-twitching. Older couples glided with familiarity and ease, lost in the music of the live band. At one point the stone floor was cleared as two young dancers, in jeans and leather boots, performed an energetic and choreographed piece of theatrical tango. Similar in height, size and appearance, they threw each other around the plaza at speed, the girl's long, dark hair flashing in the sunlight. Something very difficult was made to look easy.

It would be another two years before I could execute my steps well enough to feel relaxed and assured in such a public setting, but this time I still managed to stutter my way around the square with one or two male partners. Wearing a reliable black-and-white polka-dotted dress, purple tights and traditional, low-heeled, strapped shoes, I did not realise that soon I too would be buying leather-soled stilettos, flirty skirts and tight-fitting sweaters, all for the sake of tango.

That night, as we drove home, an enormous, pomegranate-coloured moon rose above the Sierras, golden against the dark heavens. The moon had great significance for Lorca, the poet and playwright, who included it in much of his work as signifier, observer and chorus for the emotional dreams and dramas of close-knit Andalucían society in the 1930s. At times, it is a silver orb, alone and in pain; at times, a wavering, watery reflection of vulnerability; at times, the piercing eye of unremitting vigilance, controlling the destinies of men and women.

On yet another tango evening, driving back from the coast in the early hours, I saw a single segment of mandarin orange rising from the sea. As I climbed the mountain roads, it rose with me. The moon was my partner in a magical moment of synthesis.

I had started learning Argentinian tango in England, many years earlier, but there did not seem to be any rules other than 'it's just a walk to music' or 'it's all about respect' or 'the man must make the woman look beautiful.' How, I wondered, did one progress from 'just walking' to that flowing, exciting movement that belongs not to a glittering TV spectacular but to a tawdry club, a single *bandoneón*, a low-tipped hat and a pair of stiletto heels?

Some men seem to regard their partner as a sack of potatoes, to be dragged around the floor as they demonstrate their speed and prowess; others provide no support physically, so the strong arm needed to stop one from faltering is simply not there; very occasionally one is lucky enough to dance with someone who knows what they are doing. Almost always in the past, it seemed to be my fault, not my partner's, when a sequence failed or we trod on each other's toes. I had given up.

One winter's day, however, I spotted a poster in the Pitres library: 'Clase de Tango, el miércoles, a las 18.00 horas, en el Salón de Actos.' The council were making the small theatre stage available, since it had the right kind of smooth, wooden floor and a man from Montevideo was proposing to teach the basics. I already owned a pair of simple, black, strapped shoes with leather soles, suitable for flamenco or salsa or tango, and decided that this time I must persevere.

In fact, quite a lot of people got started, mostly women, but we did have one or two German men who seemed keen. Of course, as usual, the numbers fell away rapidly when it became apparent that this was a dance that might take years to learn; cognoscenti speak of ten years for men and six for women, so only the most tenacious or long-lived were going to become experts. In addition, it was excruciatingly cold and our allurement was not enhanced by woolly leggings, scarves, trousers, and jackets. One night, I was tempted to keep my gloves on as well.

But gradually the steps began to make sense. We formed an Asociación de Tangueros and a few other teachers were brought in from Granada to develop our technique. Warmer weather arrived, yet we struggled to keep the numbers up; the economic crisis was beginning to make itself felt and even 10 Euros per month was beyond some people's pockets. One spring night, we managed an evening's dancing in the local plaza, enlivened by the presence of some dancers from Buenos Aires and the Costa del Sol, but still we seemed to be losing focus.

It took a summer of persistent yet disappointing visits to Salobreña and the coast, and to Granada, before I found my level, with a group in Granada and their splendid teachers from Uruguay, William and Carina. Here were some South Americans and Spaniards who truly wanted to learn tango, who were tolerant of my poor Spanish, who welcomed me into their group and soon made me feel part of a very special family. Only one other person from the Alpujarras, whom I shall name Carl, made the regular weekly trip to the city for these classes.

We assembled in the Centro Cultural above the Teatro Isabela la Catolica, in a room that sometimes hosted art exhibitions too, or groups of men playing dominoes or chess. For two hours we worked hard. William was the creative magician who made every woman feel as though she was gliding on silk; Carina was the disciplinarian who frequently pointed out that one's footwork was poor or one's stance ungainly.

"Juntos!" she would cry, "bring your feet together!" Or, "Keep your feet on the floor, glide, don't step - suave, suave!

"The man proposes a step," she explained, "and the woman can accept or decline. You must learn how to respond to his stimulus and wait, always wait. It is not your role to lead."

"Don't think," reiterated William, "just respond to the music and the movement proposed by the man."

This was hard after years of feminism, independence and irritation with men 'telling us' what to do. In any event, not all the men had William's skill or musical awareness to 'lead' or make a clear 'proposal.' Even the Spanish women had trouble with yielding to this extent, although we had a reprieve of sorts due to the presence of Yolanda, a delightful person who was sufficiently competent to take the role of man or woman.

"Naturally, I prefer to dance with you, hombre," was our frequent and amused response if she was asked to supplement the male team. We had a lot of fun when it was someone's birthday, as the opposite gender would each take it in turns to dance with the birthday boy or girl. Yolanda had the privilege of doing both.

After the class we would stroll leisurely to the Bar Ávila opposite El Corte Inglés, the biggest department store in central Granada, and join a throng of students, local business people, and other Granadinos, to drink a refreshing *tinto de verano* and eat delicious tapas. Despite the 80 kilometre round trip, I was benefiting from Spanish conversation lessons as well as dancing, and some cultural awareness as well as neat footwork. Later, when the group came up into the mountains for a summer party at our house, they were horrified at the distance involved and the winding mountain roads. "Linda, *guapa*, you travel so far! These bends, these terrible roads, how can you do this alone!"

"But often I come with Carl," I protested. "He drives very fast, it doesn't take too long."

In fact, I enjoyed the independence of travelling alone, of leaving of my own accord, of not being beholden to anyone. Besides, Carl was a free spirit who did not want to be twinned up with anyone, of that I was sure, even for a few tango classes or for cheaper, because shared, fuel costs. Steve declined to get involved, perfectly happy to stay at home, although he always complained that he had to dine on meagre gruel whilst I danced in the arms of other men. He was usually horizontal and asleep by the time I got back.

On one unforgettable occasion in April, when the temperatures continued to drop close to zero after dark, I returned to the village at about one in the morning, having had my night of tango and socialising, tired and ready for my bed. The whole village was bereft of sound; not even the cats were about. I parked the car and headed up our street, moving as quickly as I could in my short-ish skirt, hugging my suede jacket about me, keen to get into the warm. Casually, I pushed on the big chestnut door, expecting it to creak open as usual. Nothing. No movement at all.

"Damn it," I muttered. Steve must have locked up absent-mindedly, using our wooden wedge on the inside, as strong as any batten. I went to the courtyard door but the padlock was in place and I had no key. Round the back to the kitchen door, but that too was locked and bolted, as was the *granero*.

From the street I could see a light on upstairs. Perhaps he was still awake. I pulled the bell-rope and hammered on the door. This would rouse the whole population on such a still, quiet night, but what else could I do? No response at all. He must be in bed and asleep. What were my next options?

I went round the back again and managed to scramble onto the house roof. Tiptoeing across the *launa*, I reached the chimney stack that led down to the wood burner outside our bedroom door.

"Steve!" I called. "Steve!"

No answer. I tried calling even louder but there came no reply. Whatever the ups and downs of our life together, I knew that he would never lock me out intentionally. But he had no mobile phone, nor did we have a landline into the house, so I couldn't try ringing him. This was becoming grim. I knew that a night in the car without a rug or a sleeping bag would not be a happy one; I might even freeze to death.

What to do? The only possible access to the house was at first floor level via the balcony, but that would require a ladder or a very tall set of steps. Perhaps I could locate the village ladder, usually locked away in a basement *cuadra*, hidden from passers-by or potential thieves, but I had no idea where exactly this *cuadra* was.

I walked back into the centre of the village and began to cast about for any likely doorway or stable. Eventually, I found a possible entrance with a slatted window and peered into the darkness, aided by my little key-ring torch. There it lay, a wooden ladder of at least 3 metres, made in one continuous length. How was I going to get my hands on it?

By great good fortune, the stable entrance was chained but not padlocked. The big door groaned as I opened it, releasing a cloud of dust and a nasty smell of cat poo. Uncaring, I waded into the straw and dirt and eased it out. It was very heavy and difficult to balance because of its length, but I managed to find a mid-point and tottered back to our house with it over my shoulder. I leaned it up against the metal railing of the balcony and, with no one about, hitched my skirt up above the knicker line, clambered up and threw a leg over the railing. After that, it was just a matter of fighting my way through the jasmine, geraniums and other pot plants, to the wooden shutters. Often these were not barred and tonight I was able to push them open and get straight into the house. Thank goodness!

Steve had not only gone to sleep, but he had done so with headphones on and late-night Spanish radio trickling into his subconscious. No wonder he hadn't heard me shouting down the chimney. This time, standing by his pillow, I certainly managed to make enough noise to wake him up and somewhat crudely point out his failings, then I took the ladder back to its rightful home and made myself a cup of hot tea. It would be many weeks before I forgave him, but only a few hours' sleep passed before the courtyard key was securely attached to my car key-ring. Now, whenever I go out, I double-check that I have the entire chatelaine's collection with me, jangling as I go.

* * *

One can never be sure how the night will unfold in the remote mountain villages, especially in the summer. We have heard the singing of lone travellers out there in the darkness, maybe a contemplative shepherd watching over his flocks, or a local lass, returning home under the stars; often there are the children shrieking in the plaza until the early hours of hot summer nights; dogs barking and howling of course; and always the backdrop of the crickets chirruping. Closer to one's ear is the irritation of the mosquito's whine and the drone of a cool air fan. Romance and mundaneity co-exist in this dramatic landscape, driven by centuries of bleak agrarian survival and passing opportunities for celebration or levity.

We achieved a great deal of the latter when we went to a neighbouring village for their annual water fight, when the August sun was at its zenith and all sensible folk were planning to take a siesta. As a preliminary, about 100 people gathered under the trees outside the little white and yellow-painted church, to buy drinks from the temporary bar and eat homemade paella. This was being cooked by some flushed and sturdy men in an enormous metal pan about two metres across and set over an open fire. No cookers or gas bottles in sight. It was a case of 'bring your own plate, fork and chair,' join the queue and then tuck in to a delicious combination of saffron-flavoured rice, prawns, squid, lamb and peas. With perfect calculation, everybody, plus a few lucky backpackers, got a hearty plateful.

No one sat over their meal too long today. As soon as we had finished, the chairs, trestle tables and rubbish were cleared away and the odd youngster could be seen, casually making his or her way towards the fountain, bucket in hand. Older residents immediately slipped away, middle-aged cowards beat a strategic retreat, and we were left with a lot of 12 to 16 year-olds and a motley collection of young adults and grey-haired juveniles, ourselves included. More buckets appeared, plus a few water-pistols, plastic cups and cooking pots.

Essential attire for an event like this has to be something you don't care about, particularly a redundant T-shirt, shorts, flip-flops or trainers, and no hardware such as watches, cameras, or mobiles. We stowed our motorbike gear well away from the action, seized our cheap, pump-action water-guns and headed into the fray.

Steve's method of attack was a 'creep up unseen and get them from behind' style, which involved him crouching behind some trestles, shooting off a jet of water and then ducking out of sight. This worked well with the girls, but the boys were attuned to all of this and spotted him very rapidly; he was soon running around a large tree, hotly pursued by his opponents, also equipped with water pistols.

I, meanwhile, hesitated on the side-lines then decided to give my gun to Mariana, our 18 year-old 'flower' of the village. With her hip-hugging jeans, bare tummy and huge brown eyes, she was going to be an instant target and would need some sort of defence. As a replacement, I picked up an empty plastic beer mug and tried to make my way to the fountain as discreetly as possible, assessing my preferred targets as I went. Very unwise. I still had dry clothes on and had to be caught by someone. A laughing young man ran up and threw his entire bucketful over my head, drenching me completely. I gasped with shock, even though the water was refreshingly cool in the midday heat, but war is war and I made sure that my first ammunition load went his way.

After that it was mayhem and we all ended up slipping and sliding around the square, trying to wring out our clothes when we could, then standing in the sunshine to dry out, like so many damp butterflies. Eventually the fountain ran out of water, or someone turned off the supply. We biked back up the hill in the hot wind, drying off as we went.

Chapter 11

Steve's Story

At this point I am going to hand over some of the story to Steve. In 2011 we decided to go to the Isle of Man TT for its 100th Centenary Year, a long-held dream of his that had never been fulfilled. But he needs to tell you about his love affair with bikes first (it's always been bikes)...

* * *

Some of my earliest memories are of motorbikes. Long trips from Cheshire to Cornwall for the summer holidays, sharing a sidecar with my older brother Pete, while mother rode on the pillion. Nowadays, even with the M6 and M5 motorways, it's a bit of a hike; in the mid 1950s, on the old twisting 'A' roads, it must have been an epic journey.

My father, Frank, would sometimes pick us up from school, on his way home from work. I (aged 5), would sit side-saddle on the tank, keeping my feet clear of the exhaust, while Pete rode pillion. No crash helmets, no protection, and not much traffic in those days. It was a different world. That old Ariel, a 600cc Huntmaster I think, was a real 'man's bike', and I loved it. I loved the sound. I loved the smell. I loved the way the wind tugged at my clothes, and blew my hair about. And if I opened my lips a little, the air would fill my mouth and puff out my cheeks. Holding onto the steering damper or the handlebars, I imagined it was me in control. It was me swinging us through the bends and accelerating away from junctions. I was guiding the big machine expertly round corners and braking to a stop. It was a feeling I may never forget.

Sadly, Frank died in a car accident when I was 10. He never knew of the seed he had planted. It was a seed that would grow, a plant that would stay with me all my life.

When I was old enough and had sufficient money, I bought a moped. Not a very auspicious entry into the world of two-wheeled motorised transport, but that Raleigh runabout got me on the road and enabled me to try my hand at D.I.Y. mechanics. Changing brake shoes and oiling chains was an easy introduction into the world of spanners, but the moped was never going to replicate the feeling that the big old Ariel had given me.

It was hard to buy a good bike in the late 1960s, with very little spare money, but progress was made through a series of Honda 50s, BSA Bantams, and Honda 125s to my first, really fast, biggish bike, a Suzuki Super Six. The Super Six was a 250cc two-stroke twin, with a six speed box. It was a beast, and it was a wreck, and I wish I still owned it. Bought as a non-runner for the princely sum of £10, it took less than an hour to get it running and on the road. It was terrifyingly brisk off the line. At 4000 revs, it was as if somebody had lit the blue touch-paper.

The first time I took it round the block, the boys had gathered to watch. Not wanting to stall it and then have to face the cheers and jeering, I gave it a few revs and tried to slip the clutch. The Suzuki was having none of it. The clutch went in with a bang, up came the front wheel, and I was off like a bat out of hell. Snaking down the road, the bike was shaking its head and wagging its tail under so much power. It was all I could do to hang on. By the end of the road, I was just able to get the throttle closed and the front wheel back on the ground, and by the time I had got round the block, I'd regained my composure and was Mr Cool again.

"Not too bad," I said, casually, as they stood watching in awe. They would never know that my underpants had been very nearly the first casualty.

The Super Six was a monster of a bike, and though it served as daily transport, it was far from roadworthy, and was eventually traded with a Liverpool dealer for my first real bike. The British racing green, Norton

Commando 750cc Fastback called out to my soul in a way I can't describe. Just thinking about it still gives me butterflies in the stomach.

Without a licence, and with a young man's disregard for the law, the papers were signed, the deal was done, and I rode home in a daze. I loved that bike. It looked fabulous, and had a big bike's power and feel. I just looked at a bend and the bike went round it by itself. It was tall, solid, and it fixed in my heart a love of big, pushrod twins that has never left me, and probably never will.

I had some memorable rides on that bike and Pete, perhaps on a pillion for the first time since the old Ariel, had at least one. One day, we pulled on our crash helmets and set off for a spin. I took him on a circuit of the north-west end of the Wirral peninsular. It was a run of about eleven miles, taking in some bends, straights, small town high streets and a bit of traffic. It wouldn't take long.

We set off uphill on an empty main road and I could tell by the grip of his hands on my waist that the Norton's torque was impressing him. It was impressing me.

Now it has to be said that Pete was not a motorcyclist, though he did drive a car rather 'enthusiastically' and with very little regard for his passengers. By the time we got to his favourite Frankby bends, where the road winds like a snake between high sandstone walls, we were moving, if not dangerously fast, then at least quite briskly. The Norton did its job faultlessly as we flick-flacked through the series of short twists and it was picking up speed rapidly by the time he looked over my shoulder and saw the speedo.

"My God!" he shouted in my ear through the wind rush, "you've just come through there at eighty miles an hour."

Of course I hadn't, we'd just managed to pick up a lot of speed before he'd got his eyes open, but I never told him and I believe that to this day he thinks we did.

The rest of the run was nice, with some good sweeping curves and, for those days, fast dashes down the relatively empty straights. Overtaking was done with gusto, and he couldn't believe it when we filtered through the queue of vehicles at the traffic lights to take up our position at the front. The lights changed, and a short blast down the hill brought us home.

When he stepped off the bike he was smiling, and though I don't think we ever spoke of it again, I think he enjoyed the experience.

Having said that, we never did ride together again.

Sadly, the Norton met its maker one Sunday morning, in an incident that ended with me trying to avoid walls and lamp posts, whilst failing to control a 100 mph tank slapper. I've had better days, though I count myself lucky to have escaped with just a few broken bones. The bike never recovered, and having family commitments, it would be many a long while before I would return to such big bikes.

The years following the Norton were filled with old British Villiers-engined bikes. By now, I was living out in the sticks in Suffolk, and an old James with a 250cc Villiers two-stroke twin engine would take me the 18 miles to work, in all weathers. This was a time before decent, cold-weather clothing was available, and we used all the tricks we could to stay warm; jackets and trousers were stuffed with newspaper and we'd wipe the inside of our goggles with a cut potato to stop them misting up.

That bike ran on a wing and a prayer. It had a tool box on one side filled with bits of string and wire, odd nuts and bolts, pieces of inner tube for tying things down (perhaps the forerunner of the bungee), spanners, mole grips, clutch and throttle cables. I could usually get home, but bikes then were more simple machines to repair. I doubt that my old James had many lengths of wire that were the same colour at both ends, but it never really let me down. It was old-school biking.

I seem, at one time, to have passed through a trials bike phase. I had a couple of Greaves 197cc trials bikes, and probably enough spares to build a few more. Lord knows where they came from. Though I never competed, we used to spend hours on the Common, or on a bit of waste ground, doing slow speed manoeuvres around obstacles, bunny-hopping over empty cans or trying to outdo each other by riding up the steepest banks we could find.

I thought those bikes must be the easiest thing in the world to ride, until an Ossa 250 MAR found its way to me. Mick Andrews had just won the World Trials Championship, and this was a replica of his bike. I'd never ridden anything so light or agile, and that was in the 1970s. Whatever are the modern trials bikes like? I eventually sold the Ossa to a friend, and never replaced it.

For various reasons, I was away from two wheels for over 30 years. That's to say, I didn't ride, though they never left my heart. Once a biker, always a biker. But apart from renting small bikes while on holiday in Greece, I had no time or use for one. I worked away from home, and although I kept abreast of new developments, and read articles, papers, magazines and so on, I never squeezed a clutch lever or turned a twist-grip in anger.

But time passes, and the beast stirs.

Linda and I met one cold December day, and a new phase of life began. Folk often speak of 'life's rich tapestry', but I think a patchwork quilt more accurately describes the way we live our lives. For my part, I've been a seaman, a wanderer, a fisherman, an engineer, a Merchant Navy officer and a truck driver, amongst other things. Like most folk, I've been young, foolish, kind and cruel; been drunk, sober, brash, shy, an adversary and a friend. I've trusted people too much, and I've trusted them too little; been surprised by them, and been disappointed. At times, I thought I'd seen everything, and yet I knew that I'd seen nothing. In fact, a pretty average sort of life.

Now, with plenty of summers under the bridge, I'm moving, if not into the final furlong, then at least into the downhill section, and it was strange and pleasing not to hear someone sucking air through their teeth when I mentioned getting another bike. Quite the contrary, Linda was very enthusiastic.

Driving down a small country road in Norfolk one sunny April morning, we saw a few bikes standing outside a car sales site. Stopping, we looked them over, and a bright yellow Suzuki GS500 (a four-stroke twin), took my fancy. After a short talk with the salesman, we slapped hands on a deal, and I owned the bike. Because I had no licence for a bike of this engine size, but was now a responsible adult, he agreed to deliver the bike to our home, and I set about taking my test.

The last time I rode, it seemed as though I had been born on a bike. It was just like an extension of the body, and a different bike took only a mile or two to get used to. You think that you'll never forget, but, as I discovered, this isn't so easy nowadays.

The riding school started me off on a 600 Yamaha Fazer. I'd read the road tests on the bike, and thought I knew what to expect. Wrong again. The Norton had been considered a fairly brisk bike in its day, but still you'd twist the throttle and wait a while. The Fazer was a different beast altogether. The merest hint of throttle and it was off like a rocket. I'd kept up to date with bikes for thirty-odd years, yet this relatively ordinary machine took me by surprise. This was going to take a while. And it did.

The examiner was doing his job properly. First time out, I wasn't good enough, so he failed me. The next time, I forgot to cancel an indicator, and he failed me again. I was a motorcyclist dating back to a time before indicators, and you never forgot to pull your hand back in. I was going to have to try harder.

It took me three tries to get my licence and I'm not proud of that, but eventually I was on the road, and I was legal.

In buying the Suzuki, I had thought it was the last bike I'd ever buy. It was a fairly big bike, it was fairly fast and I was getting a bit long in the tooth. Surely it would last me the rest of my days.

Ha!

Any biker will tell you, that's not how it works. The Suzuki was, and still is, a lovely bike. Easy to ride, easy to work on. It's a twin (which gives it a place in my heart), and they go on forever. But could we tour on it?

Enter the Honda CBR1000F. Stylish in silver, complete with panniers and top box, this was a bike that would take us anywhere. It could eat continents. We could tour Europe, no problem, never mind East Anglia. But it was a heavy bike, and in fact altogether too weighty for me. A slow-speed U turn in a station car park found us both lying on the ground beside the bike, and that was enough to confirm what I already knew. It would have to go.

The CBR was replaced by a Honda VFR 800i, a lighter, more modern bike, with an engine set in a V4 formation, and in my mind I view it as an honorary twin.

This bike was, for a time, considered the best of the sports tourers, and was very easy to ride. I bought it from a black church minister in Peterborough, at a very reasonable price, and rode it home with a huge grin on my face. This was more like it.

En-route, along the A47, I spotted an R1 Yamaha coming up in the rear-view mirror. I was at the back of a line of cars, and riding cautiously on the unfamiliar machine. The Yamaha rider was 'making progress,' as they say, so I moved closer to the curb and looked long and hard into my off-side mirror, to let him know I'd seen him, and that he was safe to pass. He moved alongside me and we nodded to each other, then moving to the centre of the road, with a twist of the wrist, he popped the bike up on its back wheel, and wheelied down the line of traffic as steady as you like. Clearly not the first time he'd performed that manoeuvre, and whilst not my personal modus operandi, I was unable to suppress a smile.

The rest of the trip, of about an hour and a half, was uneventful, though I did have to stop to send Linda a text saying how much I loved the bike. She soon felt the same way. We both enjoy riding it, though for different reasons. For her, it's comfortable enough to spend several hours on at a time and she feels secure. For me, it's a great handling bike, with plenty of power for overtakes, and even two-up with luggage it has real speed. I rarely do more than 130mph, and though the bike still has some in hand, I feel that that is about fast as I can comfortably go. My old brain can't process data as fast as a younger one might.

We have had a few outings to see how we get along with it. We went to a bike show near Bristol, a round trip of about 500 miles, and enjoyed some good roads in the West Country, as well as torrential rain on the way back. Later on, we took the scenic route to Huntly, just north of Aberdeen, via York, the North Lakes and Loch Lomond, which was a round trip of about 1200 miles. We had quite a few more runs to London, Peterborough and Derby without complaints. Next outing would be to mainland Europe.

Then, in about 2005, the world began its slow decline into recession. I was a truck driver by then, mostly in the music and conference business, and our industry suffered along with all the others. By 2007, work was getting thin, and I spent a few weeks sitting at home before Linda said, "You might as well be in Spain." I got on the Suzuki, and set my compass south. Next stop would be Dover.

* * *

"I'm sorry sir," the young lady said, "but there's no space. The next ferry is in three hours."

"It's a motorbike for Pete's sake," I pleaded. "You've got room for a motorbike, haven't you?"

"I'm sorry sir, the boat's full."

I walked across the office to the Norfolk Line desk. Four minutes later, and £26 lighter, found me riding towards the Dunkirk ferry.

This was my first foreign tour on two wheels, and the Suzuki was loaded with a Lidl tank bag, a £10 tail pack (Peterborough bike show), a £6.50 sleeping bag (Tesco) and a £10 tent (also Tesco). Minimal route planning was done on a French road atlas, bought for £1.50 from a local discount bookshop. This would be touring on the cheap. No tolls, no péages and no camping fees.

I was in something of a hurry. I wanted to be in the Alpujarras for the summer fiesta season, when the sleepy little villages of the Sierra Nevada take it in turn to hold all-night outdoor parties. Street theatre, makeshift bars, live music, and food cooked on fires built in the village square. These are straight-forward, warm-hearted people, with a great sense of humour, who know how to enjoy themselves.

The first evening, I burnt the midnight engine oil, to get through the less interesting parts of northern France. Towards Chartres, with 380 miles behind me and 1,120 ahead, I found a quiet spot behind a service area and pitched the tent. I slept well.

Friday started quite early and was a good day. In warm sunshine I rode south through Limoges and Bergerac on quiet country roads, smelling the thyme and lavender, riding through fields of sunflowers. French motorcyclists have a great sense of camaraderie, perhaps even greater than the Brits. Bikers coming towards you always give a low and lazy left-hand salute. Those overtaking will kick out a right foot as they sweep past. All very Gallic and very cool. Considerate car drivers receive the same recognition, and I soon fell into line and acknowledged their co-operation.

On through Agen and Auch, into the early evening, and when a sign indicated that there was parking behind a small village restaurant, it seemed rude not to stop. The people were charming, the food was good, and one of the waitresses spoke a little English. Having had a drop of wine with the meal (it would have been an insult to go without), I asked if could I sleep in the garden.

"Yes," she said, "but it's going to rain."

I didn't care. Up went the tent, down went my head, and I was back on the road before they awoke. Lovely folk, and it's amazing how well you can communicate with so little common language.

Saturday morning was misty and cool, and the roads were tranquil as I headed towards Aragnouet, and the tunnel of the same name. What a great route it was.

Approaching the tunnel the road becomes steep, with hairpin bends winding their way uphill, layer upon layer. Just the ticket for a biker who enjoys a technical challenge. Almost at the entrance, the way was full of sheep, heedless of any traffic; an old sheepdog lay on the slope and watched me as I picked my way through them. Minutes later I was in Spain. The views over the National Park were truly spectacular, and made me wish I was a better photographer.

The ride from Zaragoza to Andalucía was uneventful, and I arrived at our house in the warm dark of Saturday night. 1,500 miles in two and a half days, and no complaints. I loved it all.

I spent five weeks of that summer clearing brambles from the land, cleaning floors, and painting the house. By day, that is. By night, I was watching how the Spanish celebrate and party. I lost several pounds doing the work and put some of it back on eating tapas and drinking local vino, but all good things come to an end, so in September I returned to dear old Blighty and the joys of the big wheelers, while the summer passed, as summers do, into a mild autumn.

Having just finished a work assignment, I was back at base, sitting in the drivers' room, and browsing the 'bikes for sale' section on the Motorcycle News website. Thanks to my love of big V-twins, as always to the fore, I started with the Honda VTR Firestorm, and having found a good-looking bike in the Carlisle region, emailed Linda to see if she could check it out in more detail.

Going back to the same website, I moved to the Moto Guzzi section. Since first seeing a Motorcycle Mechanics' report on a Moto Guzzi V7, in the late 60s or early 70s, I had fallen in love with these bikes. I loved the huge, transverse V-twin engine that dominated the bike. I loved the Italian styling, the straight line along the length of the bike, formed by the base of the seat and the tank. I loved the parallel lines created by the tubes of the frame and the front forks, and I loved the big round cylinder fins. I admired the sporty models like the T3 or the Monza, and I really appreciated the more workaday models, like the V7. But they had always seemed beyond the reach of an ordinary chap; they were exotic machines that others owned and that I could only admire.

Now, whilst browsing the adverts, my eye fell upon a 1998, two-owner, 1100 Sport, with low mileage and some service history, and at a price I could afford. These are very handsome machines, and this one was in Birmingham, therefore, if it hadn't sold, I could view it on the way home. I emailed Linda again: 'forget the VTR, look at this.'

As if by fate, the transport manager called me in and said he had nothing for me and I could go home if I wanted. I unpacked the truck and loaded my personal possessions into the car. I was going to Birmingham. I had a bike to see, and perhaps a dream to fulfill.

The owner was a nice chap. An engineer, he loved these Italian bikes for the same reasons I did. He had a file of information that he'd downloaded, and a list detailing the work he'd done. When he took the cover off the bike, it knocked my eyes out. We were standing alongside a very special, very beautiful machine.

We did the deal, yet I had not even ridden the bike. He would MOT it, and I would pick it up in a few days when Linda could drive me over in the car to collect it. So it was that, on a rainy afternoon in late October, I mounted a Moto Guzzi for the first time and rode it home. How sweet does life get?

Logistics prevented me from riding the Guzzi, the VFR, or indeed Linda's Honda C90 down to Spain. As Linda has recounted, they were all loaded onto a trailer and towed here behind the van. We did the changeover to Spanish registration with the others, as she said, but with this bike we had some serious difficulties.

The headlight, being fitted for British roads, dipped to the wrong side, and was hard to replace, but I managed it. The main problem was, and continues to be, with the Swansea-based Driver and Vehicle Licensing Agency. For reasons that are unclear, only 7 of the chassis numbers, rather than the full 17 are recorded on the registration log book, and the Spanish equivalent of an MOT cannot be awarded without all 17 numbers on the British paperwork. But DVLA require a letter from the manufacturer before they will alter their documents. Try writing to Italy, to a motorcycle company, even in Italian, and see if you get a response.

The lesson here is that if you intend to export a vehicle from the UK, check all the identifying numbers against those on the log book. Check them again. Don't leave the country without total confidence that your vehicle will pass muster in your next country of residence.

All that aside, biking in southern Spain is great. The heat of August means that even mesh jackets are too much, making spring or autumn the most comfortable seasons to ride. But in winter, during daylight hours, it's often still warm and pleasant, with well-surfaced roads, interesting vistas and plenty of roadside spots where you can park up and sample the coffee or the tapas.

The lads and lasses from Granada, Almeria, or even Cadiz often make the Alpujarras their destination for a day's ride-out and we've sat in the sunshine in Trevélez with lawyers who own shiny, red Ducati's, Bavarian dudes on BMW's and tough hombres dismounting from their Harley Davidson's, hip-chains jangling and steel tankards hanging low.

So what does the future hold for us in biking terms? Well, the Suzuki is doing sterling service for local rides, as is Linda's Honda C90 for shopping runs. The trip to the Isle of Man is coming up. A visit to Italy is on the cards, to see Linda's relatives in Milan and maybe, as a last-ditch attempt, the Guzzi factory at Mandello del Lario. The VFR will have a chance to stretch its legs as it hauls two ageing Brits into a few more sunsets. And why not? We have a bit of spare time now, and there are an awful lot of roads out there still to be ridden.

I wonder what Frank would have made of it?

Chapter 12

Isle of Man TT

So there we were, preparing for our trip to the Isle of Man. There is not much point in going without a bike, so we decided to load up the VFR with the bare essentials and make a 'grand tour' to include friends in Haute Provence and the Pyrenees. We could go out via Santander and come back overland. We reckoned that this would take as long as four weeks and the secret of success lay in the planning.

As it was already mid-January, we were about 6 months too late to be picky about sea crossings, campsites, B&Bs or any of the refinements that we might wish for on a small island that was likely to be invaded by 30,000 other motorcyclists. On a short trip back to England, I mentioned the plan to some friends in Cumbria, and the difficulties we might have in seeing it through and finding somewhere to stay.

"Oh," said Janice. "Well, of course, Robert lives there now, with Mary and the girls. You could contact him - he was an old boyfriend of yours, wasn't he? And I think they do B&B anyway."

This gave me serious pause for thought. Robert was indeed an old (forty years previously) boyfriend, but whether that justified getting in touch and what Mary might make of it, was a conundrum. Only briefly, however. We were so keen to go that I decided to write to Robert and beg for a piece of turf on which to put a small tent, hoping he would oblige. Within a week, a splendid email came flying back, assuring us of a camping spot in their two acre garden and saying how much they enjoyed the company of bikers. I wondered whether they realised that we could only get ferry tickets spanning a 15 day period, which is a long time to be anyone's guest, even behind the rhododendron bushes. We knew the Mark Twain quote about guests and fish stinking after 3 days.

Tickets booked and accommodation assured, we moved rapidly into spring and then early summer. Steve stripped down the bike, replaced anything that might give us trouble and we started to assemble our kit. We all know the traveller's mantra: lay out the items you need to take, remove two-thirds of them and then pack the remainder. When you have only a couple of panniers, a top-box and a tank-bag, and the many essentials include tools, spare headlights, a hazard triangle and loo paper, there is not much room left for clothing, a tent, and the means of brewing a cuppa.

"Don't bring anything extra in the way of clothes," said Steve meaningfully, "just your motorbike kit and a toothbrush."

I pondered on this. Southern Spain in May and June is already getting pretty warm. The same period on a small island in the Irish Sea could include snow, night-time temperatures of below zero or, by good fortune, a heat-wave. Leather jeans and lined textile jackets, with full shoulder and knee armour and a sweater underneath, although excellent for northern European travelling, would be too hot in any temperature over 20 degrees, and on the return trip we could encounter scalding heat south of Lyon. So we would need textile trousers which would be cooler than leathers and we would have to carry complete 'wets' too, to protect us from heavy downpours. None of these items count as style garments of course.

Footwear would need to be protective, waterproof, comfortable, cool or warm as required and, hopefully, look good in a restaurant. Helmets were, of course, de rigeur, and would have to be the full-face variety with ear-plugs and visors. Gloves, a neck-warmer, socks... the list was a long one.

Oh dear. The limitations of our saddle-bags presented serious problems and I began to review my options. I reasoned that if it was too hot on the Isle of Man, I could always buy a cheap top and throw it away afterwards. Keeping warm had to be the priority, which meant thermal underwear that could double as pyjamas. Keeping cool coming home was an issue I chose not to think about, but any social activity required a spare pair of ordinary jeans. Sandals or flip-flops had to be squeezed in somewhere too, but I knew that these would count as 'extra' in Steve's reckoning. Then, naturally, there was the question of knickers. How many pairs for a month? One pair to wear, one pair to wash and a third for emergencies? Or could I manage with two pairs? My friend and frequent traveller, Sue, put me right.

"Three is the minimum," she pronounced. "It would be better to have four pairs, but you can't have less than three." In retrospect, I think two is possible but only if you get into a nightly washing routine and have somewhere to dry them out easily.

I decided that a small rucksack was going to be the only way to carry what I needed and, at the same time, avoid Steve's scrutiny.

"How will you lean back against the top-box if you have a rucksack on?" he enquired, raising an eyebrow.

"Oh," I breezed, "I can just hoick it up a bit, on top of the box. It'll be fine."

So there we were, at seven o'clock on a fine May morning, loaded up and ready to depart. Steve had a kit-bag in front of him on the fuel tank with its integral, transparent plastic envelope protecting the map and SatNav; I had saddle-bags behind my knees on both sides, the top-box behind me with a padded backrest, and the rucksack.

Ah, that fearsome rucksack. By the time we had reached the main road, a matter of minutes, I could feel it pressing on my neck and pushing me forward. Fifteen minutes later I realised that it would have to be adjusted or relocated. We stopped and I took it off, placed it on my lap and leaned back gratefully against the top-box. After about 30 minutes, Steve stopped again. We had been going downhill and although not heavy, the rucksack was pressing on his spine now, instead of mine.

"It's no good," he said. "We'll have to ditch it."

"I'll try loosening the straps and balancing it on the top of the top-box," I replied. "Once we get going, the airflow will keep it in place."

This proved to be more or less correct, but unless we were doing the maximum legal, and sometimes illegal, speed, I was constantly juggling its weight and disposition. As we swept around a left-hander, I had to raise my left shoulder, pull on the right-hand strap and hope it stayed in place. This was then reversed for a right-hander. If we stopped in a hurry and I slid forward, the whole thing shot up and then fell into the small space behind me. The mechanism to correct this involved standing up on the foot pegs, like a horse-rider in the stirrups, and humping the darned thing back into position. All, naturally, without disturbing the main man at the handlebars, as well as the balance of the bike. Anyone perceiving these acrobatic feats, such as road traffic police, would probably have pulled us over. Luckily for us, during our entire trip, this never happened. There were other adventures with the rucksack however, which we will come to later.

Flying through Spain on secondary roads was a delight. So little traffic, such a huge landscape, such intense colour. We passed pink, stone-scattered hillsides dotted with herds of black, brown, and cream goats; lush, pale-green fields edged with vermilion poppies; ridged sienna-brown soil surrounded by fluttering, silver poplar trees. White houses, orange roofs, honey-hued churches, black eagles against a cerulean sky. Everything casting its long, purple-blue shadow as the sun rose higher and the light intensified.

There was no shortage of land covered by ranks of solar panels, or hilltops decorated with wind turbines. They belonged in a Miró painting, behind the farmer, his dog, the ladder against the farmhouse and the rows of maturing vegetables. A surreal world decorated by fantastical, yet everyday, shapes and patterns.

On our first night we found ourselves outside the great walls of 16th century Avila. Swallows swooped and played above the battlements, storks nested on the highest pinnacles, while the folk below took their evening *paseo* and the Plaza Mayor played host to a modern-day political protest. We found a small restaurant which, though catering to the tourists, served up a great dish of beans and chorizo, as delicious as if it had been made that instant by Mama in her kitchen. Here was Spain working through its own particular blend of history, passion, and pride.

Our second night at Riaño in the Picos mountains was a bit different. Foolishly, I had assumed that a small town on the edge of a lake would automatically be picturesque and appealing. I was utterly wrong. About 30 years ago, someone had looked at alpine chalet towns, poured-concrete high-rise flats and a selection of very ugly colour schemes, and assembled them together to form perhaps the most dismal place in Castilia y Leon. What a disappointment.

Only the lakeside position saved it from total ignominy, but that too was marred by driving rain and a very small and dishevelled touring circus positioned on the lake shore. A sodden camel and two little ponies waited for someone kind-hearted to come and take them to shelter. We almost ran over a hedgehog and regarded its survival as the only ray of sunshine in such a miserable spot. We parked the bike, bought a quantity of instant food in the local supermarket for our supper and lounged around in a dismal bedroom, watching the sparrows hopping along the dripping telegraph wires until darkness fell.

By contrast, the next morning's run was sublime. There are few greater pleasures than winding one's way slowly up and down mountain passes on a motorbike, the pastures on either side twinkling with birdsong and sunshine, the bright sky yielding eagles, buzzards and hawks, all wheeling around the high peaks and crags in the distance.

On one descent, we met a procession of russet cows heading up into the high pastures, a well-horned bull in their midst and a bevvy of dogs keeping to the verges. The farmer walked at the front, his wife at the back, both of them stepping out energetically despite the incline and the warmth. All traffic stopped, as it should, to let them progress.

"¿*Dondé vas?*" I asked the wife - "Where are you going?"

She mentioned a village we had passed through earlier, about 5 kilometres higher up the mountainside.

"*Muy duro,*" I replied admiringly, "*ustedes son muy fuertes.*"

She shrugged and smiled, and on they went.

Thus we moved north, from the Picos to Santander, out into the Atlantic and up through the Bay of Biscay to Plymouth. Then from Devon to Liverpool, where I had booked us a Holiday Inn for the night, and finally to the docks and the Steam Packet Company ferry.

"Where were all the bikes?" we wondered. It seemed remarkably quiet, even at 8a.m., with perhaps only a dozen machines and their riders lined up, tickets in hand. It was not yet race week, but we expected much more activity.

We did not speculate for long. A trickle of bikes soon became a convoy, then a flood, with engines growling, throbbing, and revving as they were manoeuvred into position. It was very chilly, but someone spotted a Portacabin with a café sign and we crowded inside. Too late. Whatever the hot drinks machine had once contained, it had been drained dry by the previous batch of passengers and we would have to go without. Congratulations to the resourceful folk who had anticipated this and brought their own thermos flasks. Nil points to the ferry company and its marketing team.

As we began to embark, we noticed a huge, electric-blue Harley Davidson waiting ahead of us, ridden by a diminutive, moustachioed cowboy in fringed leathers and glistening blue helmet. As we were all guided around a tight turn to get onto the ferry, his machine paused, tottered and then fell with a crash to the ground. Such a long and heavy bike, designed for sweeping curves and American highways, could not cope with a cobblestoned Mersey wharf. Everyone rushed to help pick it up, but the poor man must have wished he was on something smaller and less distinctive.

The Island however, was buzzing with machines of every size and type, and discretion was not a requirement. From that first day on, we saw sizzling Honda Fireblades, an old and idiosyncratic 250 Ducati single, pearl-white Buells and, of course, two-toned, red and grey MV Agustas. Steve drooled over a quite rare 175 Bridgestone disc valve two-stroke and a lovely, blue Suzuki T20. In addition, there were several Suzuki 750 water-cooled, two-stroke triples (nicknamed the tea kettle), at least one of which was very nicely customised and sporting chrome expansion-box exhausts.

What else? Well, there were classic Velocettes, BSAs, Nortons, Tritons, and a very appealing old BMW 250 single with its unusual springer frame. There must have been a bike to suit every taste. Rider nationalities ranged from French, Italian and German to four Greeks who had ridden overland from Athens; a tearful Argentinian who had not spoken Spanish for five days until he met us; two Republican firemen from Baltimore, and an Australian on his newly-acquired, bright-yellow Moto Guzzi.

"I told the wife over breakfast," he beamed, "I said it as quickly as I could, before her jaw closed. Then I got on the next plane out of Sydney, picked up the bike in London and here I am!"

We even met up with the sorry owner of an astounding, fire-engine red Honda SP2 'the bike that smashed Ducati at their own game in World Superbikes,' (Gardz, Buellersunder website), who was so physically damaged by the act of riding it on normal roads that he was desperate to sell it. We were very tempted, but managed to resist.

Robert and Mary refused to let us camp and put us up in great luxury in their guest suite. We had not expected the joys of white bathrobes, tea-making facilities, TV and Internet access, all in our spacious bedroom. It was only when some pre-booked Italians visitors arrived with their bikes for race week that we departed to the meadow and our small tent. Three days later we were back in the house again, just as the temperature fell and, briefly, the rains came.

Practice week was a relatively quiet affair and gave us the chance to wander through the Grandstand area and say hello to the 'greats' such as John McGuinness, Ian 'Hutch' Hutchinson and local boy Conor Cummins. No one stood on ceremony or gave themselves airs, although it was hard to locate Guy Martin at any hour. During this first week, practice sessions ran erratically, dependent on the weather and if the roads were clear of local traffic. Despite so many years of organised racing, someone still had to ensure that old Bill kept his sheepdogs locked up, that the children were all on the right side of Ramsey Park and that no idiot had high-sided up on the mountain just before the road was closed to the public. Each day, bikes were being stripped down and display tents put up, while the side-car teams plotted their strategies and the police embarked on an intensive speed camera offensive.

We had time to explore our sea-encompassed holiday destination, a microcosm of the United Kingdom. There are hills and dales, forests and meadows, cliffs and beaches; prehistoric standing stones and early Christian chapels; seagulls and seals and basking sharks. Much of the housing around the coast reflects Edwardian wealth and grandeur, but inland there is plenty of open space, farming and woodland.

The ports are very individual, each with their own charm and their own selection of fishermen's cottages and grey, pebble-dashed council houses. We visited Port Erin more than once, wandering the sea-shore and eating delicious ice-cream. Somewhere on a hilltop high above the sea we lay down in ancient burial trenches and listened to the larks high above. We went up over the mountain of Snaefell, on the one-way system allocated for the racing calendar and shivered as young men on faster machines than ours went haring past us.

Most days we went out to sample possible viewing spots for the following week. We were casing the joint: how about the uphill section of the Gooseneck? Or would we see more action near the Joey Dunlop memorial? How about Glen Helen? Or would there be midges? Ballough Bridge looked exciting and then there was the straight towards Ramsey... Steve was looking for potential displays of technical virtuosity, whilst I was considering how cold or windswept it might get, where the loos were, and whether or not there would be a food van. Once races began, one tended to be trapped at the chosen viewing point and if any accidents or delays occurred, that could be for several hours. Some spots had tiered grandstands, others, such as churchyards, were filled with benches. Some were isolated fields with just a stone wall between you and the motorbikes as they flew by. We selected our preferences and then waited to see what the weather would provide.

It was late May, we had come from southern Spain, yet our first Isle of Man incident was sunburn. We could have been at sea, such was the impact of wind and sunshine on our faces. It had not occurred to us to bring sun-screen or floppy hats and our noses were soon bright pink. But the island is very changeable and there were moments when spectators on the west coast sunbathed while those on the eastern side experienced hailstones, even sleet. The racing was dependent on dry conditions, so quite a bit of time was spent looking anxiously skyward, tracking the clouds and assessing their density, or listening to portable radios for the latest forecast.

Every afternoon and evening we went out to watch the practice sessions, eating fish and chips or beef burgers, drinking tea and, later, beer. Finally, the first week was over and the practice sessions completed. Sidecar combinations and motorbikes were in their final stages of preparation. Tragically, three local bikers and two competitors had died. No doubt that proportion of riders die every day on the roads in England alone, but it seemed an unwelcome, if inevitable statistic for week one.

We thought the island was packed to capacity, but another 20,000 spectators arrived over the weekend and all the roads were flooded with magnificent two-wheeled creatures, bedecked and glistening like so many horses at a latter-day jousting tourney. Let battle commence.

The racing was fabulous. Men, and occasionally women, with whom we had been speaking just a few days earlier, were now racing each other down the Sulby Straight at speeds of up to 200 mph, or chasing each other over the mountain and daring to overtake, flying shoulder to shoulder through impossibly fast, sweeping bends, their bikes squirming and bucking on the uneven road surface. If you've never seen this type of racing, you would not believe what these particular individuals are capable of, their audacity, their courage and, for some, their foolhardiness.

The TT lost its MotoGP (Motorbike Grand Prix) status in 1976 because it was deemed too dangerous, and in Steve's opinion, rightly so. Nobody should have to race on that circuit. It should be reserved only for those who want to race there, by choice.

But we were hooked. We watched all the races, then we watched the highlights on the pub TV in the evenings. We watched the ¼ mile sprint races down on the promenade, and we watched the vintage racing at the southern end of the Island, where the bikes of our childhood, the G50 Matchless', Manx Nortons, Ducati's, and other ancient exotica, carried on the battles they had fought in the 1950s and '60s, as if they'd never stopped.

We rode the circuit several times ourselves, following in the tyre tracks of such greats as Stanley Woods, Geoff Duke, Giacomo Agostini and Mike Hailwood, and, of course, the king of the mountain, Joey Dunlop. It was two weeks of motorcycle-steeped bliss, and though we may never return, it left us knowing that we had seen something very special. As Steve says, those who come to race nowadays on the Isle of Man are not ordinary people; they may look like the rest of us, but they're not.

So, back to Steve and the latest episode in his love affair with these fiery beasts.

* * *

A while later, I bought another bike.

A friend of mine, Declan, who had been a biker in a previous life, heard the call and was reborn. Having searched for a while, he found a bike locally, in Spain, a 125cc trail-style Yamaha 2 stroke single, which was duly purchased. It proved to be a nice machine and, along with riding it on the highways, he could often be found on the mountain trails, exploring inaccessible places with wild abandon and no apparent regard for his own safety. Biking was back in his blood and there was no point trying to fight it.

If necessary, making a quick trip to his green and native land, he would ride to Málaga airport with his luggage strapped to the pillion seat, or we would sometimes go out together for a run to Jerez or Puerto de la Ragua, or across the Contraviesa on the scenic route to the Mediterranean. These rides were rarely more than five or six hours, always pleasant and unhurried affairs, and we'd stop for coffee and a chat when we felt like it, or for a cooling drink when the summer heat became unbearable.

Inevitably, after a while, he decided that the Yamaha, whilst a nice little bike, didn't quite do everything he wanted, and that he needed something a bit bigger, with touring possibilities. So the search began.

To narrow the choice down somewhat, he laid out what he required of a new bike, and eventually he called me saying he'd found something that fitted his needs, and asked if I would like to go down with him to the coast to see it.

We arrived in Motril one Tuesday evening, as it was cooling down a bit, and after some searching through the narrow streets, we located the address. The bike was a BMW F650 CS single in powder blue, in lovely condition and, to be honest, it looked better than it sounded. The chap selling it was a family man who found he no longer had time to ride, so it had to go. Perhaps he needed the money too. We asked all the usual questions and felt that we were getting honest answers; when he asked us if we'd like a test ride, Declan looked at me, nodding his head and raising his eyebrows, so I jumped aboard and went for a spin.

I've never been very keen on BMW as a manufacturer, although in the past few years it has made one or two interesting bikes. Its HS2 is a horizontally-opposed flat twin with a very sporty look, a real eye catcher, and the 800 twins were turning out some quite impressive performance figures, but BMW's main line was still 'adventure' bikes and large tourers, some of which are just too ugly to describe. Though it may keep you from the wind and rain, there is nothing attractive about a combined fibre-glass tank and fairing unit with a surface area the size of the Isle of Wight. Motorcycles are all about stripping out the superfluous and leaving only what is essential to get the job done. Their beauty is in good design and functionality, not in how much crap you can hang on them, or what you can cover up with plastic.

In this instance, I'd been on the bike less than a few minutes before being struck by how comfortable it was. One of the main things about touring bikes is that you will be sitting in a position that you're prepared to stay in for quite some time, and I'm talking here about days or weeks. In this instance, somebody had spent a good bit of time working on the relationship between seat, footrests, and handlebars, and it had been time well spent.

The F650 CS had been conceived originally as a motorcycle for non-motorcyclists. The target market was people who had never ridden a bike before, so the company had put in several user-friendly features that bikers wouldn't normally have - the seat height had been deliberately set to the minimum to accommodate the vertically challenged; the petrol tank had been put under the seat to keep the centre of gravity low and thus direction changes easier to handle; and because it was driven by a toothed rubber belt, there was no oily chain to deal with. It was designed as a city bike and day tourer, something on which businessmen could filter through the rush hour traffic during the working week and then play about on at the weekends.

"So, what do you think?" asked Declan on my return.

"Well, if you don't buy it, I think I might," I responded.

He bought the bike and I was envious.

A few weeks passed without incident and though we talked about a ride to Cordoba and Sevilla, no plans had been made. Before too long, it was time for his annual summer visit to Ireland and having decided that this year he would go on the bike, we agreed that I would ride part of the way with him. The beloved Suzuki was prepared and off we went. Linda and his wife, Topsy, and their two daughters happily waved us off - peace for a little while!

The national roads up through Spain are a treat to ride, with good road surfaces, fast bends and a varied and interesting topography. We swept along like happy children, at one point swapping bikes briefly, and again I was impressed by the way the BMW rode. The night was spent in a B&B located in the huge church in Teruel, so in the morning we awoke to the sound of the faithful giving praise to the Lord. We ate a meagre breakfast and fled. Later that day we parted company in the foothills of the Pyrenees. Snow was clearly visible higher up, the temperature was dropping and I hadn't come prepared for cold weather. We bade each other farewell, and while he headed into France, I turned and rode south to enjoy once more the way the little Suzuki swept through the bends in an easy and uncomplicated manner. I had bought wisely those seven years ago and I still loved this bike, but a BMW seed had been planted too.

Without making a conscious decision, the Internet search engine seemed to be accessing F650 CS pages with increasing regularity, and I found myself thinking, *that looks cheap*, or, *nice bike, I wonder if it has any service history?* There were quite a few available and I started an elimination process that narrowed them down. The bike that was left and seemed to fulfill all requirements was a metallic yellow, 2 spark version with low mileage, some service history, ABS, a few factory options and a dedicated luggage package. The price being asked was very fair and it was hard to find a reason not to buy it. After all, we had space in the courtyard for one more bike, and it was only a little one. A deal was struck, the bike was bought and easyJet transported me to London to collect it.

At first sight, the bike proved to be everything the vendor had said, clean and well cared for. Documents were checked, money was passed and counted, hands were shaken, and a very happy boy rode his new steed out into the busy streets of London town. The sun was shining, God was in his heaven and all was right with the world.

Because there was still a need to sort out the Guzzi log book, I had arranged accommodation in Surrey at a very reasonable price via Airbnb, and Thursday morning found me in the local DVLA office, trying to persuade them to rectify their administrative error so that I might once more experience the pleasure of the mighty V-twin before I shuffled off this mortal coil. It was hard work and I left their office feeling less than hopeful, only able to set my compass east for Dover and the 3 p.m. ferry to Calais. Once again the road to the south was beckoning and I was too weak to resist it.

Before leaving Andalucía, Linda had taken a forecast and predicted good weather for the trip with the possible exception of a light shower in London. As I parked that night in a lay-by south of Paris the drizzle was turning to rain, and by the time the bed was set out it was little short of torrential. The night continued with thunder, lightning and heavy rain from which the trees offered very little protection, and by morning everything was wet, but at least it wasn't cold. All day I employed different clothing configurations to expose as many items as possible to the warm air, and it wasn't long before I was dry again.

The journey continued in the usual leisurely manner, cruising down country roads, stopping to eat at an inviting restaurant or snooze in some cool and shady spot, or making a diversion to see the odd interesting place. The border was crossed south of Pau, and the length of Spain passed beneath my wheels until Sunday morning found me riding into the *pueblo* with the latest addition to the stable.

The VFR is a great sports/touring bike and in its day it was the best, but I'm not getting any younger now and am becoming ever more aware of its weight. Though it's light enough whilst riding, if it ever fell over it would prove to difficult to pick up without the aid of a surgical appliance, and these days I don't often feel the need to do 150 mph. It has served us well on many trips, getting us to the TT and back in safety and comfort, but I think the BMW may be taking over that role now. I've loved having the Honda, but it's time to stop racing other people and start acting my age, before it all ends in tears. I shall be sad to see her go, but perhaps it's time she brought a smile to some other face and put a twinkle in another's eye.

The Suzuki too will now be vying for the same place as the BMW. They are too similar in size and weight for me to use them both and it's a sad thought, but she may also be moving on to bring somebody the same pleasure she has brought, and still brings, to me. I still clearly recall the first time I saw her whilst driving down that country road in Norfolk, the joy with which I bought her thinking she'd be the last bike I'd ever buy. She's never given a moment's trouble, brought me down through France and never missed a beat. Truly, I shall be sad to see her go. Now, in my sixty-fourth year, with this BMW, a bike that covers all the bases, I can without fear of contradiction state that this will definitely be the last bike I will ever buy. I think.

Chapter 13

Tree Felling

So, from bikes to... trees. I mentioned earlier that Steve had bought two pieces of land from Jack. The smaller piece contained one ancient, but still living chestnut tree, albeit yielding very small fruit; only a short distance away we also had a forty metre high, lightning-struck, dead one. There had been a third tree, but at the exact moment that Steve was signing the contract it was felled by an unseen hand and much of the wood removed. Later on, we discovered the culprit, someone who objected to its presence interfering with a fine view of the valley. Without reference to anyone, Ninette simply chopped it down and kept the family warm on the proceeds. Luckily, we arrived on the scene in time to salvage a small part of the main trunk and for Steve to explain the laws of land ownership to the vandal.

However, both of the standing trees, alive and dead, needed attention. Drastic pruning for the living one, since it had many redundant branches at the top, and complete felling for the other. This latter giant would not be an easy matter; some of the branches overhung an electricity cable, the whole tree leant uphill and towards our neighbour's new and expensive swimming pool, and there was no access whatsoever for a cherry-picker, fire-engine or lorry that might help us deal with it. On one side of the land we had a small, stony *barranco*, on the other ran a public footpath. This was a task that would need much looking at before chainsaws were raised in anger. This was men's work.

"When will you cut it down?" asked our French neighbour. "It could fall onto my pool at any time."

"In November," I replied sweetly, taking care not to say in which year that might be. In fact, six years passed before it assumed a horizontal position on the ground.

Almost all our male friends and acquaintances took a serious interest in the problem. From builder Emilio to our hilarious Glaswegian pal Stevie, and from local villager Augustín and his helpful wife Incarnación, to anonymous backpackers passing through, everyone had advice to give. Steve wanted to do the job himself and had already thrown a rope or two over some branches and hauled himself up for a better look at the problem.

"I'm getting too old for this," he acknowledged, after a 25 metre climb and many rotten branches falling to the ground as he put his weight on them. "When I was 14 or 15 you wouldn't have been able to keep me out of it, but these days I'm beginning to lose my nerve."

I was relieved to hear it. I didn't want to scrape him off the rocks down below. By good fortune, a chance meeting with a young Englishman called Guillem finally resolved things. We had gone to an informal literary gathering and found ourselves chatting to a friendly, toothy chap of about thirty, dressed in a check shirt and jeans. I asked him what he did out in the Alpujarras and as soon as he let slip the word 'arboriculturalist', I knew that we had found our man.

"What sort of trees do you work on?" I asked.

"Mostly fruit trees," he replied. "Around here I prune olives, almonds, sometimes apples and figs. A lot of people want their land cleaned up but don't have the time to do it themselves."

"Do you do bigger stuff?" asked Steve.

"I used to," he said, "and I did some training at Kew gardens on tall trees, but there's been nothing out here for quite a while now."

We explained our problem and he seemed interested, so we exchanged phone numbers and email addresses. That was in high summer and we were in agreement that we should wait until autumn. Little did we know that to get Guillem actually on your land, armed with all his equipment and ready to start work, was regarded as a considerable achievement. As another friend said later, "Even to get a date written into his diary is something." We waited patiently for the season to change, while he ordered new safety boots from England and had his chainsaws re-calibrated.

Some of our neighbours were getting official permission to have bonfires, so we took the opportunity to have our tree felling approved as well. Two men from the regional Junta walked down to the land with Steve and agreed that he could prune the live chestnut and remove the dead one. They were not concerned about any fire risk. Perhaps the adjacent swimming pool reassured them. However, this particular danger is so great that, even in the cooler times of the year, every precaution must be taken to avoid setting the sierra alight. What starts as a glowing cigarette butt or small camp fire can soon develop into a major *fuego*, destroying thousands of hectares of forest. Quite recently, 60,000 hectares was lost near Granada due to someone's naivety and foolishness, and many years ago our own village was encircled by flames thanks to a shard of glass and bright sunlight.

Land-owners are expected to keep undergrowth and dry material to a minimum and may have to pay for the fire services if neglect can be proved. Everyone is expected to report trees being struck by lightning and we have seen villagers rushing out with buckets and hoses to put out a sudden conflagration by the roadside. In the summer we see helicopters doing their afternoon reconnaissance of the hillsides and there are several heliports in remote parts of the mountains, usually positioned alongside huge water cisterns, to enable a quick response.

Finally, in late November (as promised to the neighbour), Guillem arrived on the doorstep and set off with Steve to 'just have a look.' I went off to my Spanish lesson, expecting to return a couple of hours later and find them sitting on a rock and mulling over the problem. Instead, I could hear the buzz of the chainsaw as I parked the car, so I ran to the house, put on the kettle and made up a basket of coffee things, biscuits and some chocolate cake. By the time I reached the footpath, I could see Guillem's orange safety hat up in the branches of the living tree and realised that about 7 metres of canopy and dead branches had disappeared from view. As I turned the corner and reached the scene, there was a mighty roar and a particularly massive branch dropped to earth, crushing all the smaller pieces already lying there. This was going to be fun.

Throughout the day, Guillem worked with disciplined application on the various branches of this monster. By the time he had finished 'up top', the tree looked like a giant octopus caught out doing the macarena, with some of its arms swinging across its body and a few severed limbs scattered on the grass below. He and Steve set about reducing these to lengths that we could barrow up the path, their chainsaws whining in harmony. The biggest pieces were left whole, so that no casual passer-by would be tempted to add to their own fuel store. I got the car as near as I could to the site and undertook many trips to fill the boot up. The delight of having our own firewood was tempered by the gruelling task of getting it to the house, uphill all the way.

One down and one to go. We agreed with Guillem that the dead tree would have to wait until the New Year and a date was pencilled into that highly-prized diary. He admitted that it would be a challenge, but felt more confident now that he had done the first one. We said that we would get the electricity cable lowered for the day, having had some reassuring messages from the electricity company earlier in the year that this could be facilitated quite easily.

"Just ring us," they said cheerfully, "and someone will come out straight away."

But January came and with a week to go, this turned out to be a serious stumbling block. Neither we, nor our Spanish neighbours, could get through to anyone by telephone who seemed able to help. We found ourselves in lengthy answer phone queues, spending a small fortune on mobile phone charges, until we managed eventually to speak to a call centre operator in South America who had no idea what we were talking about. "A minor cable somewhere in the Spanish mountains needs to be lowered? Why? To cut the branch off a tree? Why? To fell the tree itself? Well, just cut the tree down for goodness sake, branch and all!"

In the end, we decided to take our chances and do just that, with the cable in place. The locals also seemed to think that nothing could possibly go wrong and even if it did, well, it would only affect 3 or 4 houses. So there we were, all in place for the event, including various neighbours higher up the hillside, loitering out on their terraces, binoculars in hand. We were equipped with 4 chainsaws, many ratchet straps, three large wedges, a sledge hammer and plenty of rope. Guillem wore all his safety gear and used a prussicking device to get himself up the first 10 metres or so, to a central 'v' in the tree. His height to weight ratio, plus good upper-body strength, made this look easy.

When Steve had made his earlier reconnaissance, he had managed to tie a rope securely onto the branch nearest to the electricity cable, and it was this branch that Guillem decided to cut first. With luck, and some tension on the line, it could be cut in such a way that it would pivot away from the cable and rest against the main trunk. If we had no luck, the whole project would be compromised and we would have no electricity and some angry neighbours and officials to deal with.

"Take the strain," shouted Guillem, having sawn through two-thirds of the branch, close in to the tree trunk.

"Taking strain," shouted Steve from below.

I stood on a rock at some distance, fingers and toes crossed.

Guillem made the final cut. Elegantly and gracefully, in slow motion, the branch spun around, dropped a few feet below the cable, then hung there, waiting to be lowered to the ground. It was like watching a ballerina complete her pirouette, pause to rest on the arm of her partner and then sink slowly to the floor. She was due a standing ovation.

Next came a whole section of the upper canopy, bare of leaves but full of weight. In its present 'Y' formation, we needed the shorter arm to come down first, again at risk to the electricity cable, before we could fell the entire tree. Guillem re-positioned himself securely in the 'Y' crux, attaching his ropes and safety harness afresh while Steve threw a tensioning length around an old almond tree. I held a video camera but was very unsure whether I could track a fast-moving, falling object with any kind of success.

"We have an audience," shouted Guillem.

It was the first time that he had noticed the spectators, out on their terraces and even far away in Pitres, all there to have a good look at the show.

We had little time to prepare the stage. "It's going," shouted one of us, and with a sudden crack, the branch fell, twisted slightly, hit the cable and dropped to earth. The cable, still in my view-finder, twanged and bounced, but did not break. Silence. Then a cheer, as we realised that we had managed not to cause any disruption either to our neighbouring *vecinos* or to the Endesa electricity supply.

"Well done! *Bien hecho!*" I called as Guillem descended from the tree, which now stood like a defeated sentinel, stripped of its armaments and decorations. We all paused briefly for a very British cup of tea and to consider the next stage.

"We'll put in a cut on the side we want it to fall," said Guillem. "About a 70 degree angle should do it. Then we'll need wedges and a sledge hammer for the other side."

He knew exactly what he was doing.

The cut was made about 1 metre off the ground, using his largest chainsaw. One horizontal slice to the centre and one diagonal cut to the upper 'jaw' at approximately 70 degrees, taken out like a slice of cake, revealed the pale yellow and very solid timber at the heart of the giant. Now, even if the tree fell of its own accord, the weak point was away from the swimming pool and towards various clumps of brambles, small trees and the footpath. All was safe. Yet the tree did not move. Time for the wedges.

Guillem hammered them in on the opposite side to the cut - one, two, three. Did the tree waver? We were not sure. He took up the sledge and began to attack them with energy, a smallish man throwing himself against a mighty tree. Still it did not move.

"We'll need more wedges!" he shouted.

"I'll go up to the house for something we can use," I offered, grabbing my jacket.

"No, hang on a minute," said Steve, hunting around. He came upon our short club hammer. "Try this."

In went the club hammer. Guillem gave it a couple of bashes. The tree wavered once again, but this time took up a decided lean and then slowly, gaining momentum, it crashed down and laid its length on the grass. Like a dead elephant or a beached whale it lay there, glistening silver-grey, no longer breathing. It was positioned perfectly, obstructing nothing and no one. We were quite subdued at first, paying our respects to a fallen warrior, but soon I yelped with delight and raced up and down the trunk, balancing on its curves. The job was done.

Over the following days we cut up and removed all the smaller branches for firewood. The wood-store filled up very quickly but we knew how rapidly we would get through it on winter evenings. The really massive pieces were safe where they lay, and Steve had a mind to take some central planks for a table or two. Our neighbour was delighted as well. I think she imagined we had done it purely for her sake, but we allowed her that conceit. How much worse it could have been if it had fallen into her expensive pool.

Chapter 14

Walking the Mountains

We were living in the mountains but we had not really learned to live on them. Even at 1100 metres, we were in habitable terrain and surrounded by the evidence of normal, daily life. Within our view were pine forests and rocky outcrops, and just down the road we could see the high peaks of the Sierra Nevada, often partially covered in snow, but we had not even begun to explore these higher regions. Low level walking was relatively easy and the paths familiar. What about the rest?

I had made two expeditions on horse-back, up towards Mulhacén and the Siete Lagunas (7 lakes), both of these in high summer and with a small group of friends. Despite having done some rock-climbing in the Lake District and North Wales in my youth, and a lot of road-running in later years, I did not fancy the gruelling slog involved in climbing mountains carrying a rucksack and provisions. Steve had never done any hiking or mountaineering to speak of, his wanderings in the 1960s being mainly focused on getting from one end of England to another without wearing out the soles of his feet or succumbing to an overload of marijuana or LSD.

So it came as a shock when our French friend Tomás turned up on the doorstep one day and asked if we would like to go into the mountains for a day or two with himself and Bartho, the father of Roque from the *molino*.

"Overnight," we asked, surprised, "with tents?"

"Not necessarily with tents," responded Tomás in Spanish, this being our only common language, "it's warm enough to sleep outside in a sleeping bag."

"Well, it's not for me," I responded, "but you Steve, what about it?"

There was little hesitation. A new experience beckoned and he could not resist the idea. "Yes," he said, "I'll give it a go."

"Vale, we'll drive to Capileira on Friday morning at 8 a.m." nodded Tomás. "Bring enough food for 3 days."

That was my perception. This is Steve's version:

Whilst chopping logs in the wood store, I was hailed by a voice with a heavy French lilt. Tomás is a tall whip of a man, with a strong beak of a nose and a shock of black hair that resembles nothing so much as an explosion in a mattress factory. We had met three or four times previously, and, whilst he had a reputation for not being the most sociable of chaps, I liked him. He and a friend were going to the mountains for a few days, and he asked if I would like to come. I said yes, and asked what else I should bring.

"It's up to you, but a sleeping bag, some good boots and a warm jacket would all be sensible," he replied, and with a hearty "*Hasta luego,*" and a wave of the hand, he was gone.

Tomás and his wife Isabella are a very special couple. On one of my first visits to the village, Marianne took me to see a 'secret garden,' tucked away in a remote part of the valley. The owners were away but, she assured me, they would not mind if we sat among their huge lavender bushes and admired their collection of semi-tropical trees and shrubs, their beautiful stone-built house and studio, and the ceaseless bubbling of a natural spring.

Sometime later, as Steve and I were out walking in that area, we saw a deeply-suntanned man, not far from the path, vigorously clearing out a stream with his mattock, a shock of hair standing out like a dark halo around his face.

"That must be Tomás," I whispered, neither wanting to disturb the work in progress nor seem to be spying. We passed on.

Occasionally thereafter, in the market place or at a fiesta, we would see this handsome pair in the distance, and gradually discovered from other people that they were artists and not particularly sociable. Why should they take an interest in us? It was not until Marianne's 70th birthday that we sat at the same table with them and worked our way into a satisfying conversation. Isabella and I got on well and I admired her vivacity as well as her elegant black jet earrings. A few days later, the knock came at our door, and there stood Tomás with his invitation.

Steve's preparations were cursory. It was August, he did not have any mountaineering kit or any particular knowledge of camping out. All he owned was an old-ish rucksack, our tiny 2-person tent, a very thin and lightweight sleeping bag and his well-worn, Doc Marten steel toe-capped boots.

"They'll be too heavy," I protested, "and the bag is too thin. It will be cold up there at night."

"It'll be fine," he replied. "I don't need much and I'm used to cold nights in the truck. I just need to take some food and a jacket."

Steve:

A short search located my old work boots, and what I had always called my 'big' rucksack, which was stuffed with £20 worth of Tesco's finest: a cheap sleeping bag, what food we could muster, a jumper, a pair of jeans, some spare socks, a bottle of water, and an inflatable sleeping pad for a little added comfort. That would do me.

When we opened the door to Tomás, he looked down at the steel toe-caps poking through torn leather, and said, in Spanish that even I could understand, "Are those your boots?" He then looked at my relatively diminutive rucksack, and must have wondered if he'd made a mistake asking me along. We put the backpacks in the car, and headed for Capileira.

The plan was that I would drop them off and then await the call on Sunday to collect them. As we stood in the main street, I looked out over the Poquiera valley and considered what a perfect day they had chosen. Cool, clear, pristine. I felt quite envious.

Bartho drove up in his battered Renault 4, tooting the horn. A small, whippet-like man with spectacles, white hair and an intellectual aspect, he proceeded to haul an enormous rucksack out of the back, chatting vigorously as he went about it. A discussion took place concerning tents. He had a 3-man tent, Tomás preferred to sleep in the open, Steve might be carrying enough for a novice - did they need a tent at all? In the end, they agreed to travel light and leave the tents behind. Delightfully ignorant, I waved them off and then departed myself, planning my two days alone as I went: a visit to a garden centre, a book that I wanted to re-read, some interesting wine to savour.

Steve:

Bartho turned out to be a very active Spaniard, who, like Tomás, carried not an ounce of fat. He did, however, carry a HUGE rucksack. He too looked at my boots, but said nothing. He looked at my rucksack and asked if I had a sleeping bag in there. I was starting to wonder if there was something wrong with these people.

Whilst having coffee, Bartho nipped off to the bakers and returned with an enormous country-style loaf, which he slid easily into his bag. Over the next three days I would be amazed at the capacity of that bag. It was like a magician's hat. He would produce fresh fruit, salad, cake, pasta dishes, boiled eggs, tomatoes, cheese, ham and salami, the bread, of course, and I wouldn't have been surprised to see white rabbits and flocks of doves too. Lord knows what it weighed, but it didn't seem to bother him.

We said goodbye to Linda, and boarded the bus. I was off for my first walk in the mountains.

The bus ride was quite remarkable for a Suffolk boy. I suppose it carried about twenty-four people, and travelled on a road that I think of now as normal, but at the time seemed a little rough for a mini-bus. As we climbed higher, the view opened out, revealing the Mediterranean to the south, and aspects beyond the nearer mountain tops to distant ranges, each with another tier behind it, until they faded from view in the haze. A watercolour painter would have enjoyed putting down the overlapping layers of blue.

The bus put us down at about 2300 metres and we started walking. If you don't know what to expect up there, and I didn't, it's quite a revelation. What looks from below to be one large piece of rock, turns out to be a mix of scree slopes, broken ground, cliff faces, and boulder fields. The patches of green consist mainly of inhospitable, low-growing, spiky shrubs, and the tree line is a long way below.

The weather stayed fine and early on Sunday evening, three days later, Steve re-appeared in the house, very sun-tanned but somewhat wobbly around the knees.

"Did you have a good time?" I asked. "Where did you go?"

He may never quite bring himself to describe this expedition in any detail, but the gist of it was that he enjoyed this first outing enormously, nearly froze during the two nights out, and his legs lost all co-ordination after the second day. Like an unprepared marathon runner, the muscles had simply failed, especially on any downhill sections. The pace set by Tomás and Bartho had been too fast and too extreme for a beginner; his boots had been too heavy and too slippery; the sleeping bag totally inadequate for the overnight temperatures. But he was ready to do it again.

Meanwhile, Isabella and I had agreed that while the men walked, we could amuse ourselves with idle gossip, long lunches, and getting our respective homes re-decorated with the ubiquitous white emulsion. In fact, I think that is something that she actually does endeavour to do, whilst I can find a hundred other activities that are more important than anything involving a bucket of paint and a stepladder.

Isabella is a perfectionist in all things and we have enjoyed many excellent evenings in their stone-built *cortijo*, with Liszt or Schumann playing in the background, drinking fine wine, consuming fabulous food, and enjoying lots of laughs despite the language difficulties. Sitting on cobalt blue cushions and using delicate, bone-handled steak knives, we have eaten home-made tapas of marinated garlic cloves alongside wrinkled, sun-dried, crimson pimientos and crisply-roasted almonds; delicate salmon and spinach hors d'oeuvres, layered like little cakes; baked rabbit with tiny, roasted turnips; wild boar casserole enhanced by whole chestnuts and baby carrots; green salad decorated with the pretty blue flowers of the borage plant; home-made crème caramel in terracotta dishes or physalis and mulberry trifle in fluted glass bowls; and, of course, French cheeses followed by chocolate-dipped, crystallised orange segments.

Such culinary delights have been followed by wickedly-strong, locally-brewed liqueurs and interesting teas. Perhaps the odd unusual cigarette has been passed around too, but as a non-smoker for over thirty years, this is one compulsion that I can ignore.

Following such gourmet feasting, in winter we have retreated to the cosiness of the fireside, and in summer lolled back admiring the ordered chaos of their garden - jasmine, lilac, roses, and even banana trees, with green grapes clustering above one's head. The perfume of lavender and the distant sound of goat's bells. All that is missing is Le Douanier Rousseau's lion, lurking in the undergrowth. And I don't know how, but there is a lot less dust here than in my house, that's for sure.

Healthy arguments flowed just as vigorously as the plants:

"This terrible economic crisis," protested Bartho, who can talk on into the early hours while everyone else dozes off, "we have to take to the streets, let the government know where they are going wrong."

"We need another political strategy," agreed Anna, his wife, a firebrand of the Left, "and more responsive politicians."

"It will be just as bad, no matter which party they belong to," murmured Tomás. "They are all the same, deep down. They start out with good intentions and many promises, but they soon lapse into corruption and lies."

"We need a new system."

"We need to deal with the banks, the bonuses, the secret deals."

"There's nothing we can do. Like Voltaire's Candide, we must tend our own gardens."

"We must have more coffee," said Isabella, prosaically, getting up from the table.

We all acknowledge that our generation may be the last to benefit from reliable jobs, decent housing, pensions and free healthcare. It will be our children and our grandchildren who will suffer, not us. No wonder the Spanish hang on to their land. When not used simply for kicking, the campo can defend against starvation and homelessness.

"Why have you chosen to come and live here?" I was asked on one occasion in a bar, by a young Spanish businessman.

This is still a good question, and similar to asking someone why they have chosen their husband or wife or life partner. Simply to say, "We fell in love with the place," is not quite enough.

"We didn't want to retire and grow old in a familiar country," was the first response, "we wanted the warmer climate, the challenge of a new language and culture, a last adventure."

We might have said also, "Because we could afford to do so, because Britain does not command any serious degree of loyalty, because beautiful places such as the Lake District or the Cotswolds or the Brecon Beacons would be beyond our means, because we feel that we fit into a simple, rural backwater."

In addition, we might have mentioned the Internet and Skype, new ways of communicating with the family who can be accessed from anywhere, and brings a sense of remoteness coupled with the ability to observe the world in all its crazy variety. It has been said that in the event of a worldwide collapse, be it nuclear or natural, economic or political, the Alpujarra is one of the seven safest places in the world, and the first in Europe. We haven't given that as a reason yet, but are saving it for the moment when Armageddon strikes.

But when I am out riding or walking and looking out across the vast distances towards the sea and the Atlas mountains, or as the dawn evolves into a perfect day of blue, green and gold, or when I saunter through Granada towards the fountains and marbled plazas of its historic centre, then I know that I am here for the wonder that Spain inspires. Just having the good fortune to be here is sufficient.

We sit outside our little village bar on a summer's evening, supping a cool *tinto de verano*, while aged Angelina nods over her walking stick and the men inside are concentrating on their card game, and we know how fortunate we are. These are people who have relatively few needs or expectations, whose interests are mainly limited to their families and neighbours, their land and their vegetables, so it is easy to slip into the same mode.

We potter along at our own pace and are pleased with the sight of a soaring eagle or the taste of a ripe fig or the hee-hawing of a donkey. We have time to inspect our village existence at leisure, noting every oddity, every flaw and every moment of harmony. We see the peeling cement beside the fountain, we notice (and clear up) dog messes in the street, watch as a new litter of kittens peeps out of a stable doorway, hear the distant sound of some youngster's drum kit, note the new moon rising above the trees and the stars coming out. Our daily life acquires its own timelessness and meaning.

* * *

Back to the walking. We started doing longer and more strenuous expeditions together, just the two of us, taking a compilation of newly-acquired, purpose-designed gear. Steve did a lot of online research and began to realise that there was yet another world out there, inhabited by serious walkers with very specific requirements. The first of these is to travel comfortably but lightly, only taking the essentials. The terms 'liteweight' and 'superlite' are themselves often misnomers; one needs to know what the item actually weighs, be it sleeping bag or rucksack or even a plastic spoon. For example, some backpacks put 3 kg on your back before you add essentials such as food and water, never mind warm clothes. Cumulatively, every item takes one further away from the desired target: to carry as little as possible up the mountain.

So the hunt was on for the most suitable, but lightest, kit on the market. We made some mistakes along the way, which is why we now possess 8 or 9 rucksacks, not just two, but they all have their uses. They range from Steve's 20 litre Terra Nova Ultra which weighs in at a mere 121 grams, to his more generous Zpack at 380 grams, my Gossamer Gear Mariposa (615 grams) and the 'heavier' Osprey Exos 46 (1.118 kg). We both have OMM waistpacks (244 grams) which, despite their appearance, can accommodate a complete set of overnight summer gear plus food and water. They take the burden off the shoulders and put it on the hips, which is the aim of most backpacks anyway.

Following all the surgery in the area of my right armpit, I discovered some unexpected problems out walking. Going uphill, I had no trouble with 5 or 6 kilos on my back. Descending was a different story, however. The lack of lymph nodes and a 'cording' of scar tissue seemed to be linked somehow to reduced blood flow; my forearm began to ache and go numb, and my fingers tingled. Eventually I had to slip the strap off that shoulder completely and support my right forearm with my left hand until the aching stopped. Using a walking pole made no difference either way. My intention was not to whinge, so I kept quiet, but often on the last few miles downhill, Steve would offer to carry my sack as well as his own. Heroic and much appreciated. Not long afterwards, I discovered that my troubles were not solely due to previous surgery; other things were happening to my body that would take me back to the cancer clinic.

Another walking requirement is the interest value. Most of our walks were 6 hour affairs, ranging between 14 and 20 kilometres, but we never hurried, as we wanted to observe the butterflies, identify the flowers, and admire the many fabulous views. We walked up steep, stone-laid *escarihuelas*, the mule-tracks of bygone travellers which zig-zagged their way up the perilous valley walls; we plodded through mud and sometimes snow alongside the water courses; and we sampled the abundant wild fruit as we passed underneath or alongside it. Mostly we walked alone and in silence, but when friends came to visit - and I am thinking of Carlos the Singing Postman and his wife Pennie, from deepest Suffolk, and a variety of wild-eyed Scots of both genders - the mood changed.

"Can one eat bracken?" or "Does water take longer to boil at altitude?" stimulated light-hearted arguments.

"What would you take back to the Berbers of 1400 AD that a) they could make good use of and b) they could find a way to reproduce with familiar materials?" provoked much thought and debate.

Of these three questions, the answer to the first is, "Only if it's young enough and then in moderation," and to the second, "No, it simply boils at a lower temperature." For the Berbers, we conceded that a bicycle would meet the criteria, more or less, but some medicines or painkillers would have played a valuable role.

Us girls enjoyed some fun too, usually when the group was trying to locate a specific hilltop or look-out point. While the men got out maps, compasses and satellite navigation devices, took readings and sun-sights and wore deep frowns of concentration, we simply looked around, glanced at the map and pointed, "It's over there, isn't it?"

Up on the mountain, the phrase 'they're like two old women,' invariably applies to middle-aged men who find they have much to discuss and can only do so from a stationary position. This happened frequently with two good friends from Glasgow. Whilst Lynn and I strode ahead, the two Steve's would fall further and further behind; when we looked back, there they would be, at a bend in the road or on the crest of the hill, face-to-face and, in wee Stevie's case, waving their arms about to emphasise a point.

"Whatever are they talking about?" Lynn would murmur. "He never stops moving when I go out on the hills with him."

"It must be important," I would suggest. "Perhaps the relative weights of their bootlaces or whether politicians have any integrity these days."

I hoped it was the former. Getting started on politics in such sublime surroundings and so early in the day, without a tot of whisky in sight, was not a good idea.

* * *

Soon enough, a single day out was too short to get Steve and I where we wanted to go. We began to make a plan to do an overnight trip, just the two of us, up into the high Sierras, but as soon as we looked at the maps, this evolved into a 2 night, or 3 day outing. Nothing worth doing at altitude could be achieved in less time.

We watched the weather forecasts and picked three days that would be dry and fairly warm at altitudes over 2,500 metres. I had stated clearly that 5°C was the lowest temperature in which I wanted to sleep outside, even though my sleeping bag was good to -6°C.

We set off in the late morning from Treveléz, the highest inhabited village in mainland Spain. We parked the car in the Barrio Medio, changed our footwear from flip-flops to walking boots, shouldered our backpacks and strolled up the narrow streets towards the Barrio Alto, passing beneath white-washed walls and abundant flowerpots, crammed with red, pink and white geraniums. We were not going to rush - this first outing required perseverance and a steady pace.

Walking north up the river valley to El Horcajo, we encountered some cream and brown cows with their calves, chewing heartily on lush green grass and, tucked into a rock crevice, a fat green frog. Water gushed liberally down the path, over the low-lying river banks and into our boots; the last slabs of winter snow were melting somewhere high above us and filling the water courses. Hummocks of pink flowers and small swarms of blue butterflies accompanied us as we worked our way slowly uphill, from an altitude of 1400 to 1800 metres.

Steve had been this way before and had already identified a good bivi spot for our first night: an island of sorts, bisected by small streams, without cow pats or prickly shrubs. Buttercups adorned the grass and a convenient acacia-like tree provided a suitable wardrobe for hanging up surplus clothing and food, well away from bugs and, during the night, Zorro the fox. Although we had a couple of hours before we would lose the June sun behind the steep-sided valley slopes, this was the last bit of moderately flat turf that we would encounter for some time. Also, of course, one cannot pitch camp and cook supper in 15 minutes.

"Where do you want to sleep?" asked Steve. "Choose as level a piece as you can."

Once we started to look at the disposition of the ground, we realised that there were not many such areas. Sliding into a stream during the night was not a desirable option, and neither was ending up, roly-poly fashion, a good metre away from one's sleeping mat.

"I'll go there," I said, pointing towards a small space that looked adequate. Not too near the clattering rush of water, hopefully not on top of an ant's nest and as soft a surface as I could find. Steve picked a similar spot, parallel to mine but about 3 metres away. All my notions of snuggling down together, nose-to-nose, faded away; a good night's sleep was more important than a romantic encounter out in the wilds.

We still had plenty of daylight left in which to make up our beds. The sequence, from bottom layer to top, and outer shell to inner, went thus: a full-length sponge beach mat with the insulated foil coating facing the ground and closed-cell foam coating topside up; then a 3/4 length Thermarest Neoair mat, the Holy Grail of outdoor comfort; then a car windscreen sun-shield, to trap as much of one's body heat as possible. Of the latter, mine was newly-bought for the princely sum of one euro, but we found Steve's abandoned in a car park on the coast and decided that it needed a good home. By good fortune it was lorry-sized and well suited to a tall man. Next came a waterproof bivi bag, and inside it the sleeping bag (mine is a Cumulus Pertex 350 goose-down tea-cosy), and inside that, a washable silk liner to take up most of the dirt, sweat and condensation. When I finally climbed in, I was wearing merino wool base layers, a beanie, and warm socks. Although the temperature never fell below +7 C, I wasn't taking any chances.

As my other stipulation for any overnight expedition was a hot cup of tea at the start and end of each day, we were able to locate enough dry roots and small pieces of wood for Steve to get his home-made stove going. It may have taken some time and involved considerable puffing and blowing, but tea followed by instant noodles made for a delicious supper. We had rations for every meal, kept to a minimum and weighing as little as possible. Heavy items such as oranges and sandwiches had already been eaten at lunchtime; now we were down to dry food, muesli bars and water, always water. We had the means to filter this too, as those fresh, tumbling streams are visited by wild and domestic animals at all altitudes and only rarely does one find a spring coming straight out of the ground at one's feet, pure and uncontaminated.

As darkness progressed it was easy to fall asleep, but something woke me at about 1 o'clock in the morning. At first, with my beanie acting as an eye pad, I listened blindly for any unusual sound, a fox perhaps or a wandering badger. A fresh breeze was blowing, so perhaps that was what had disturbed me. I decided to have a look around. Peeping out, I saw with astonishment that the tree nearest to me, and the hillside beyond it, were bathed in a pale, luminous light. Yet the hills on my left were darkly black, looming over us and yielding no secrets. I looked again at the shining, wafting branches, then turned back to the darkness. This time a beam of silver flashed out from the hill-top, followed by a segment, then a complete orb, of glittering argent. A full moon was rising over the mountains, a Spanish moon belonging to warm nights and wild gypsies, to nightingales and ebony-coloured bulls, to love and death, to Lorca and Miró, Rodrigo, Almodovar and Picasso. Seemingly, all the compelling mysteries of Andalucía were contained in this sphere of burnished beauty.

As I lay and watched, the light moved across our small island of grass, glinting off rocks and water. The wind eased again and one felt that the whole of the Sierra Nevada was caught in speechless, silent witness, a submission of the earthly to the unearthly. Knowing that humankind had reached that far into space and walked on that glowing surface, did nothing to diminish its pagan power.

I fell asleep again, or perhaps into a state of bewitchment, and when I awoke there was a dawn chorus of sparrows in the bushes and a bearded chap brewing more tea. Time to be 'up and at it,' with plenty of walking ahead of us. By 8 a.m. we were on our way, picking a route straight up the hillside towards a distant *cortijo*. The grass held a small amount of dew, which the sun would soon burn off. At times, the going was so steep that I had to use my hands to steady myself, or pick a zigzag route that would give me a more secure foothold. Luckily we were still in shade, but not for long; as we moved higher, so did the sun, and soon it was time to put away the fleece top, don a hat and sunglasses, reduce long trousers to shorts and rub sun-blocker onto our arms and faces.

We were making our way towards the valley of the Rio Juntillas, along the contour lines below Cerro Pelado, when we saw below us a horseman and his dog, heading in the same direction and slowly gaining on us. He wore a straw hat and rode in the Alpujarreno style, one hand on his hip, one hand holding the reins, every part of him relaxed and comfortable. He was looking intently at the streams and *acequias*, but occasionally glanced up in our direction. When we waved, he raised an arm in salute. An hour or so later he passed even closer, heading east, and then dismounted, mattock in hand. Leaving his horse to graze, we could see him dredging a water course, heaving out clumps of weed that might block its smooth progress towards distant fields and villages.

These ancient water systems owe much to the early settlers, the Phoenicians and Romans, and later, the Arab Berbers, or Moors. Capturing the snowmelt and natural springs at their highest levels, these hand-built channels work their way slowly along the valley sides, dropping very gently in altitude, carrying fresh water to underground cisterns or overground *albercas* and, eventually, the golf courses of the Costa del Sol. Some channels are only 50cm wide, but others span 2 or 3 metres and need low bridges for livestock or walkers. They may be lined with 500 year-old rocks and slabs, or by 20th century concrete, and often pass through dense undergrowth, along the tops of dry-stone walls and across precipitous rock faces.

As mentioned in an earlier chapter, anyone with a scrap of land benefits from this age-old supply. There is a local view that maintaining one's personal kitchen garden is far more important than providing some distant good-for-nothing with a round of golf; additionally, there is great sorrow that recently some of the *acequias* have been replaced by black plastic tubing. The sound of bubbling water and the magic of dragonflies, water snakes, frogs, toads and little birds have all been lost. Perhaps the authorities in Granada or Madrid have never read about killing the goose that laid the golden egg.

As it happened, we were criss-crossing over the Acequia de Treveléz, eventually leaving it far below as we advanced higher towards the Laguna de Juntillas and the stone-shattered hillsides of the surrounding Hoya del Muerto. We came across a large herd of cattle, once again coloured cream or tan or speckled grey, and all enjoying their high, summer pasture. The river provided large swathes of emerald grass, strewn with deep-blue gentians and white *estrellas de la nieve* (stars of the snow), where the sharp-horned mothers could lie placidly in the sun while their youngsters gambolled about. One juvenile male eyed us suspiciously, his flanks heaving, his shiny nose quivering. He was big enough to give us trouble so Steve picked up a small stone or two, just in case, but fortunately he did not dare to leave his mother's side and we passed by unhindered.

Finding the laguna proved tricky. On the map it looked obvious but on the ground, picking our way over the glacial moraine and climbing as we went, it seemed to be a figment of the map-maker's imagination. Each time we saw a barrier of rock ahead, we were sure that it must be the lip of a water-filled hollow. Scrambling up, we were confronted by yet another stretch of barren stone, its ferrous-red blocks often the size of small houses. Still no sign of water. We would need to refill our drinking bottles before nightfall and this could be the last source for the next 24 hours, so it was not a matter of choice but of necessity.

Eventually Steve decided to stop and take a compass reading. I wanted to give the next ridge a looking-over, convinced that the lake could not be far off as we were almost at the head of the valley, but by now we had reached about 2,800 metres and the cooler air forced me to stop and put on my fleece before I plodded on. I was disappointed again. A flat and muddy area presented itself, as though a small tarn had existed briefly and then dried up. How old was our map, I wondered? What was once a significant lake might be no more than a puddle now.

Perseverance was rewarded. As I moved on, the ground levelled off again and there, unexpectedly, nestled at the foot of two steep ridges, was a water-filled lake about 50 metres in diameter. On one side it still had the remains of a glacier spreading across its surface, large chunks breaking away in the heat of the afternoon sun and sinking into its dark, chilly depths. A miniature Antarctica. On the other side, an ice-covered slope dropped down to the water's edge, a fast bobsleigh run for anyone keen to have a dip. Rising above it, to the north, was a forbidding 200 metre hillside, all rock, up which I knew we would have to climb.

But first things first. I called and waved to Steve's distant figure, still mapping our course, and soon we were settled by the laguna, snacking on muesli bars and drinking as much of our existing water as possible.

"Camel-up, girl, camel-up", he said. "Whatever we take on board now will keep us going until nightfall. Tomorrow there'll be no supplies and we'll have to conserve as much as we can for the walk back."

Between us we had 2 half-litre bottles, a 1 litre bottle and his 1 litre Platypus, an ingenious, soft plastic container for cyclists, walkers and runners, lightweight and collapsible. Although it took us almost an hour, we drank everything we had left, then pumped the rather dodgy-looking and cloudy lake water through a ceramic filtration unit.

"Which way out of here do you fancy?" Steve asked, nodding towards the ridge, Puntal de Juntillas, ahead of us.

"We could go across and up on a diagonal line," I replied, "but it will take us longer than a direct attack. What do you think?"

I knew what his response would be.

"Straight up I reckon. Let's get it over with."

We advanced at our own individual pace, picking our own lines. I knew that he would reach the top before me, but we have never been in competition with each other, so I was happy to just keep going upward. On part of a previous walk (Cerrillo Redondo, 800 metres of altitude over 1.5 kilometres of distance), I had kept going by counting my footsteps. This time I did it in Spanish: *uno, dos, trés... diez, veinte, treinta... ochenta y cinco... cien... quinientos...* and was pleased to find how effective it was in distracting me from the effort involved. At 500, I allowed myself to stop and look back down at the laguna. Now it was a small brownish-red circle with ice-white fringes, turning first turquoise and then deep blue towards the centre. It seemed very far away and I was surprised, yet again, at how rapidly one gains or loses height in these mountains and how deceptive distance can be.

As soon as we reached the top of the ridge, a fierce wind rushed to meet us, blowing hard from the north and the hills beyond Granada. To the west stood proud Alcazaba, inaccessible on our side, its shaded slopes still covered in patches of snow and ice. Ahead, we could see the Pico de Jerez and an even longer ridge of dense snow. To the east, and in our direction of travel, lay Piedra de los Ladrones (the Robbers' Outcrop) and another ridge running towards Cerro de Treveléz. But first of all we needed to kit up again.

Crouching in a man-made stone enclosure (for sheep, for walkers or, once, for militia perhaps), I zipped my trouser legs back on and we both pulled out warm, down jackets from our rucksacks. I found my beanie, gloves, and a neck-warmer and put on all of them. It was late June in southern Spain, but at 3000 metres it felt similar to a very chilly afternoon on Holkham beach, with the wind coming off the North Sea in relentless gusts. When we walked on, I could barely stand upright and was glad of my walking pole. The hero, or Hierro Hombre (Iron Man) as one of our friends dubbed him, barely changed his stride and resisted putting on long trousers. Good for him, I thought.

This is a suitable moment to remind hill-walkers everywhere of the difference between a hot, sunny day down in the valley and the impact of wind and altitude up in the mountains. Even a few hundred metres can turn a pleasant stroll into a miserable or dangerous outing, and many people die due to lack of appropriate clothing and exposure to the elements. On a longish walk (or cycle ride or horse trek), always assume that it could become wet, cold and slippery, with poor visibility, and that you may be stranded overnight. Sensible footwear and a jacket goes without saying, but usually one needs more than that.

On this particular trip, I wore every item of clothing that I took, except for my waterproof poncho. We had moisture-wicking T-shirts, warm mid-layers and nothing made of cotton except underwear. In addition, I used my head-torch to make up my bivi bed on the second night and my little whistle came in handy at the dawn of the third day (which sounds a bit like something from The Lord of the Rings). We ate all our food and drank all our water. Steve used his satellite navigation system, compass, cooking implements, firelighter and water filter; we both had maps and our own emergency knives, plasters, pain-killers, and, in my case, antihistamines in case of wasp stings. Neither of us carried more than 8 kilos, but we had tried to cover most summer-time eventualities. In winter, crampons, warmer clothing and a tent would have been sensible, even at lower altitudes.

By now, it was past five o'clock and we needed to locate a spot for the night, out of the wind if possible. Striding out towards Piedra de los Ladrones, it was obvious that this would be difficult. There was no shelter that we could see and the ground was too rough and too exposed to make any kind of camp. We still had plenty of daylight but we were getting tired, another danger signal. I think we walked for more than 4 or 5 kilometres along the ridge before we saw some rocky outcrops that presumably gave the ridge its name. As we got nearer and began to explore these huge lumps of stone, part of the landscape moved in front of our eyes and a group of wild mountain Ibex eased themselves to their feet and trotted away. Invisible until you stumble upon them, these creatures fear humankind and will disappear down outrageously vertical rock-faces to get away. We must have been downwind of them or they would have vanished much sooner.

This first clutch of rocks proved useless, but the next set, facing out over the northern plains towards Jerez de Marquesado and Lanteira, looked hopeful. We dropped down amongst them and found an overhanging slab that, with some effort, could accommodate one of us. A lot of goat poo was spread around but it was dry and could be swept away; besides, one is glad of any kind of insulation and who could say what thermal properties this manure might not have?

"You start levelling this off and I'll see if I can find another spot," commanded the Hero, leaving his kit tucked into a safe cranny.

I knew that I was exhausted and longed for a hot drink and something substantial to eat, but I set about locating some reasonably large, flat stones to make a level sleeping base, and some bigger ones to prevent me from slipping downhill during the night. I didn't want to wake at dawn, hanging off a rock pinnacle over a precipice. Although the overhang meant that I would be protected from the wind, I had to hope that there were no earth tremors on their way. Being squashed under a hundred tons of solid stone could be terminal.

When Steve re-appeared, he brought the good news that he had found somewhere for himself and that he too was starving, so we should eat. To conserve our water, we agreed that we would forego tea (this cost me a deep pang of misery) and have noodles instead. No ablutions would be possible and only dry toothpaste before bed. Hastily, we started foraging for dry roots and bits of wood, anything that would enable a small stove to be fired up. There wasn't much of either lying around, but quite quickly we had sufficient kindling for our needs and Steve got the water to boiling point in his home-made, ex-dog food tin.

As we sat there, spooning up our supper from collapsible rubber bowls, the colours went out off the day and a greyish dusk crept over the landscape below. Little twinkling lights began to appear, indicating the towns below and the vast expanse of wind turbines on the plain behind them. It was strange, observing these towns and speculating on what people might be doing with their summer evening, whilst we huddled high up in the mountains above them, communing with the spirits of their robber ancestors.

We did not linger long over our supper. Steve buried the remaining food stores under heavy stones, took his backpack, gave me a kiss and disappeared into the gloom. I couldn't be bothered to change clothes and decided to sleep in all but my boots, keeping my torch, whistle and walking pole beside me in case of any night visitations from Mr Fox or even, although unlikely, a wandering wild boar. In fact, thanks to my gloriously-warm sleeping bag, I was soon too hot and had to sit up and take off a few layers. With my head jammed against the overhang and trying not to slide off the sleeping mat, I managed to wriggle out of my fleece and trousers, then went through the laborious process of re-arranging my bivi sack, liner and bag so that everything aligned comfortably.

As I settled down, I heard a loud roaring from somewhere far to the east, like a train arriving at Leicester Square underground station. It got nearer and louder. The toe-end of my assembled bedding began to shake. The wind that comes off the sea as the day ends had finally reached the high Sierras; starting in Alicante or Valencia, it had worked its way inland and found us in our mountain eyrie. I will never get off in this, I thought, and promptly fell asleep.

Once again, I awoke in the early hours and in moonlight. Once again, I looked around at the fabulous landscape, marvelling at its stillness and, by then, utter silence, and once again I had no trouble in getting back to sleep. At first light I watched the sun coming up through layers of mist and low cloud, and heard a distant whistling. Someone else was awake. I responded to this human dawn chorus with my mechanical whistle and soon we were busy eating our muesli and packing up our gear. A long day's march lay ahead.

Standing on Mulhacén or other high level areas above Trevélez, one looks east towards the Loma de las Albardas and the Tajo de Breca ridges, which run consecutively from north to south, and one thinks, *that all looks pretty easy, just gentle ridge walking.* In fact, it is a long and gruelling task, with some steep uphill sections and, eventually, a knee-breaking downhill run to the valley floor. It would take us all day, with only limited water and under a relentless sun.

As we cut across to the ridge we collected up a cyclist's water bottle and, in a superb, stone-built, roofless bothy, someone's elegant sunglasses case. Had we known of the bothy, or *refugio*, we would have bivvied there for the night; someone else had laid out enough good, flat stones to make a generous sleeping area and the wind was minimal. The landscape around was harsh and barren, made up of broken stone, spiny hummocks of tough grass and little else, but we did not linger, moving on and soon meeting up with a solitary young cow, all horns and energy. She came quite near, which worried us a bit, but then lost interest in us as we ploughed uphill; every so often I would turn back and see her trotting towards the stony horizon, evidently seeking out her companions.

Peñón del Muerto II became Peñón del Muerto I, where we clambered amongst towering pinnacles of harsh, red stone and marvelled at the effect of wind and weather on dolmen-shaped pillars, as well as Nature's seemingly perfectly-cut handiwork. On a flatter part of the route, quite suddenly, we could see a small group of cattle, brown, black and cream coming towards us. First just one or two, then five or six, all advancing with familiar ease along the open *cañada* or drover's track. Six became sixteen and, finally, thirty or more. A grey horse and his *caballero* came into view, accompanied by four dogs. The horse's saddle and bridle were well-polished and adorned with silver studs and some leather tasseling. The rider wore his gaucho hat, a green check shirt and blue jeans with real style.

"Hola," I called, "have you come far?"

"Sí,sí," he acknowledged politely, "from Berchules."

"Could we borrow your horse for a while?" we joked. "Just to get home?"

"I have to get across the mountain with these animals," he protested with a smile. "It's a long way."

"*Buen viaje, hasta luego,*" we responded, and with a nod, he rode on.

"If he and the other horseman are the only folk we meet," said Steve, "I'll be very pleased."

So it turned out. Although the popular lower routes were likely to be busy, this eastern edge remained the province of local farmers, going about their business quietly and efficiently in time-honoured fashion. We took several hours on the descent towards Trevélez until, much later, before we reached the main road below Peña de los Papos, we saw an old man tending his kitchen garden, hoeing between perfect rows of onions and broad beans. He, his mule, and his two cats, all ignored us; his Alsatian guard dog, however, looked as though it was desperate to tear out our throats, but was restrained by a length of chain and a high fence. *Time to get into town and have a cold beer*, we thought, hurrying onward.

* * *

Steve made other, solo, overnight expeditions during the summer and we had a fine day out climbing the highest mountain in mainland Spain, Mulhacén. Named after one of the last Berber kings, Muley Hacen, it is reputed to have been the site of his burial. He wanted a quiet resting place, but now it is the most popular route in the Sierra Nevada. On a busy summer Sunday, or during the night of the Romería, a religious festival in early August, the mountain entertains many enthusiastic walkers, horse-riders, and even cyclists, all tramping over the king's bones.

The most peaceful creatures up on the very top are the Ibex, but in this location they seem to have grown used to humans and do little to avoid them. Reclining on the very edge of precipitous drops, they serenely watch us humans as we puff our way to the summit. Even their youngsters ignore us as they gambol about. The Ibex that haunt the lower slopes are much more easily spooked. On a long day's walk across the southern Sierras, somewhere above Castarás, we startled a fully-grown male with resplendent, curving horns, who leapt across a ditch, then paused, a deer at bay, against the cobalt skyline. Later, I was told by a Danish friend that she had seen a wolf in that area, but I feel sure that the local farmers and shepherds would have hunted it down if that were so. The Spanish men take pride in the wild boar they shoot and would not tolerate an animal that preyed on their sheep or goats.

One baking August day, we thought we would escape the heat and wall-to-wall fiestas with a little stroll in the mountains, maybe for a couple of nights, and duly packed our rucksacks with sleeping gear, some food and water, and plenty of sun-blocker, neither of us carrying more than 4 kg. We decided to drive as high as we could in the early evening, bivi near the car and have the benefit of 2 meals 'out of the boot' which would mean less to carry on our backs.

As we drove slowly up the winding and un-surfaced road, we met a few vans coming down, the men at the wheel looking swarthy and severe, probably very tired from a day in the *campo*, but not too friendly either. This bothered me a little, as we would be sleeping near the car and the road, and, as it turned out once we had parked up, my selected spot was some distance from Steve's. I pondered on this as we ate our cold chicken and home-grown tomato salad, washed down with a plastic bottle of vino tinto.

We returned to the car in the gloom, just to put a few things away, and were hailed by a voice only a few metres away, "Buenas noches. Are you going anywhere near Cadiar?"

A young man materialized, lightly-clad in cut-off khaki trousers, a loose shirt, floppy hat and sandals. He carried a rucksack and walking stick and was certainly not Spanish, although that was the language in which we all conversed. We were reluctant to say too much.

"We're not going that way tonight," I replied, "but that's your direction for Cadiar," pointing out the route downhill.

"Oh, I know the way," he said, "I just thought you might have space in your car."

After he had walked on and we went back to our camp, I wondered aloud, "Was he real, or have we just seen the ghost of Gerald Brenan, returning from Granada?"

"He'd have wanted a mule ride to Yegen, if that was the case," joked Steve.

I decided that there were too many people about on this lonely road and moved my sleeping quarters closer to Steve. Better to be kept awake by his familiar snores than the arrival of a bunch of thieves and brigands. Of course, nothing occurred other than a starlit and meteor-streaked night sky, and we slept well until the dawn.

That morning we delayed long enough to walk up a nearby hill and have a nice chat with the fire look-out man in his watchtower, or Casa Forestal. We could hear his radio chattering as we arrived, followed by his head peeping out at us from a high window. He soon came down the narrow stairway, a smiling man of about 70, his face brown and wrinkled.

"I've been doing this for 27 years," he said, with some pride. "Four months of the year, through the summer, every single day from 8 till 4."

"Do you ever meet up with the other look-out men?" we asked, knowing that each valley had its own watchtower.

He laughed. "No, no. Some of them I know as friends, but we don't meet up in an official capacity. We can speak on the 2-way radio instead."

We told him where we were heading and he had already noticed the car. As we walked away and up towards the high Sierras, I felt sure that he could monitor our progress for some distance, and would notice if we didn't return within a few days. I always left a note of where we were going on the kitchen table at home, in case of accidents, but this was a more personalised bit of caretaking.

As usual, the first two hundred metres was hard work, adjusting to the altitude of around 2000 metres, the heat and the gradient, but we soon acclimatised. Initially, it was just a long slog up a wide firebreak, once upon a time the cattle driving road over towards Granada. At Alto de las Chorreras, at 2,647 metres, I stopped to sit in the sunshine and a refreshing breeze while Steve went scouting for water. We carried ¾ of a litre each but this could be our last chance over the next 24 hours to fill the 1 litre Platypus. Running out of water is not an option in these remote areas.

I watched a couple of black eagles playing on the thermals, their wings tipped with a creamy-gold, and a few young cows ambling down the slope towards the valley below. I must have snoozed for a short while until The Man returned with good news. He had found a small spring to the east of our spot, only 10 minutes walk away, where uncontaminated and cool liquid trickled out onto a grassy sward, dotted with gentians and clumps of reeds. With the help of a silver foil spout and some ingenuity, we managed to extract over a litre, drinking as much as we could as well. We felt satisfied that this would keep us going on the outward journey and prove useful coming down later on. We continued towards Peñon de Puerto, another 100 metres or so of gentle climbing, our tummies sloshing with mountain water.

As usual at this altitude, the weather began to change, the wind getting much stronger and cooler, funnelling up from the south-west. It was beanies and wind-jacket time again. The towering crag of the Peñon loomed above us, where we found a herd of horned sheep nestled into the lee, perched on narrow ledges like the monks of Mount Athos. They were not going to share their 'island' with anyone, so we decided to press on westward, to the Loma de las Albardas and Puerto de Jerez, before looking for a bivi. It was only six in the evening, with another 3 hours of good daylight left and we knew of a small building, an old *refugio*, that could house us for the night, but this was not how it turned out.

It is easy to underestimate distances and timing, especially towards the end of a long day, and after a steep descent, we had to ascend again, going diagonally across another 300m or so of steep scree and stone, blasted by the wind. This was very hard work and took much longer than we expected. Sometimes I had to stop and lean into the sweeping arc of air, just to keep my footing. At one point, Steve was about 50 metres above me and to the left. The next time I looked up, he had vanished, so I plodded on, willing my feet to keep going. Then I heard a shout. It seemed to come from my right, but as I scanned the skyline, I saw a figure seated on a rock over to my left. I waved, but there was no response. How strange. The person wore the same black and grey clothing as Steve - surely it must be him?

Another shout came, again from my right. This time it was Steve, not far off. I angled across, "Who's that, over there?" I queried, pointing.

"A Spanish chap," he shouted into the wind. "Got a bit of a shock when I appeared, I think he thought he had the whole Sierra Nevada to himself."

Later on, we decided that he might have been a local guide, as he asked Steve if he was sleeping out and did he have warm clothing and water - the priorities for a night in the wilds.

A few hundred metres further and we decided that we had done enough. Forget the ruined *refugio*, a large rock with shelter from the wind would do nicely. We hunted about for places to sleep and somewhere sheltered to get the little stove going. Once more, we found some dry roots to fill the dog food tin and get the water boiling, while the wind roared past us on its way to Guadix and Alicante, over what looked like the plain of Mordor far below. The views were spectacular, but we were too tired to pay much attention.

Our respective sleeping quarters turned out to be a fabulous cave for me, of easy standing height and with only one side exposed to the elements. I laid out my kit. Steve selected the only other option, an absolute coffin about a metre off the ground and formed by some casually-assembled but massive lumps of stone, with no room to do more than slide in, feet first and stay put. This was heroic sacrifice of the highest order as he is a lot taller than me and could have done with more space.

In fact, neither of us slept very well due to the ceaseless, increasingly ferocious wind and, in my case, the sound of stones clinking outside the cave as the fox hunted about for our food cache. This was well buried, so he made no headway, and all remained intact in the morning.

We made an early start, at first light, when the sun was struggling out of the pale haze in the east and the temperature must have been about 5 Centigrade allowing for the wind chill factor. We fought our way off the ridge, the relentless hammering of the gale pushing us sideways. The hummocks of spiky grass under our feet and the occasional miniature Scottish thistle were undisturbed, having developed horizontally rather than vertically. We came across a small group of black and brown horned cows, searching diligently for whatever nourishment they could find, but we waited until we were back down at our water source before we stopped for breakfast.

This was a luxurious meal of hot muesli, tea, coffee, and the remains of a home-made walnut cake. The sun shone, the wind abated, and we got out of our jackets, fleeces and thermal hats. We could see the faint shadow of Africa across the sea, then the much nearer, pristine slopes of the Contraviesa, and closer still, a flock of sheep with their shepherd, slowly working their way up the hillside. What a difference 800 metres can make. Indeed, how could we know that by lunchtime we would be sitting in a walnut-shaded café garden, wafted by a hot breeze and grateful for ice-cold beer; or that when we got back to the village, the neighbours would be saying, "A COLD wind, are you sure?"

Yes, we were sure.

Chapter 15

Horse Riding and Other Matters

Although I had done a reasonable amount of horse riding as a child, I had lost my courage after a succession of bad falls and damaged body parts. Trying to control a Welsh Mountain pony with a mouth of iron, or find a secure perch on a fat Lakeland Fell horse, had seen many a tumble. Yet how could one live in Spain and not ride? I decided that I would have to overcome my fears and try again.

I started by joining up with a small group of women who had come out from England for a week, specifically to ride. I was just there for the day. They wore jodhpurs, check shirts, leather gaiters, and their own hard hats; I had some lightweight trousers, a long-sleeved top and a straw hat. They seemed somewhat hostile and I realised how difficult it can be to join an established group who have already worked out their modus operandi. This would be a one-off trip up towards Mulhacén, to round off their holiday, and it was pretty clear that they did not want some casual holiday-maker to join them. They comprised two mining experts, a veterinarian, an engineer and an accountant, and they all took themselves quite seriously. They were keen to know what I did.

"I work in the National Health Service," I replied, climbing onto my large, grey mare.

"Great," said one, genuinely pleased. "You can patch us up if someone breaks a leg."

"Not a bit of it," I replied, "I'm not a clinician, just a paper-pusher, an administrator."

That more or less terminated the conversation for the rest of the day. And it was a long day, as I recall. We rode up steep and rocky paths, crossed damp meadows strewn with clusters of buttercups and clouds of blue butterflies, and finally reached a small tarn where we had a picnic lunch. On the homeward route, we put in some flying gallops and I lost my straw hat. As I was right at the back and reluctant to stop the whole cavalcade for such a trivial item, I endured the hot sun for the rest of the afternoon. No one seemed to notice, not even the leader.

By the time we got back to the stables and I dismounted from my high, Spanish saddle, I discovered that not only could I hardly walk, but I had bad abrasion burns on the inside of each leg. Five or six hours of gripping with my knees and calves, wearing the wrong clothes, had left their mark.

But one thing was clear. I was not as frightened of riding as I used to be. An unexpected exhilaration gripped me and I knew that I could do this again, and better, than in my childhood. Several years later, once we had moved to the area permanently, I took another ride, this time at the invitation of a Danish friend, a tall, beaming woman named Susanna.

"We go up to Siete Lagunas," she explained in her halting English. "We go with Antonio from Trevélez. He has some nice horses and we make a group of five or six."

It was August and very hot. I had eaten tapas containing tuna the night before and my stomach that morning alternated between extreme gripes and an uneasy laxity. However, there we were at the stables - myself, Susanna, Carla (who rode with admirable calm and elegance), a woman named Alice, Antonio the leader, and his fourteen year-old son, Jorge. We took an extra horse, laden with a tent and sleeping equipment which we were to leave at the biggest laguna for some overnight mountaineers. I thought I looked a bit more like a rider this time, with leather boots, black jeans and waistcoat, a striped blue-and-white shirt, and a red bandana. Because of my sore legs last time around, I had placed gauze padding against each knee, held in place by copious webbing and surgical tape. As it turned out, the state of my digestive system meant that the gauze padding eventually substituted for a nappy. A practical solution for an embarrassing state of health.

It was a long ride up, zig-zagging our way across the face of the Loma de Peñón Negro (black rock hill) above Trevélez, crossing small *barrancos* and streams, passing by windswept copses of pine and the occasional abandoned farmhouse.

"Only thirty or forty years ago, there were thousands of sheep and goats up here," explained Susanna. "People lived here all year round, their children didn't go to school and many were so poor that they had no shoes on their feet. It took much work by Franco and his government to bring in electricity, better mountain roads and local schools, to make life less harsh, but then the people changed their character and expectations, and now no one wants to live so remotely all year."

I remembered the impoverished and isolated Spanish villages of the late 1950s, not that far from Madrid, when whole families would turn out to show us their sacred church and stare in wonder at these foreigners who could afford to drive a car all the way from England, just for a holiday. The children there had no shoes, the men were lean and hollow-cheeked, the older women always dressed in black, the streets were often unpaved and dusty. Donkeys and carts could be found, late at night, piled high with grass and caught in the headlights as they plodded wearily home. Anyone straying across private land was liable to be shot first and questions asked later. That was old Spain. A page has been turned and this is a new country, blessed with medical centres, municipal swimming pools, pensions and, of course, tourists, although the economic crisis from 2007 onwards has threatened even this level of modernisation.

Riding in single file, we crossed the top of a dried-up, stone-laden waterfall, so close to the edge that I could see the perilous drop below. This would be a dangerous place in winter when the snow was down. When we reached the Siete Lagunas, the heat of the lower altitudes had dropped away, a cool wind began to blow, creating little waves on the Laguna Hondera and then the rain arrived. Munching on our lunch of bread, cheese and ham, we huddled in the lee of a big rock. I stuck to a few mouthfuls only, refusing the tomatoes, oranges and nectarines, sure that my stomach would rebel even more. Carla unwrapped a plaid jacket from around her waist, put it on with the collar turned up and lay down to sleep.

"I'm so tired," she complained, "we were in the bar in Mecinilla until very late."

The horses were happy enough. We had taken off their saddles and bridles and turned them loose with just their halters on. They rolled joyfully in the grass and trotted about, drinking at the lake, heedless of the weather and a cluster of horned cattle. Antonio seemed unperturbed that they were loose. "They won't go anywhere," he said. "They have been coming up here for many years and they know that there will be apples and carrots for them before we head back."

On the way home, as we reached the lower levels, we passed various walkers and back-packers. Sometimes they overtook us, going even faster than we could on the steeper sections. At times we dismounted and led the horses down, going in front of them without a backward glance, holding the reins at full length. They were so sure-footed, we did not have to worry about where they placed their feet or if they would slide into anyone's back. At 2000 metres, the sun came out again and the heat returned. Susanna and I agreed that we should do some more riding, soon, and even began to talk about a combined riding and tango trip to South America.

Over the next year, we managed several half-day outings and I found myself with a regular ride named Lola who was stabled in Bubión. This sweet-natured, sometimes frisky, bay mare suited me very well. Standing at about 14.2 hands, she had a willing energy but would stop when I needed her to. Often, she and I would lead a ride, as she had no fear of cars, strange machines or new paths. She belonged - still belongs - to Rafa, a riding instructor and stable owner who does indeed give instruction.

"Don't go to him," I was told by several people. "He always shouts at you and tells you how to ride."

"But that's what I want," I said. "I can do the basics, but no one has ever shown me how to get better."

In fact, Rafa only shouted when some element of risk was involved, either to the horses or the riders. Being in control of the horse and not vice versa meant having a good seat and upright posture, good hands, and connection with the horse - heels down, legs bonded to the horse's flanks. He had little time for slouches who made no effort.

"Only ride with one hand holding the reins," was his first command to me. "The biggest risk to you is if the horse falls and you are crushed. With only one hand on the reins you are more likely to be thrown free and not get injured. Unless you are stopping or turning the horse, or maybe going fast, you don't need two hands. That is the English style, but you don't need it here."

Much later on in my riding adventures I wished very much that I had had a third hand, to grab hold of the mane and prevent a bad fall. One hand or two, it's a long way down when one topples off.

The second piece of useful advice was for ascents up steep, rocky and narrow paths that had previously been used by the shepherds. "Lift your bottom out of the saddle, reach forward and grasp the mane with your free hand, as far forward as possible, give your horse a bit of slack and she will do the rest."

This worked extremely well and I had the comforting knowledge that I was helping the horse to get up the slope safely, not handicapping it in any way. Going down felt more perilous and involved an opposite stance, leaning back over the horse's rump, with one hand on the rear crest of the saddle. However, although I had moments when Lola slipped onto her haunches, I never felt vulnerable to being thrown off.

One of Rafa's favourite riders was an elderly gentleman named Harry. He had been in a Ghurkha equine regiment and was accustomed to riding for several days at a time, always upright, with his sabre at the ready. Nowadays, he and Rafa would set out across the sierras, laden with bedrolls, food, hay and plenty of water. Neither of them knew how far they would go or for how long. Harry was full of interesting anecdotes and stories of his time in Nepal, so their trips were never boring and I could easily imagine the two of them in some sort of Don Quixote mode, Rafa looking macho in his brown leather waistcoat, long chaps and Spanish hat, and Harry in a braided and buttoned period costume, ready to hurl himself at full gallop against the enemy.

As autumn gravitated towards winter and the vague conversations about riding in Patagonia began to develop into serious plans, Steve surprised me by announcing that he too might give riding a go. He had read a Simon Barnes book, *This Horsey Life*, and his friend Tómas had had a good day out riding with a local shepherd, so he decided to try this new mode of transport: *sin frenos, sin papeles, sin nada* (without brakes, without papers, without anything).

"You'd better have a proper class first, in a riding school," I suggested.

One bright October day, he booked himself in for an hour with Rafa. When he returned, he was not exactly hooked, but he had certainly learned the basics. Being a man who likes certainties and technical exactitude however, his main concern was to know whether he was taking the horse for a ride, or vice versa.

"I don't want to kick the horse and make it do what I want, against its will," he explained. "These trekking horses are very obedient, very safe, but I need some rules that will work with other horses, with other temperaments."

"I think you'll find that the general training methods don't change very much," I replied. "You need to do more riding so that you start to feel comfortable and in control on any horse."

He got more advice and training from our friend Nadia, who never neglected her bright-red lipstick even when she was riding, and although he would never make a keen horseman, he had a better understanding from then on as to how they functioned.

* * *

Meanwhile, time had caught up with me. I began to notice a new, not-so-small lump in my right armpit, and some pimples along the operation line of my right breast. What I had assumed to be scar tissue began to look and feel abnormal. Could the cancer have returned?

"I think I should visit the doctor," I told Steve, "just to be sure."

Our medical centre is located in a small village, in a converted house, and consists of no more than two clinic rooms, a single waiting room, and a bathroom. There are no secretaries or receptionists, just the doctor and the nurse. You simply turn up, ask who is *el ultimo* - the last in the queue - and wait your turn. Sometimes there are only three waiting, sometimes ten; sometimes the nurse is still in the village bar round the corner, having his morning coffee and cognac, or the doctor has been asked to attend an emergency. Your visit may last 5 minutes or you might wait for an hour. Always, I take a book to read.

On this occasion, I waited in turn to see a locum, my usual doctor being on her annual holiday. It was just myself, two elderly gentlemen, and a plump woman with her child. The be-spectacled and serious locum was dubious about the lump - "it's probably just scar tissue," - but decided to refer me to a specialist in Motril hospital anyway. Two days later, we made our way there and began to learn how the Spanish health system works and how it differs from the British one - noisier, more chaotic, less administratively-based, and more informal. Arguably, however, more efficient.

We needed to book the actual appointment day and time ourselves, so the ground-floor booking hall was the first stopping point. It was crammed full and people jostled to grab a numbered ticket from a machine on the wall. There were two TV screens that showed the next available number and which desk was free. As only two of the four desks were manned, the industrious booking clerks waited less than 20 seconds for someone to wave their ticket and dive in front of the desk, before they moved on to the next number, so we stood, alert and nervous, watching the numbers as they flashed up. Woe betide anyone who had slipped out for a cigarette or a cup of coffee and missed their turn. Mind you, with casual insouciance, they usually managed to persuade the clerk to slot them back in again without delay; after all, they had done the requisite queueing, hadn't they?

We soon learned which appointments required a booking clerk and which did not; where to go for a blood test, and how that system worked (get there before 8 a.m., grab a ticket, watch for your slot in the *cola* and you'll be out again in no time); where X-rays and scans were done; and how to nab the medical nurses as they materialised outside the consultants' doors, to show that one had arrived for the scheduled appointment.

Because my referral mentioned cancer, I was given my first consultant appointment within a few days. We drove down again on that hot September morning, apprehensive but, in my case, as ever, optimistic. In the waiting room upstairs, unlike the hushed atmosphere of a British hospital, large groups of people chattered away, almost shouting, in true Spanish fashion. Mobiles rang, children played... I was surprised that *bocadilla* sandwiches did not appear, or a trolley with beer and tapas.

The consultant, a woman in her fifties with bright red trousers, a blue silk shirt and an efficient, pleasant manner, did not like the look or the feel of my little lump and referred me for an ultrasound scan. This took place almost immediately, just down the corridor. The specialist there did not like what she saw either, and during the next hour or two I spent time under another scanner, in front of an X-ray machine, had a blood sample taken and endured three biopsies. We were delighted at the immediate response, at the attitude of 'let's do this now,' instead of being fobbed off because the next person could not wait more than 10 minutes. From then on we learned to be patient ourselves, when other people were being passed through the necessary system of tests.

After this full medical morning, we thought we thought we would go off down the coast road and have a look at Salobreña castle. We had only been gone a couple of hours when my mobile rang. Could we return to the hospital immediately for a consultation?

"We can confirm that your cancer has returned," the surgeon told us, using clear Castilian and speaking slowly. "We need to act fast, to try and prevent it from spreading. I can remove the lump under your armpit, but you are going to need chemotherapy, maybe radiotherapy, for other tumours. This big one will reduce as a result of chemotherapy anyway, so it's up to you whether you want surgery or not."

"Is the cancer just in that area, in my armpit?" I asked apprehensively.

"No, it has spread to your ribs and your shoulder blades, into the bone."

As soon as she said 'bone', I knew that I was in trouble. Always an optimist and not too interested in medical programmes or magazines or internet sites, nonetheless I realised that bone or organ cancer was inoperable and often terminal. I had granted myself a drug-free couple of years in the sun, but left myself open to this potentially fatal recurrence.

I decided not to bother with minor surgery. The horror of chemotherapy would be enough, and the sooner that started the better. Another appointment was made for the following week, to see a medical oncologist, and as Steve and I descended in the lift, we were both near to tears. Another kind of dust had appeared in our paradise, one whose cellular structure was running out of control and would overwhelm our lives. I knew that the thirty years I had hoped for, with this big-hearted and special man, might be reduced by half.

"What would you like to do now?" he asked.

"Go up into the mountains," I replied, unhesitatingly.

So that was what we did. We picked a remote area in the lee of a mountain known as El Caballo (the Horse), checked the weather forecast and packed our kit for two nights out in the wilderness. We would have to drive as high as possible near to Granada, then strike eastwards, to gain altitude. This is an extract from a blog post that I wrote afterwards:

'We've been three days/two nights up in the wilds and had a great time of it. We took the battered road up behind Niguëlas and drove (or bumped) for at least an hour to reach our car parking spot, had a quick picnic lunch and then set off towards El Caballo, rearing its 3000m head high above us. We had enough bivi kit and food to last the two days, and thanks to Steve's obsession with 'liteweight' we carried 4.5 kg and 5.75 kg respectively (he had the stove, water filter, more food than me...). Not such a lot considering.

'It took 3 hours of leisurely 'look at the view' climbing to reach the summit, with a sharp wind at our backs, but the sun and the effort kept us warm. We didn't linger too long up there... the wind was even stronger (35 or 40kph)... and soon wound our way down into the valley on the other side, where there's a great *refugio* and laguna. It was good that we had enough warm gear for outdoor sleeping as 4 people and 3 dogs were already in occupation. As it was, we dined off noodles and tea and snuggled down as soon as the light had gone. Slowly, the wind backed off, the stars came out and I slept... not sure Steve did, but then he only does 4 hour stints anyway.

'Just before dawn I woke up to a perfect, almost new moon and the laguna as still as a sheet of polished metal. Gradually, light began to seep over the high peaks of Tajos de los Majos and by about 08:30 we were dancing about in the sunshine. We took our time over breakfast (the dreaded muesli) and then set off northwards, towards the top of the valley with Veleta in the distance. It's an exciting walk, often on well-laid stone but at one point crossing a deep ravine, where we clung onto chains that had been fixed to the rock wall. Not one for people with vertigo!

'We saw eagles and vultures, falcons and ravens - and mountain goats of course. That night, deep down in the valley, Steve improved on an existing ruin with a spot of wall-building and we settled down for a much calmer and warmer night. We were lying side-by-side, chatting and looking at the stars, when I saw, two feet above his head and tiptoeing along the wall... Zorro the fox! Or Zorra, perhaps. Silhouetted against the darkening sky, s/he had no fear of us at all but was clearly looking for the source of the chorizo and cous-cous that we had just eaten. Of course, the creature ran off as soon as we sat up, but was back sometime later, as in the morning we found various empty packets thrown around, even T-bags!

'We decided not to walk up to the Elorrieta refuge but to stay in the valley, and then we climbed almost vertically up towards Pico de Cartujo to reach the high ridge, stunning views of Granada and the wide plains below, the sea and other distant mountains . I could just make out the rosy terracotta of the main Alhambra tower. It took us several hours to wind our way back down to the car, stopping to 'chat' with more mountain goats and about 12 horses, leaderless and unroped, that were heading north in a very determined fashion. They seemed to know exactly where they were going.'

We did not know exactly where anything in our lives was going, but the following week we made another trip down to Motril. We had an appointment with Señor Jurado, the medical oncologist, a tall, slim, serious man who had a sniffly cold and, thankfully, spoke excellent English. He opened a small window of hope.

"First we will try hormone therapy," he said, "for two months. If it reduces the tumours, you might not need chemotherapy. Also, we will send you to Granada for a bone density scan. The hormone injections can be given by your local doctor or nurse and I will see you in six weeks time."

He sat down and wrote out copious prescriptions, all in triplicate, all for the same drug, to be given every two weeks. It took us several trips to purchase this from the pharmacy in Orgiva, but eventually we had enough prepared syringes in the fridge for three sets of double injections, one in each buttock. I remembered with dread the anti-Tetanus jabs of my youth and the shooting pains in my legs afterwards. This was not going to be fun.

In fact, the nurse in our little medical centre, though matter-of-fact and dressed as though he had come straight from his kitchen garden, delivered the injections with care and a light hand. I hardly felt them. We had arrived on the Suzuki and we departed again by the same method, without any discomfort at all. Then it was a case of waiting for the side-effects to kick in.

Days passed. I scrutinised many cancer websites, including the ones that tried to answer the question 'Why and how does cancer kill you?' and I sent forlorn messages to my closest friends and family. I cancelled a group walk into the mountains with Steve and some English folk in case I couldn't manage it. I put myself on a low carbohydrate diet: no bread, little wheat or grain-based fodder, more proteins and lots of fresh fruit and vegetables. Alcohol didn't appeal, even well-watered wine and I already had caffeine-free tea in the cupboard. However, on day three, having drunk two glasses of pure orange juice, I developed a headache and my vision slid away; the computer screen became distorted down the right-hand side, as though watching a Predator-type dissolve. *This is it*, I thought, *I'm entering a new world and I don't like it at all.* It hadn't occurred to me that I might not be able to use my eyesight.

Luckily, it must have been a temporary migraine, since an hour asleep on the sofa put it to rights. I awoke, with clear vision once again, to a knock on the door. Steve was out on the land, watering the young olive trees, so I went to answer it and found Emilio, suntanned and solid, waiting in the street.

"I've come to fit the new water meter in the wall," he announced. "Well, I'll come on Wednesday, but we need to decide exactly where it will go and how much piping will be needed."

I ushered him into the courtyard, where the white jasmine had begun to flower, draping itself over the motorbikes.

"So, how are you?" he asked, in a genial way, as he always did. He knew I had had cancer before.

"I've got bad news," I said, looking him in the eye but probably speaking a bit unsteadily. "The cancer has come back."

"Oh, Linda," he sighed, shaking his head, "I'm so sorry." He put his arm round my shoulders and gave me a big hug. He felt warm and reassuring.

"*Soy una mujer fuerte*, I'm a strong woman," I said. "I'll just take it day by day, *día por día.*"

He nodded and we got on with the business in hand. I liked the male response to medical ailments; my women friends were thoughtful and sympathetic but for too long. The men gave me kisses and strong hugs, pressing me against their manly chests, then they reverted to normal.

Beyond this, no one changed their essential character in terms of their response - Marianne was charmingly empathetic but quickly got back to the topic of her awful ex-husband and recalcitrant son; my riding friend Susanna told me "You will beat this," and then wanted to discuss the trip we were planning to South America; Isabella was practical and kind, bringing grapes and other delicious titbits; Juanita amazed me with her concern, a big kiss and yet more grapes, from her own *huerto*. Friends from Scotland rang, expensively, to see how I was faring and my sons offered to come out to Spain if a hand was needed. "Of course not," was my response. "I'm not going to become an invalid if I can help it."

So there I was, digging away in the sunshine, clearing weeds and admiring the fat worms and shining brown millipedes, and wondering how many more seasons I had before me. Perhaps not a lot. Perhaps only 3 or 4 if I was lucky. I had started to die, as all creatures and plants do, but in such a paradise that it had taken me some time to acknowledge the fact. Fortunately, I had been given the opportunity to savour my life while it slipped inexorably from me, and the reasons to find joy were magnified by the knowledge that it would come to an end sooner than I might have anticipated.

Five days later and still feeling good, I went to my tango class in Granada. I had cancelled a number of sessions whilst waiting to get through the initial treatment, so they knew broadly what was going on. To my surprise, their welcome was effusive, their warm sympathy and geniality outstanding. How had I managed to stumble across such fine people? The women wanted detail, but the men, again, were happy just to dance. Carina, one of the teachers, gave me a shock. "I have got many benign tumours," she whispered. "In my breasts and my ovaries. I am being monitored for the next six months to see if they change or become malignant."

I looked at her pale and slightly pensive Uruguayan face. She needed more concern than me, I thought. Even now, she did not look too good.

"Is it in your family?" I asked. "Your mother or grandmother?"

"No, nothing," she replied.

I hugged her. "We'll get through this together, *juntos*," I said.

* * *

The next time we discussed our ailments, a couple of months later, we were standing in the overcrowded Bar Avila in Granada, just after a tango class. This small, brightly-lit, L-shaped room caters for students, shoppers, the occasional foreigner and certainly many of the city's roaming tapas population. Famed for its grilled pork slices and little dishes of *callos*, or tripe, it seems impossible for the place to make any kind of profit. A modest glass of wine or beer is accompanied always by a generous plateful of food, with two or three people beavering away in the kitchen and two barmen as well.

"You look very well," Carina said. "How is your treatment going?"

"The tumours are subsiding, it's quite astonishing," I said, grinning. "I feel fantastic."

It was difficult not to be so cheerful. Contrary to my expectations, I had had no further side-effects, the lump under my right arm had diminished to the size of a small pea and I had a sense of renewed energy and vitality. Even though the monthly X-rays had revealed a tumour hotspot on my left lung, or *pulmón*, this too was beginning to reduce.

But I had read enough on the internet to know that secondary cancer rarely goes away forever. One day the medication stops working, or the disease moves to a new site, or some horrendous side-effect begins to take a hold. So I was not surprised to discover that my bone density scan was the harbinger of bad news - I was losing minerals and calcium from my bones, a process of leaching which can become fatal. Interestingly, when I had asked the question, "What is it about cancer that actually kills you?" an excessive amount of calcium in the bloodstream was the first answer that I found.

My oncologist was grave. "We will start you off on some treatment for this as soon as possible. Follow me."

We swept out of his neat office and down the squeaky linoleum corridor, around the corner and through a pair of swing doors, into a fairly large day-room, scattered with comfortable chairs, a few screened beds and some busy folk in white coats. There were lots of drip-stands. Steve muttered "I'll wait outside," and vanished. I wondered if the start was going to be made immediately; this was obviously a treatment room for people on chemotherapy or other types of intravenous medication.

A plump woman, escorted by a young nurse, sat down nearby. She had a fixed, frightened stare and one sensed that she was in some sort of shock. "They've just given her some very bad news," I thought, "I wonder if I looked like that a month ago?"

I was ushered over to a high desk.

"Do you have any allergies?" asked a senior nurse, dressed in a pale blue shirt and white surgical trousers, as the oncologist gave me a casual wave and disappeared through a different set of doors.

I began to say "No," then remembered the ghastly business with the iodine contrast and quickly described what had happened. "I blew up, like this," I gestured, "like a balloon." I did not know the Spanish for pufferfish.

An appointment was made for the following week.

"Shall I book her in for another one after that, next month?" the blonde receptionist asked the nurse.

"No," I heard the reply, "we'll see how this goes first."

That should have warned me straight away. Later on, as I began to read of the 'hell that is this medication' and 'how my jaw broke thanks to prolonged bisphosphonate infusions' and 'nausea, vomiting, migraines and weakness are common side effects,' I realised, once again, that I had stepped onto the wide escalator of chronic diseases. There are many of these: diabetes, heart disease, osteoarthritis, and even clinical depression, for example, and the treatment is often as unpleasant as the actual ailment. Chronic means that these diseases rarely, if ever, completely vanish.

In terms of Stage IV cancer, many others had been there before me and suffered horribly; a minority were lucky and became NEAD (no evidence of active disease), but one had no way of knowing until the ghastly business was well under way. My first round of treatment might yield suddenly to other debilitating conditions that I had never considered. The rosy glow of dealing with a 'bit of cancer' could, like a chocolate-box Renoir painting of flowers, turn into a Hieronymus Bosch nightmare at any moment. Indeed, as the poet Jason Shinder wrote: 'Cancer is a tremendous opportunity to have your face pressed right up against the glass of your mortality.'

The next day, which was unusually redolent of December chill and drifting hill-fog, saw us coming out of our local shop and bumping into our builder Emilio again. We had not seen him for a couple of months by now, so it was a real joy to recognise his burly form clad in rain jacket, hood and beanie.

"Emilio!" I shrieked. "Where have you been?"

He grinned like a child and gave me a big *abrazo* and kisses to each cheek.

"I'm very pleased to see you," he said. "We were talking about you only yesterday, the chaps and I, wondering if you were OK. What's the latest news?"

We gave him the good, and the less good, medical information. He only heard the first bit and clapped Steve on the shoulder. "She's going to be around for a bit longer! You won't get rid of her quite as soon as you thought!"

Often people think that foreigners come to Spain only for the sun, but we knew yet again that we had come for the human warmth as well. Without artificiality or false bonhomie, these friendly souls drew us into their circle of existence, metaphorically sharing their fireside and their food. Emilio typified all of that, inheriting and passing on values that had sustained remote communities for hundreds of years.

* * *

So, what next?

"Let's get into the hills again," I suggested, and Steve had no hesitation. We spread out the maps and considered our options for a winter walking trip.

"We'll go south," he said, "towards the coast and those limestone Sierras that look so interesting, up behind Nerja. It'll be warmer at the lower altitude."

We had walked in this area with our Glaswegian friends Stevie and Lynn, but that was in high summer heat, when the glare of white stone and the incessant attention of flies made it hard work. We had a notion that this time we could go further and higher, and have the place to ourselves. Out came the kit: sleeping bags and mats, warm down jackets and thermal underwear, cooking equipment and dehydrated food, and assorted emergency items - torches, knives, plasters, aspirin and tiny cut-off toothbrushes. Even with water, we were aiming for backpacks weighing around 5 kilograms. In the event, we were closer to 6 kg, but that is still considered lightweight among the cognoscenti.

Food plans were worked through in detail. If we spent two nights and three days out there, we would need 2 breakfasts, 3 lunches, 2 suppers... lots of water... and something for emergency rations. We settled on the ubiquitous muesli, noodles, soup, clementines, chocolate, and a bag apiece of assorted nuts. I took half a lemon for my hot drinks and Steve brought instant coffee mixed with dried milk. Folding cups, snap-lock plastic bags, plastic spoons and forks... someone jokingly said that God's big message was 'more plastic' and maybe they were right.

"Let's get away early," I suggested, "perhaps by about eight o'clock. It will take us two hours to get to Nerja or Frigiliana, have a coffee and set off."

We had bargained without two difficulties; my alarm clock failed to go off - "Shit, shit, it's already 08:30," and the very cold night meant that the car wouldn't start. Even the portable jump-starter couldn't get the engine to turn over.

"We'll have to try the motorbike," said Steve, vanishing in the direction of our house. Five minutes later he emerged astride the VFR, parked it alongside, removed the seat to expose the battery and we attached heavy-duty jump leads from it to the car. At that moment José wandered into view, on his way to collect some mules to work his land.

"*Qué pasa?*" he asked, drawing deeply on his first cigarette of the day.

I explained the plan and he shook his head in disbelief.

"In summer, yes, but why do you want to sleep outside in these temperatures?"

Another acquaintance appeared, Mad Mike and his dog Goldie, with a different perspective. "I did that too, about 5 years ago," Mike nodded enthusiastically, his brown and gold Moroccan skull cap slipping to one side. "I had a bit of a crisis and wanted to purify myself in the snows of Mulhacén. I took my kukri sword, a rucksack of logs and wore my favourite Scottish kilt."

We began to laugh. "A thermal kilt, hopefully," I smiled.

"Why logs?" asked Steve, "There's plenty of wood up there."

"I wasn't sure," Mike grinned. "If I got to the snow line before nightfall, it would be too late to find any."

"And did you make it?"

"No," he replied. "I stopped off at the Buddhist monastery, where they took me in and gave me a bed for the night. I think they were a bit shocked that I had only got sandals on as well."

"Saved your life, mate," said Steve. "It's probably about minus 15 Centigrade up there right now."

Mike comes and goes to the village, depending on his finances and his work in England as a painter and decorator. A kind-hearted bachelor in his fifties, he has adopted Goldie, a bright-eyed, long-haired retriever who appeared on his doorstep one morning, hungry, unkempt, and wagging his tail with optimism. Rightly so. Since then, he has been cleaned up, micro-chipped, trained (a little), and familiarised with a collar and lead.

"He's my talisman," Mike explained. "I needed something permanent in my life."

Sometimes Mike's Italian friend, Francesco, who hails from Sorrento, also arrives in the village and together they take themselves off to Granada or Málaga in search of thirty-something goddesses who might offer a night of passion. Goldie assists in this quest, a sure-fire way to attract tender-hearted females, including the four-legged variety.

One upshot of all this was, the local vet told us later on, that Mike took Goldie to be 'done,' with unexpected consequences. Having given the dog an anaesthetic, he asked Mike if he wanted to hold him during the operation.

"Sí, sí," Mike replied in his limited Spanish.

The vet made the first incision, heard a groaning sound and looked up to see Mike reel against the wall and then slump to the floor. So there he was, surgical knife in hand, with two unconscious patients rather than one. Needless to say, he attended to the dog first, completed the procedure and then checked Mike for signs of life. A fainting owner was not entirely new to him.

Francesco always arrives with his old car loaded to the gunnels with Italian delicacies. He doesn't want to trust his digestion to his perception of the poor quality of Spanish cuisine, although my Seville orange marmalade has been given the seal of Italian approval. He is a slight, silver-haired man, very dapper in black jeans and waistcoat, and a complete contrast to Mike in his baggy cords, alternative headgear and unshaven visage. They do throw good parties though.

Today we were leaving them to their New Year celebrations and heading off to the Sierra de Almijara. Our destination was a ruined property named Cortijo del Imán, which we had seen through binoculars, lying on a small plateau at about 700 metres, encircled by high, bleached limestone peaks. We had been told that the path to it was difficult to find and very overgrown. I packed secateurs, while Steve wished he had a machete.

Leaving Frigiliana behind us, we made our way up the Rio Chillar, following a well-trodden route that skirted around La Presa, an old concrete dam. So far, so good. We knew that the *cortijo* path was on our right, heading north-east and north, but somehow we managed to miss it and continued along the rock-strewn river bed. There were fresh streams and occasional mini-waterfalls, but nothing that we could not negotiate. We passed tall eucalyptus trees, wild oleander and mature, knotty retama bushes. A few birds whistled above and we felt as though we were a lone expeditionary force, seeking the source of the river. It was perfectly clear however, from the enormous boulders and wrenched-up trees, that when the river was in spate it would be a very dangerous place to be walking. Twice we found ourselves clambering up these boulders, with Steve going first on his longer legs, then holding out a strong stick for me to grab hold of.

"Pull!" I shouted, like a clay-pigeon marksman, "Pull," as he hauled me up the rock face.

After a couple of hours, we found ourselves in a narrow defile with high walls and dripping vegetation. Around the next bend we reached our terminus: two or three waterfalls pouring, one after the other, over smooth rock walls, with no possible chance of getting past them. Far back, beyond this marbled cleft, I could glimpse a pool of water and sun-filled woodland. A magical spot, I was sure, if only we could reach it.

We retraced our steps and got the map and compass out. There were several steep *barrancos* that might lead us up in the general direction of the *cortijo*, but which one to choose?

"Let's try this," I suggested, looking up at a stony, dried-out ravine. "It doesn't look too severe."

Famous last words. The first couple of hundred metres were a scramble alright, but we managed. Then we found ourselves hedged in by vicious, thorny plants with no obvious escape route. It was difficult to see beyond a few metres and we were still climbing.

"Don't go too far ahead," I begged Steve, realising that if I got into a vulnerable or dangerous position, I might need him nearby to haul me to safety.

Finally, we reached a clearing of sorts, but the cliff looming above us was not to my taste at all. Steve might manage to climb up there, but I knew I could not. Old memories of a bad fall whilst out rock-climbing in the Lake District in my twenties came flooding back; I didn't want to be hurtling through space like that again. Having cancer does not suppress one's survival instincts.

Our other predicament was the retreating daylight. This was not the place to spend the night. There was no useful level ground, no open space to lay out our sleeping kit, only a 60 degree slope bristling with spiky bushes that would puncture our inflatable sleeping mats instantly.

"We'll have to go down again," Steve said, regretfully.

"Yes, but not through all that gorse! Let's try the next ravine across."

We turned to survey our options.

"There's the *cortijo*!" I pointed. "There it is!"

Out on the horizon, beyond several rose-red cliffs and pinnacles, we could see the creamy, stone pediment of the building outlined against the fading light of the sky. We had no chance of reaching it tonight, but we were able to get our bearings for a second attempt.

Down we went, sliding and stumbling over loose rocks and large pine cones. We could hear the river burbling below, a welcome sound. As soon as we reached its banks we began to cast about for two sleeping areas - preferably level, no spiny grasses, protection from the coolness of the water but also from any pending rain, with a few large stones to make a cooking range. Soon we found a good site and set about preparing our beds as quickly as possible. By the time we were done, each of us had a head torch switched on. Darkness had fallen.

"What do you fancy for supper?" asked Steve, setting up a stone slab and breaking up small twigs for his home-made stove.

We settled on instant dehydrated soup followed by instant dehydrated noodles: chicken flavour for him, prawn for me. We had enough river water for boiling plus two litres of spare, uncontaminated drinking water. Packing his twigs and Vaseline-coated cotton wool into an adapted beer can, complete with ventilation holes, the master chef soon had a brisk fire going and a cone-shaped wind-buffer made of aluminium foil to keep it alive. Carefully placing a smaller can on top, filled with water and topped off with a lid, it was only a few minutes wait before we had a rolling boil. Not a shop-bought camping stove in sight.

One of the problems with winter bivi-ing is that it's a long night. There's no point in shivering in the dark, waiting for one's usual bedtime, but you know full well that at two in the morning you'll be wide-awake and ready to get up. This time, however, we had a few disturbances to enliven proceedings. Something startled me awake about midnight - was it a rock falling on the other side of the water or an animal moving about, closer in? Then I heard the hooting of an owl. Or was it a call sign? Were there people nearby, moving stealthily up the river-bed? Steve appeared to be a motionless lump, silhouetted against the dim glow of the river. I lay awake for some time, straining to hear any other sounds, then drifted back to sleep.

Light rain disturbed both of us around 5 o'clock. Our down sleeping bags needed to be fully protected, so we shuffled about, hauling our waterproof bivi sacks higher and spreading our ponchos out on top for extra protection. I turned my boots over, which I had forgotten to do earlier and pulled my duck-down jacket into the sleeping bag with me. We lay there, listening to the pattering of the drizzle on our heads and hoping that it wouldn't last long. I speculated on how much rain might be falling higher up in the mountains and at what point our stream would become a raging torrent. Then I went back to sleep again.

When I woke, the sky was clear and just a few drips fell from the pine trees above my head. Peering out into the pale dawn, I could see Steve's trousered legs and hear the sounds of more twig-breaking. This was no time for the feminist agenda, I decided; much better to lie back and think of, well, English Breakfast teabags at any rate.

We didn't dawdle long over our morning preparations and were soon packed up and ready to move on. Looking back at our overnight bivi spot, I could see that apart from a few compressed grasses and a fire-blackened stone, there was no evidence of our presence. Just as it should be.

We crossed the stream and looked up at a ridge about 300 metres above us.

"That's where we want to be," said Steve. "Shall we try the direct approach?"

"Let's give it a go," I agreed, and up we went.

Again, the first part was fairly easy going, climbing up a small *barranco* with plenty of shrubby trees to hang on to. We reached a tall pine tree and realised that we would need to strike left to find any possible route; very quickly the incline increased, the shrubs vanished and we were left with limestone rocks that came away in our hands or from under our feet, with little else to hang on to. We should be roped, I thought. If either of us slips here, we could fall a long way. But we had no rope. These thoughts made me extra careful. I recalled lessons from the past: maintain three secure points of contact at all times; don't look down; ensure a good centre of gravity. Also I remembered my own personal mantra: no whingeing. On we went.

"It gets better up here," Steve called down from a few metres above me.

Indeed it did. We were able to stand upright, the shrubs returned but were less spiky, and then we saw olive trees, definitely part of an old, semi-terraced orchard. The outline of the *cortijo* reappeared. It was set on a flattish apron of land, about a hectare in all, encircled by high limestone peaks and scattered, stunted pine trees. To the north stood La Cadena at 1,600 metres, to the east, Navachica at 1,800 metres, whilst the greener Sierra Enmedio ran down the western flank towards the distant sea. It was an extraordinary location with outstanding views.

We agreed to approach quietly, just in case someone else was there, but the building and its scattered ruins were empty. We found the main 'room,' roofless but with three walls intact, and the remains of a rough-and-ready fireplace in one corner. Parts of the floor looked compressed as though someone had slept there recently and a few items of gear were stuffed into various gaps in the stonework: a cheap inflatable air mat, a black biker jacket of dubious quality, a rolled-up sleeping pad, a tub of damp salt and, amazingly, a three-quarters full bottle of Limoncello liqueur. Who had left that there? Was someone coming back? Had he or she, or they, made a base camp and gone off for a day's wandering in the high peaks?

We thought we'd better look for our own sleeping area immediately, away from this apparently requisitioned part of the site. We wandered through the more ruinous outer rooms and became conscious of a swirling, chilly wind. It was midday and although the sun was out, at 700 metres it was none too warm.

"Look at this," called Steve's voice.

I followed him and turned a corner at the front of the building, facing down the valley and towards the distant sea. A small, stone-built lean-to huddled against the main wall, without a door but with an opening at waist height, just big enough to crawl through. I stuck my head inside and discovered a dome-shaped, internal roof, a flat pamment floor and scattered pine fronds. It was the old bread-oven, big enough to function as a bakery. There was definitely room inside for two.

"This is our bedroom for the night," I announced. "Absolutely fantastic!"

We couldn't understand why the owner of the kit that we had found had not laid claim to this wind-proof, snug little space. No matter. We hauled our rucksacks inside, stuffed pieces of foam into the odd hole and congratulated ourselves on our find. We nibbled at a bit of lunch, sitting in a sheltered spot in the sun, and then walked downhill through the olive trees to see if we could find the start-point of the correct pathway out again. We would not be climbing down the cliff-face, of that I was sure. I wanted the rest of the trip to be as stress-free as possible. Steve took a slightly different direction than me and soon called out that he thought he had found the path; sure enough, half-hidden by young trees and undergrowth, there was clear evidence of a stone-laid route, wide enough for a mule or a donkey. We followed it for half a kilometre, to be sure of it, and reached one of the dried-up *barrancos* again, but this time we could see the way ahead and the path continuing south, cutting across the hillside.

"Perhaps that was the main reason to abandon the *cortijo* long ago," I suggested. "No water."

We turned back and as the winter sun began to dip, we laid out our sleeping gear in the bread oven and collected bigger pieces of wood for the fireplace next door. I put on another layer and a beanie, preferring to anticipate the inevitable drop in temperature, and wandered away through thickets and shrubs, hauling out anything substantial that looked dry enough to burn well. I noticed the remains of old stone walls and a low-lying area of natural grasses and reeds; perhaps there had been a water reservoir or *deposito* here at some point in the past. A swirling wave of crows passed overhead and a pallid mist began to obscure the mountains. Time to make another brew and light that fire.

In the growing darkness we could see the glimmering lights of the distant coast and hear the wind soughing down from the heights above us. In the angle of the walls, already blackened with previous use, we piled up brushwood and a few big branches and lit our New Year bonfire. Immediately, the flames leapt up and the sparks flew crazily around the 'room,' driven by strong gusts. We had no anxiety about starting a serious campo fire as it was well-contained and this was January, not July or August, but we kept a good watch on things nonetheless. The last person that we knew of to start a major fire in the Alpujarras had received a stiff fine and four years in a Spanish prison.

We thought we should try the Limoncello and gave ourselves a couple of tots out of the screw-cap, toasting the new year, our happiness and the solitude of our surroundings. A fine night-cap to another exciting day. Then we headed to our boudoir.

One thing we had not reckoned on was the location of the bread oven on the other side of the wall from the fireplace. Visible in the torchlight, smoke was filtering through small cracks and giving off a noticeable smell of charcoal.

"Kippers for breakfast," I thought.

Steve went out and banked the fire down as much as he could, while I stuffed some grasses and bits of foam into any holes I could see. Nonetheless, a spark actually made its way through and landed in front of me. That was something we did not want on our beautiful, goose-down sleeping bags with their delicate outer layers.

Within a short time, the smoke had dissipated and we were tucked up as snugly as two rabbits in a hole. Steve got out his iPod and we played Sudoku for a while, but I could feel my eyes closing even though it was only about eight o'clock. He would sleep and wake, sleep and wake throughout the night, but I had a feeling that nothing would disturb me. This luxurious bedroom was just the ticket.

In fact we both slept through our nocturnal visitor, Señor Zorro again. This time he managed to make off with three of Steve's nylon stuff-sacks, all located near to the small doorway. Just like a Beatrix Potter watercolour, I had visions of a handsome four-legged fellow running through the Spanish villages, attired in improvised polyester bootees, held in place by shock cords and toggles. We made some hasty searches in and around the building but could find nothing, and set off without delaying for breakfast; we knew it would be a good 5 hour walk back to Frigiliana and our water stocks were adequate but not excessive. Best to get going while the day was fresh and cool.

On the walk in, we had not met anyone at all, but this time, perhaps because it was the New Year holiday, we were almost tripping over other walkers on the lower stretches of the valley. We counted 53 in total. On a very steep and narrow uphill section, we stepped off the path to let a troupe of English and American walkers come down.

"Are you English?" asked the walk's leader, genially.

"We try not to be," I could not resist replying.

She was closely followed by another woman. "Oh, we've caught you up," she said, brightly.

Steve was more polite than me.

"No," he smiled, "we're heading uphill, in the other direction."

We were a bit surprised that no one in this large party thought of giving way to us, the ones who were tackling the gradient, as is the usual custom whether on foot or in a vehicle, but perhaps it's like that going up the Langdale Pikes nowadays, as well.

A short time later, when we were on a downhill section, we met a ginger-blonde Dutch family, struggling their way up from the river and looking particularly red-faced from their exertions. By now it was about two in the afternoon and very warm. The man paused beside Steve.

"Do you think we will get to the Nerja caves in an hour or so?" he asked.

We must have looked shocked.

"Not a chance," Steve replied. "It's a good two hours to the main picnic area and another hour at least down to Nerja, maybe more. It'll be dark before you get there."

"We'd be better to go back, then," he said, reluctantly. "Look, we have this little map from our hotel and it says 4 hours in total."

We explained that, in our opinion, these calculations were usually wrong.

"They send out some fit young men and ask them to time themselves over the distance. No doubt there's a beer at the end of it, or a girlfriend waiting or a day's pay, so of course they strike out and go as quickly as they can. You can add another hour at least if you have children or older people in your party."

"I shall write and complain," he said, stubbornly. "I hate it when they give the wrong information."

His pink-faced wife looked relieved that they were turning around. Her tight, black, leather-effect trousers must have been boiling hot. We moved swiftly on, but we could hear the children jumping from rock to rock as they retreated back down the path behind us. Much later, as we sat in the last of the afternoon sunlight, in the town, we saw them come through and gave a wave. It was a relief to think that they were not going to be caught out, as the warmth disappeared and the light faded, still plodding their way through the darkening countryside.

* * *

I had my first intravenous bisphosphonate infusion soon after this expedition. A simple enough process, it involved sitting patiently in the hospital day-care room with a drip running into my left arm, waiting for the medication to go in first, followed by a saline solution. I had been advised to drink plenty of water too, to ameliorate the impact of a new drug in my body.

Around me sat other patients, also in high, wing-backed armchairs, their drips and bottles attached. Some were much older than me, their faded, wrinkled skin appearing to be as thin as tissue-paper. One or two of the women wore head scarves, often the insignia of cancer and chemotherapy. I felt strangely youthful and energetic beside them and that evening we went for a meal with friends and I forgot all about the medication.

Remembrance came at dawn, when I awoke to a sensation of nausea and dizziness. "Here we go," I muttered, staggering to the bathroom.

I spent that day in bed or on the settee, shivering weakly under a duvet. Steve was the perfect nurse, offering me weak tea, banking up the wood-burner and generally hovering about. By the next day, I felt pretty good again; if this was the only after-effect each month, we could cope.

Four weeks later, while Steve was away in England, I prepared myself for a day of sickness on my own - plastic bowl and towel by the bed, bottle of water at the ready, warm dressing gown to hand. All unnecessary. This time, I felt a bit weedy but nothing serious. My body had adapted to the presence of the bisphosphonate. From then on, I had no particular trouble with the infusions, although I always took care to eat very little for 24 hours afterwards and to drink plenty of water. When I heard about other people's experiences, yet again I felt myself to be extremely lucky.

I read Siddhartha Muckerjee's book *Cancer: The Emperor of all Maladies* and understood how changeable this disease could be and how varied the treatments and their efficacy on different people. Several friends and acquaintances tried to steer me towards alternative remedies: herbs, concoctions, supplements, psycho-babble, guru-speak et al, but if a clear evidence base was not available, I ignored them, every one. However faulty medical analysis can be, I prefer science to speculation and control trials to quackery.

I began to feel stronger too, so much so that when our friends wanted to firm up the trip to South America, I agreed willingly, but my oncologist looked grave.

"Mmm, you will not be here if anything serious occurs," he murmured.

"We will only be going for a month," I said, stubbornly.

His eyebrows went up, his spectacles dropped lower over his nose.

"Only a month!"

But we worked out some new appointment dates and I said that I would have my injections done privately in Argentina, to keep everything regular and on target.

"Enjoy your holiday," he smiled as we departed.

Chapter 16

South America

So it was that we flew out of a cold, wintry Spain and into a warm, summertime Latin America. Although Buenos Aires was our first landing point and would be a final destination at the end of our trip, we lingered only long enough to change terminals and pick up a southbound flight for San Carlos de Bariloche, the Bowness-on-Windermere of southern Argentina. Here we would meet up with Susanna, my horse-riding friend and her Tyrolean husband Giorgio, a man of deceptively serious demeanour and a delightful sense of humour.

This tall, energetic, and resourceful couple turned out to be the ideal guides in this part of the world, as they had visited before and knew how to book buses, campsites, and local guesthouses. Very organised, very Teutonic. Whether they intended to land themselves with somewhat carefree, often accident-prone and, in my case, diminutive Britishers was another matter. We all learned a thing or two about each other over the next 18 days.

Giorgio, thanks to living at the junction of several countries in the Tyrol, knew that pathways had existed in mountainous areas for hundreds, if not thousands of years, passing from one country into another, so he had already researched routes going from Chile to

Argentina and back again, all in the area known as Patagonia. Thus it was that on our second morning we took a small, local bus down to the lakeside and caught a tourist ferryboat heading towards Puente Blest, a scenic waterfall shrouded amongst mighty trees, and then on to the cul-de-sac at the lake end, where we would disembark and vanish, like early explorers, into the dense forests of the hinterland.

To our surprise, despite the beauty of the pale-blue lake, the snow-capped mountains on the horizon and the impenetrable green of the hillsides, our fellow travellers, all South Americans, were interested only in feeding the seagulls that followed in our wake and dive-bombed the boat. A piece of bread or biscuit was held out at arm's length and if someone was lucky enough, it would be snatched away just as the camera clicked. Our jaundiced European view was that these 'rats with wings' held no charm whatsoever. Familiarity had bred contempt.

The tourists were equally amazed when we gathered up our backpacks, stepped off the boat at a narrow jetty and set off on our trail. Who would want to walk back to Bariloche in this heat, when they could comfortably travel over water? Little did they know that we would not be back in that area for almost 3 weeks.

However, we managed to get lost within 10 minutes. Our friends had not been on this precise route before and with no detailed map - an oversight surely - and no obvious signposts, we were not sure where the correct trail began. We plunged up a steep footpath that seemed to lead in the right direction, but it soon petered out. We stumbled over fallen, mossy tree-trunks and pushed through low foliage. Quickly, too quickly, we had lost sight of the lake.

"This doesn't feel right," someone muttered.

"Let's go back down to the water and start again," was the suggestion.

As we headed downhill, it occurred to me that if we got lost in these dense woods, no one would ever find us, and caution had to be the best bet. If in doubt, admit it and re-trace your footsteps, literally or, in the wider world, metaphorically.

As we reached the lakeside, three young men came into view from a more northerly direction and it became very obvious that they were on the path we wanted; they had walked through from the Chile side of the border and reassured us that it was not too far and very easy walking. We shouldered our packs and set out again, this time passing by a statue of the Virgin that we had missed previously. A good luck symbol perhaps, or a warning to over-optimistic hikers.

We were travelling as light as possible: three Osprey backpacks and my Mariposa. I doubt if anyone's weight exceeded 10kg including sleeping gear, riding helmet, jodhpurs and gaiters, other clothes and waterproofs, a cook stove, and assorted medical items. My total pack came in at about 7.5kg which seemed very acceptable, although later on, staggering up to the Paso de los Nubes, I would willingly have reduced that by half.

We walked all afternoon, overlooking eau-de-nil lakes and their cream-coloured stony beaches, cascading rivers bordered by wild fuchsia and bilberry bushes, and always above us a clear, blue sky. We passed the border marker, the first of several, following a route that wound its way along the valley side. We had to clamber over many fallen trees and teeter our way across bridges that consisted predominantly of a single tree-trunk with a rope handrail. Or just a tree-trunk, no rope. At times the water was only a metre or so below us and not too deep, at times it was more extreme than that. We were very careful, as none of us wanted to soak ourselves and our backpacks so early on in the adventure.

We had been warned about the horse flies, or *Tabanus,* that arrive in swarms during the warm season and I used liberal amounts of DEET on my clothes and exposed skin. Steve, manly to the end, eschewed such nonsense but soon came to regret it. He put his hand down on something - a log or a branch - and got stung. Probably even DEET would not have protected him. Within minutes, his hand was swelling up and he began to feel unwell.

"I'll have to stop for a second," he said, looking anguished and pale.

"I think this is anaphylactic shock," I said, and hunted out an antihistamine. It was a bit early in our adventure to have medical problems, but gradually he began to improve and we moved slowly on. Around about then, we discovered that his bush cap, featuring a protective piece for the back of the neck, had gone missing, perhaps on the ferry or when we went ashore for lunch. It was the first of several 'English droppings' as Susanna referred to them.

"It will be dark in 2 hours," said Giorgio. "We need to think about a place to sleep."

Those who pitch tents out in the wilderness will know that finding level, reasonably clear ground is not easy. The same applies to bivi-ing: you cannot just lie down on the pathway; wet areas are unpleasant, tree roots uncomfortable. As we walked on, it seemed as though the forest grew thicker and places to sleep less apparent. We needed to stay fairly close together too, so we could make a good start in the morning.

We passed some open, marshy land and could hear the bullfrogs croaking. Too damp, too many mosquitoes. The path rounded a crest and we looked up towards the top of the valley, facing east, where we could see a long, glacial ridge topped by thick snow and ice. The tropical temperatures down in the valley had made us forget, briefly, that we were at latitude 41 South (not so different from Barcelona in the Northern hemisphere) and climbing at about 1000 metres (similar to Andorra la Vella in the Pyrenees). The setting sun lit up the edge of the ridge and some distant peaks beyond it, but the snowline below was already turning grey as it moved into shade. We must find a place to stop.

By great good fortune, we came upon a clearing very soon afterwards. Two rivers met there and we found plenty of grassy spaces to put down our mats. Steve set up his cook stove and the prospect of tea, followed by soup and biscuits, gave us the necessary energy to prepare our 'bedrooms' in record time. The midges and mosquitoes homed in on us, so we donned our head-nets and defiantly drank our delicious evening meal before turning in.

I slept well, but during the night was woken by a loud rumbling. Thunder, I thought. If there was heavy rain somewhere up in the mountains to the north, we could be swept away by a river torrent very easily; the same anxiety that I had had in Spain. Should I wake the others? I was still pondering this as I dozed off again.

We were all awake and getting packed up by seven. No brews this morning, we would breakfast higher up, at the Paso.

"Did you hear the thunder in the night?" I asked the others.

"Not thunder," responded Giorgio. "Glacial avalanches! Pieces of the ridge up there will be falling off all the time. The bigger the slab, the louder the noise. The mountains behind too, have avalanches all the time."

I looked up at the skyline. Now, I could see gushing fountains and spouts of water falling continuously from the snowy ridge, down onto smooth rock faces and ledges, then on into green crevices and the forest below. An endless supply of water, flowing down to the rivers and lakes that we had passed the previous day. Close to the skyline and these cascades, I noted huge birds, eagles or condors, swinging through on the thermals, spiralling up and down in a leisurely way.

We began to climb steadily upwards past yellow orchids, pink-flowering rhododendron bushes and tall evergreens, with a forest floor that was dry and tinged red, a natural layer of rich, organic compost. The Paso de los Nubes (Pass of the Clouds) lay ahead. A sign said '200 metres' but made no mention of the fact that this was the vertical distance; we climbed about 400 metres at an unrelenting angle, the hot sun beating down. I let the others go ahead. Could I do this? I thought about the 'hot spot' on my left lung and acknowledged an unwelcome weakness in my legs.

Steve waited at the next bend and gently ushered me on. We would get up there eventually, for breakfast and the picture-postcard views if nothing else.

It was much easier descending the other side and I felt sorry for a young couple we met going upwards, toiling away in the midday heat. The girl gave me the kind of despairing look that I must have worn in the morning. Finally, we ambled into Pampa Linda, a green valley nestling beneath the mighty Mount Tronador (the Thunderer). Its snow-covered peaks glistened in the afternoon sunshine; much later we were told that 90% of the time it is hidden in cloud, so we were very lucky during our 2 days to have clear sight of it. This was the mountain I had heard rumbling during the night.

We bivvied at one of the three campsites, using the shower facilities, rinsing out our sweaty walking clothes and sampling the local cuisine. We drank locally-brewed ale and a Chilean liqueur similar to Pisco, made with lemon juice, fermented fruit, and topped with egg white. Also a bottle or two of La Linda red wine. We had to be careful as we made our way back to our sleeping bags, zig-zagging through the open meadow, as we shared this with a number of un-tethered horses and foals. Wandering about in the night was a potential hazard. Their dark outlines loomed up unexpectedly and one wondered if they would take fright and stampede. However, a horse's night vision is a lot better than that of humans, so if anyone was going to run away it would be us, not them.

We took some of these same horses for a ride the next day to the Black Glacier, or Ventisquero Negro, the scene of a dramatic rescue some years ago when such a large piece of melting glacier broke off and plunged into the valley that people had to be airlifted to safety. Many trees, livestock and buildings were lost. Now it's a tourist attraction, a dark-grey ice block of immense size, overlooking a gloomy lake of smaller icebergs and floating debris. The discolouration comes from volcanic ash and rock minerals.

Our ride took us through young, sparse woodland, then along the river bed, its wide and stony expanse showing very clearly how glacial valleys are formed and the type of residue that is left behind. Torn-up trees, boulders, and layers of smaller rocks were spread across the entire valley, bisected by icy rivers that we had to wade through on horseback. Many of these rivers changed colour as they merged, from icy green to pale brown, depending on the minerals seeping out of the stone.

It was amusing to watch the dogs that accompanied us as they tried to negotiate these fast-flowing streams: they would plunge in beside us and then paddle vigorously, battling the current as they drifted inexorably away downstream. One could see them drag themselves out 100 metres further down, then race frantically back to keep up with us, shaking out their dripping coats as they ran.

Our destination the day after this was quite different. Leaping on a small, local bus we made our way to the nearest centre of civilisation, finding ourselves in a frontier shanty-town named El Bolsón, full of collapsing 1960s Cadillac cars, cruising motorbikes, hippies, hobos and yet more frantic dogs. The streets were unsurfaced, the parks strung with fading fiesta lights, the pavements over-flowing with debris, and yet it was there that we ate some of the best *parilla*, or barbecued meat, of our lives. The accompanying salad was delicious too, embellished with circles of finely-sliced grilled aubergine.

A party spirit pervaded the whole town and it was only with difficulty that we found beds for the night, but it was pleasant to sleep on a proper mattress. Steve was sorry to leave so much excitement the next day and celebrated this fact by leaving his iPod on our bus out of town, then breaking Susanna's (loaned) reading spectacles and almost losing his favourite MontBell jacket in the little Chilean town of Futaleufu, our destination. More droppings.

We stayed in a variety of cheap hotels as we headed further into Chile, this being more convenient than finding campsites and rolling out sleeping bags. Some were solidly-built private houses, some were timbered cabins with walls almost as thin as paper. In one of the latter we passed a near sleepless night, waiting for our landlord and family to finish their supper in the garden below, their son to get his motorbike engine to turn over and our fellow guests to complete their ablutions in the communal bathroom. As this was on the other side of our partition wall (painted apple green to complement the pale blue curtains, apricot skirting boards and bare ceiling light), I soon got the hang of each person's routine and how vigorously he or she brushed their teeth, flushed the toilet or ran the taps.

This familiarity was renewed at 0700 hours when the cockerel crowed beneath our window and everyone rushed for the loo. The sunshine streamed in; it was going to be another hot day.

Thanks to good planning, we managed to catch a sequence of buses and taxis to get ourselves on the trail of the hidden valley of Alto Paleno. We walked for about four hours, wading through several fast-flowing rivers and across swaying, planked bridges, until, at about nine in the evening, we reached the pretty blue and yellow farmhouse of Arturo and Gemilia Casanova, our hosts for the next 3 days. This paradisiacal spot turned out to be the highlight of our trip.

Arturo's father had come here as an Italian immigrant in the 1930s, walking and riding into the interior until his horse died of fatigue and the winter snows forced him to stop. Land ownership at that time was so uncertain that anyone who cleared the forest, through burning or felling the trees, could lay claim to that specific area. Señor Casanova and his fellow adventurers soon set about it, opened up the valley and brought in their wives and children from the coast. Wagons arrived with stoves, bedding and agricultural implements, and each family selected their own area of farmland. It seemed as though each one had done enough to acquire many hectares of prospectively verdant grassland.

In a book owned by Arturo and Gemilia, by Bernadita Hurtado Low, entitled *Alto Palena* (Valdivia 2010), I found some poems and quotes that came directly from these original settlers and their children, and that I have loosely translated:

'*Mi padre dejó un tesoro en la huerta unas melgas de papas, un arból de manzanas febreras. En el campo dejó trigo para que siempre hubiera pan y sol en nuestra mesa y párajos entre la siembra.*'

'My father left a treasure in the kitchen garden: a medley of potatoes and a vibrant apple tree. In the fields he left wheat so that there would always be bread and sunshine on our table and birds in among the seeds.'

Also, reflecting the scale of their undertakings:

'*Y esa lejanía infinita, marcando el límite de nuestro térritorio...*'

'And that infinite distance, marking the limit of our territory...'

Arturo was a lean, energetic man in his early sixties with a black moustache, expressive hands and hollow cheeks. His wife could have stepped straight out of a Goya painting with her alert, dark eyes and small Spanish mouth, but she was shy and much less talkative than him. They made us very welcome, sitting us in their small kitchen next to an Agatype stove and offering excellent tea, scones smothered with home-made plum jam, and sugary biscuits. Arturo got out his *mate* cup and sipped on this South American brew of hot leaves and spices - an acquired taste and reputedly highly addictive. He said that if he was going away from the farm for a day or two to collect up the cattle, he wouldn't bother to eat, just take his *mate* with him; it kept hunger at bay and had a soothing effect at night, when he was sleeping out in the woods.

We learnt that Gemilia had come to the farm when she was only five years old, because her own family could not afford to feed another child. Arturo was nine and had the responsibility of keeping an eye on her. Somehow this childhood friendship had blossomed into love and here they were, still together in their older years. They had three children, but one was living in a disabled facility in Santiago, one was in the south of Chile and the youngest, a teenager whom we met briefly, appeared to suffer from that cruel condition Proteus Syndrome, or Elephant Man disease. At the time, I wondered if this genetic disorder came down through the male or the female line, but it seems that it is not an inherited condition but one acquired through individual gene malfunction.

Poor Arturo had had a difficult time finding somewhere for his eldest child to be looked after. He had gone to Santiago with a quite a lot of rural naivety and ignorance, only to have his money stolen and the big city disinterested in a country lad far from home. Eventually some kind-hearted strangers had taken pity on him in his anguish and helped him to find doctors and a care home. But it highlighted for us that even paradise - and Chile is something of a damp Garden of Eden - has its dark side and its share of sadness.

Also divisiveness, even among visitors. At an almost definable moment, soon after we arrived at the farm, I sensed a change in Susanna's attitude to Steve and myself. For some reason, perhaps because she and Giorgio had found this beautiful place on a previous visit, she seemed to develop an air of possession that deliberately excluded us. A frisson of hostility was generated and I felt disappointed, as though a jealous child had come into the group, where previously we were all adults. This sensation did not diminish until sometime after the holiday was over. Perhaps it was a good thing that we elected to bivi outdoors at the newly-developed little campsite, while they slept in the house, thus creating a degree of distance and independence on both sides.

However, there were plenty of distractions, including two-legged ones. Strange birds with long, curved beaks flew, shrieking, up from the river and across the meadows; chickens busied themselves around the cattle pen and the kitchen garden; hawks and eagles cruised up above. Naturally our hosts had horses, their only form of transport, as well as the cattle and, in the distance, a strange type of woolly bison.

On our first morning, Steve helped Gemilia to milk one of the cows - after Arturo had lassoed it and tied it up to a rail - then we accompanied her and her bucket to the small, cool, bamboo-lined dairy where she made fresh cottage cheese. Using simple utensils including two rounded stones to weigh down the muslin bags, she soon had her cheese 'setting'. She brought some of the harder, aged blocks back to the house for breakfast, which we ate with homemade bread rolls and more delicious jam. It all reminded me of my childhood on the farm at Skelwith Bridge and my mother busy in her dairy.

Over breakfast, we planned a 2-day riding trip to Lago Azul, a remote lake only accessible by horse, foot or helicopter. Giorgio wanted to do some fishing there but it was a bit too far to walk just for that, Susanna and I were keen to ride and Steve was happy to ride and fish, so we asked Arturo to organise an expedition. By liaising with his friend Hugo from across the river, he soon established that there were enough horses for everyone and half a sheep could be taken with us as dinner the first night. One of the horses needed new shoes, or *herraduras*, so Susanna and I rode with him across the river to Hugo's farm, where this would be done. There are no blacksmiths in this region; everyone learns the basic skills and helps his neighbour to get the job done.

Hugo turned out to be a small, muscular, round-faced man of about 50, with a jolly smile and an impressive black stallion that he controlled with ease. His numerous grandchildren, perhaps on their summer holiday, attended to some of the horses tethered in the yard, even the 8 year old sitting astride a tall chestnut, with his little bare legs hanging loose. Chickens scratched around in the dirt and the dogs lay panting in the shade of a couple of dilapidated and weather-beaten old barns.

Hugo and Arturo soon had Paloma, the grey mare that Steve would ride, hitched to a rail where they tested different sizes of horseshoes for her feet. She stood patiently, allowing her hooves to be picked up in turn, completely confident with the process. Hugo held the shoe in position and knocked in the nails, then Arturo produced a small wooden hammer and a fearsomely sharp knife, about 25cm long, with a wooden haft. With Paloma's feet presented to him one at a time, he dextrously angled the blade against the excess 'toenail' that overhung the metal horseshoe, tapped the haft with his hammer and trimmed it off. His hand and eye never faltered. Soon the job was done and Paloma had a new pair of shoes with exquisitely-trimmed hooves to match.

As we rode back, across the river again and into Arturo's fields, he asked us to help him gather up the young cows that were wandering about, to move them into another meadow.

"Get round the side, over there," he gestured to me, "to block them in."

This principle was familiar to me from years spent working with sheep. I knew exactly what was wanted and how to occupy the open space that the cattle might escape into. So, of course, did my horse. Together we swerved around the animals, trotting back and forth, and I found that the riding part became instinctive, as I focused exclusively on the cattle. What fun! I could have spent all day out ranching, I decided.

The following morning we were up early for a quick breakfast before setting off. We numbered seven: 4 Europeans, the 2 Chilean men, and Hugo's 14 year-old grandson, another Hugo. Gemilia had decided not to come as it was too long a period spent in the saddle for her preference.

Arturo selected a specific horse for each rider and I was pleased to be told to ride one of Hugo's horses, a bay mare, perhaps 15 hands, with bright eyes and a gentle mouth.

"What's her name?" I asked Hugo.

"She doesn't have one," he shrugged.

"Then I shall give her my name," I responded, "and call her Linda."

He smiled at this and nodded. Linda is Spanish for 'pretty,' so it was as good a name as any and would work well after we were long gone and back in Europe. Like the others, she was tacked up with a fleece-covered Western saddle and a rope bridle. Hugo would be riding his stallion and leading a pack-horse loaded up with our bedding, a chainsaw and the requisite portion of freshly-slaughtered young sheep, wrapped in sacking.

It was a hot day as we trekked up through the high pastures, riding past ever more remote farms with splendid horses grazing freely and groups of yapping, excited dogs. Picking our way through red-flowered shrubs and silvery, fallen tree trunks, we finally reached the Portizuelo de Casanova, named after Arturo's father, and the pass over to Lago Azul which we could see in the distance, glowing like a sapphire in its wooded setting. Grey and pink quartz mountain peaks formed an outer band above the tree line. We stopped for a picnic lunch, then slowly rode downhill through mossy, primeval forests and along gently flowing streams, the horses picking their way with care.

Occasionally, our way would be blocked by a fallen tree, so Hugo would dismount, get out the chainsaw and clear the path. Smaller branches were removed with a machete that he carried tucked into the back of his waistband. Sometimes he couldn't be bothered to stow the chainsaw away again but simply carried it in front of him on the saddle pommel, guiding his stallion with one hand, all done with total ease and control. His grandson, by contrast, rode his fidgety young mare as he might a café-cruiser motorbike - slumped over the handlebars, his cap on back-to-front, feet hanging low, Mr Cool himself.

Finally, we reached the water's edge, passing a weather-boarded, white and green Guardia outpost and its three lucky militiamen. They had been allocated this place for a month-long tour of duty, very close to the Argentinian border, and were happily spending their days fishing, building barbecues, and rowing around the lake perimeter. We moved another few hundred yards down the shingle beach and found a large log cabin where we could base ourselves. It was very primitive. The interior consisted of one big room with a large wooden table, the ubiquitous wood stove and various bed-sized slabs of thick polystyrene. The toilets were wherever you chose to go in the surrounding forest.

Once the horses were settled - which seemed to involve merely short-tying them to a tree, each at a reasonable distance from the other - the Chileans gathered some dry wood, lit a small fire outside and unwrapped the lamb. They hacked off the shoulder portion and hung it up against the cabin wall, out of reach of dogs and pumas, and while Arturo held the remainder, consisting of the back leg and the ribcage, Hugo went into the cabin and came back with a metre-long steel blade. This he proceeded to thread through the animal's ribs a couple of times, then the pointed tip was driven into the ground, right beside the glowing fire. The carcase, angled slightly towards the heat, soon began to spit and a delicious smell pervaded the evening air.

Steve and Giorgio went down to the water to try their hand at catching fish. Steve had his tiny pen rod, while Giorgio carried a simple plastic ring, looped with fishing line to which he had fixed a large red and yellow spinner with three hooks, which he called El Terrible. Whirling it around like a lasso, he threw the line far out into the deeper part of the lake; Steve's line, with a smaller lure, was in shallower water. Neither had any luck on this occasion, but a few days later, in another part of Chile, at a different Lago Azul, they each caught several trout big enough to cook for our supper.

Tonight our meal consisted of roast lamb and home-made bread. Hugo carved big chunks off the sizzling meat and handed them around; he gave me the succulent lower part of the leg which pleased me mightily. My favourite cut. We all had second helpings, washed down with cheap red wine straight from the carton. As darkness fell and the conversation slowed, we debated where we should sleep, in or out. Susanna and Giorgio opted for outdoors, on the shingle beach, using some extra polystyrene 'mattresses,' whilst Steve and I chose a corner of the log cabin, sharing with the Chileans and using our Thermarest air mats and usual lightweight gear. It didn't take long for everyone to turn in and fall asleep. We were awake again within a couple of hours: a thunderstorm had rolled across the mountains and heavy rain was falling. The dogs began barking loudly.

Pumas? we all wondered, but it was only Susanna and Giorgio, coming in to collect up some waterproof covers for their sleeping bags.

I think Hugo went outside to check on the horses and cover up the saddles, then all was quiet again and the storm moved on. I slept well the remainder of the night and awoke while it was still dark, to the sounds of Arturo and Hugo moving about quietly, lighting the stove and brewing some tea. I got myself dressed as decorously as possible, inside the sleeping bag and then wandered out into the dawn to find a 'green' toilet, wash my face in the lake, brush my teeth and return for a light breakfast. Slowly we began to get ourselves organised for the return ride.

The sky was festooned with low cloud and as we departed we looked back at what was now Lago Plata, a silver pond rather than a blue one. The long-suffering horses were full of energy and enthusiasm to get home, so we made excellent time, trotting and cantering whenever we could, reaching the farmhouse in time for lunch and a brief siesta. This was important as we had a second ride to do in the late afternoon, crossing the main river again, to get ourselves back to 'civilisation' and the next stage of our journey.

It turned out that Arturo's uncle, as a young man, had set out in winter to go and visit some neighbours, or perhaps a girlfriend, and had to wade across a particularly wide stretch of water to reach them. He never arrived and it was some time before his body was found, washed downstream and frozen solid. The fast-flowing current and icy waters had claimed another victim.

Escorted by our hosts and Hugo and his grandson, we did not have to take such risks. The horses waded across without hesitation, showing no signs of fatigue, so we soon reached the nearest road and our motorised taxi ride into Palena. This was an ancient pick-up truck, so Steve and I travelled in the back, sitting in the fresh air with the luggage. It was farewell to this remarkable area and these delightful, unassuming, hard-working people. We would not forget them.

Our journeying continued in and out of Argentina and Chile, through grand, beautiful scenery and ugly little towns, past *cumbres* recovering from the ash-layers of the most recent volcanic activity and across endless grass-gold pampas. On foot we traversed more high passes, sometimes in sunshine, sometimes in pouring rain. We stood in a small border control office, dripping individual puddles of water, while the *carabinieri* stamped our passports, and we also waited, sweltering, on a cross-border coach while everyone's ticket got double-checked in case we had illegal migrants on board.

We observed drunken villagers staggering past, leading ox-drawn carts laden with barrels of beer and followed by miserable-looking womenfolk; and we watched little piglets huddle round their sleeping mother in the corner of a windswept, dirty shack on a lonely hillside, waiting for the rain to stop. We kept an eye out for the rare and mysterious *pudú*, a tiny South American deer and tried not to fall into the many streams that we had to cross (though I did manage it at least once, much to everyone's irritation I am sure).

We spent a day at the so-called horse races, in an open space the size of three hockey fields, surrounded by beautiful *caballos* and their handsome riders, with the rain still falling. A gigantic cascade of water dropped from the rocky heights above, adding its spume to the low-hanging clouds. Chile is a wet country for 10 months of the year, so we were the only ones who were disappointed with the downpour and the limits it placed on the racing opportunities; the locals were philosophical and simply sat, dripping, on their steeds and drank more beer.

The following day, Susanna, Steve and I took another ride ourselves, this time with a man named Don Giraldo, sporting a notable moustache and thin as a whippet. Somewhere during the three hour ride, Steve lost his lightweight waterproof jacket out of his trouser pocket. It was compressed into a tiny, red stuff sack and highly visible. I could see the look of despair on Susanna's face: these wretched English!

"I'll come back tomorrow on foot, while you're fishing," I said. "I'll go the other way round but it shouldn't be too hard to find the same path and the stuff sack will be easy to spot."

I was wrong on both counts. Setting off in a drizzle, wearing my long, green poncho, I had difficulty recognising the path when going in the opposite direction. After traversing two fast-flowing rivers, with the icy water swirling around my knees, and then wandering through isolated pastures, or *corrales*, of pigs, cows and a few horses, I had to admit that I could not find the track and, more seriously, I could easily become lost myself. No one would know exactly where I had gone and in this vast, overgrown terrain, I could walk for many days before I found a road or a house or a human being. It would be highly irresponsible to continue.

The constant rain, especially further north, was swelling the streams and rivers very rapidly and as I turned back, I realised that those two rivers would have to be crossed yet again, but they were now deeper and fiercer. Each time, I had to put my poncho in my small backpack, remove my trainers, tie them together, and drape them around my neck, roll up my trousers, find a stout stick to supplement my walking pole and plunge back in.

I knew that if I lost my footing I would be swept away and that I would have difficulty getting upright again. The glacial waters turned my feet, ankles and lower thighs into painfully frozen limbs in seconds; full submersion could be fatal but I had to get across. I tried not to think of Arturo's uncle.

On each crossing, somewhere in the middle of the stream, where the current was fiercest and my foothold weakest, I found myself growling and screaming, using a hitherto unknown, primeval force to drive myself to the other side. Somehow I made it and with it came a sense of achievement. I had never had to summon up that kind of demonic energy before. It was a relief when I got back to the familiar scenery of our campsite and let Don Giraldo try his luck with the local radio handset and bush telegraph. No joy. No one had seen anything along that route and Steve would have to go without his jacket.

The last stage of our trek took us back by bus to El Bolsón and then Puerto Varas, where our routes divided. Susanna and Giorgio were heading to Puerto Montt, then Santiago and back to Spain; Steve and I had Buenos Aires in our sights. We each took our own memories with us and, in my case and Steve's, a few fleas as well - Don Giraldo's guesthouse had provided some 'little friends' that did not disappear completely until we got back home and I had machine washed every single item of clothing.

It is true to say that I had begun to find our foursome increasingly restrictive and I longed to break free from it. The obligations imposed when travelling in a group, especially an artificial construct where one is 'led' rather than 'leading,' can soon create problems and a sense of antagonism. The leader resents the hapless followers, just as much as vice versa. I thought about Sir Ranulph Fiennes and his Antarctic treks, when he and Dr Mike Stroud developed a (temporary) mutual loathing, purely connected to stress, isolation, and physical weariness. I pondered on different types of horses - the plodding, yet willing variety and the highly-strung, headstrong ones; those that need a kick to get them going and those that are hard work to restrain. Humans, like horses, have their temperamental and cultural differences, which are not necessarily compatible after more than a few hours or days.

Many years ago, a work colleague told me of a holiday she had taken with her husband John and another couple, the Smith's, in Greece. Although they did not know each other very well - just a chance meeting in the Canaries the year before - they decided to share a sailing boat and cruise around the Greek islands together. Both men had done some sailing before, their wives got along very well and all seemed set fair for a pleasant two weeks aboard. They met up at the local marina and boarded their luxury yacht, enjoying a bottle or two of wine and a hearty supper.

The following morning they emerged on deck, ready to motor out into the Mediterranean and then hoist the sails as they headed towards Mykonos. My colleague and her husband, dressed casually in shorts and pullovers, were astonished to see Mr Smith emerge clad in white trousers, a reefer-type jacket with gold buttons and a nautical cap.

"Someone has to be captain," he cried gaily and seized the wheel. "You ladies had better go aft and you, John, can go forward and act as look-out while we negotiate the harbour wall."

This set the tone for the next two days. Captain Smith continued as he had begun. It was too much for Anne and John. At 5 a.m. on the third morning, when they were moored in Mykonos, the two of them quietly packed their bags and crept away. They left a fairly polite, yet mutinous note, found a taxi and had themselves transported to the other side of the island, to the biggest and most luxurious hotel available. There they enjoyed a private and romantic holiday, swearing that they would never, ever make such a terrible mistake again.

* * *

The switch from rural Argentina to its capital Buenos Aires was a cultural leap too. Arriving quite late in the evening at Jorge Newbery airport (named after the pioneer of Argentinian aviation), we took a taxi to the Palermo district, where we would be staying with Isabella's French daughter Chloë and her Italian/Argentinian son-in-law, Dino. How lucky we were that they had a house conveniently placed for the city centre and, in addition, were keen to have some Euros as rental, to offset the limitations of the Argentinian peso.

Chloë, fair-haired, smiling and 7 months pregnant, welcomed us in; we had met her before, in Andalucía, but only very briefly. Dino, chunky and humorous, arrived a little later on, tired from a long working day on site, but full of bonhomie. Together we spoke a mixture of Castilian Spanish, Argentinian Spanish, French, and English.

With their combined architectural knowledge and training, they had turned their apparently traditional house into a simple, white-washed and modern space, enlivened with individually-selected pieces - the iconic Mies van der Rohe chair; Dino's colourful, plastic fruit-box lampshades; elegant, stainless steel kitchen units and a glass wall opening out onto a verdant courtyard. Some of the interior pillars and beams had been left exposed, smoothed to the texture of marble but retaining the dimples and cavities of rough-cast concrete; the floors were polished grey cement; a single zebra-skin rug defied one to walk on it. We loved every bit of it.

To reach our accommodation, we stepped out into the courtyard, went up an outdoor flight of steps to a large roof terrace, and then into an en-suite bedroom and bathroom, with TV, cool-air fan and more polished cement flooring. We quickly arranged our luggage, had a cup of tea and got to bed. Tomorrow we would look at maps and find out about the city highlights.

We awoke to a warm, humid morning and the intention of visiting the central landmarks: La Casa Rosada (Government House), La Plaza 25 de Mayo (since 1810, the hub of political life in Argentina), followed by the Puente de la Mujer (Woman's Bridge) and, of course La Boca football stadium, home to the coaching skills of the extraordinary Diego Maradona. Chloë had begun a series of exquisite hand-drawn maps for us, each one with specific details about good cafés or interesting shops. Her local knowledge meant that we should not waste too much time in the wrong streets... or at least, that was the idea.

We dawdled our way around La Plaza 25 de Mayo, looking at the placards against the British occupation of Las Malvinas ("They mean the Falklands," said Steve) and the desperate images of *los desaparecidos*, those young people who vanished during military rule in the 1970s and whose mothers are waiting still, 40 years later, for an explanation and information about their children.

Inside La Casa Rosada, we photographed each other standing beneath paintings of Che Guevara, Eva Peron and other significant figures from Argentina's past. We behaved as tourists do and soon found our way to the Rio Plata, inspecting a nineteenth-century sail-training ship and eating the ubiquitous pizza, before wandering our way along the recently-modernised and pedestrianised riverside walkway.

By about three in the afternoon, we found ourselves a couple of blocks inland from the river, on pavements milling with blue and yellow-clad youngsters.

"We must be near La Boca," said Steve excitedly, "perhaps there's going to be a game."

We stopped to ask directions from three old boys at a newspaper stand. One of them turned out to be from our part of Spain, a small village near Jaen, north of Granada.

"You need to be very careful around here," he said and pointed at my little nylon rucksack, hanging off my left shoulder. "There are many thieves and rascals who will snatch your bag."

We had anticipated this to some extent - Steve had no wristwatch and my bag contained very little money and no passports, but I did have my favourite black and green tango shoes inside and, for obvious reasons, my Spanish medical card. The old man's warning made an impact however, so I twisted the straps around my wrist and carried it like a sack; it would be difficult for anyone to grab it without taking me too.

We reached the stadium and had a brief look at its simple concrete exterior, covered with graffiti; the match or training session appeared to have finished rather than started, so we did not linger, but wandered on, down some quiet backstreets and through a rather neglected part of town. Once-elegant colonial buildings with decorative verandas and Italianate proportions seemed dirty and unkempt, with lines of washing and closed-up shutters. The occasional child screamed or a dog whined, but we saw very few people. I was not sure whether we were walking towards, or away from, the river. Somewhere nearby we should find the famous and colourful architectural gem that is La Boca harbour.

Because the sidewalks were littered with paper and because there was no traffic, we chose to walk on the unpaved street instead. Steve was on the inside, I was more towards the middle of the road. Sitting on a low wall ahead of us were two young men in loose T-shirts, their small Honda motorbike beside them with its engine running and headlight beaming. As we drew alongside, I began to construct a light-hearted phrase in my head, in Spanish, along the lines of 'you'll run down the battery soon,' but then the older, dark-haired lad asked Steve, "*Que hora es?* - What time is it?*"

Steve pointed to his wrist and shook his head - no watch.

Unthinkingly, in best Girl Guide style, I glanced at my inexpensive timepiece and replied: "*Son las cuatro menos quarto - It's a quarter to four.*"

As I looked up again, I saw the lad pull up his T-shirt, whip out a semi-automatic handgun from his trouser waistband and make the sliding, cocking motion so famous from the movies. He pointed it at Steve and said something in rapid Argentinian, perhaps, "This is a robbery," or "Hand over your money." His friend moved towards us menacingly, a pale-faced, bespectacled young man of about twenty, thin and desperate.

For a moment we were immobile and shocked; this was not a movie, this was for real. Then I went straight into 'mother-of-teenager' mode.

"No, no, no!" I shouted angrily, moving forward and waving my finger at them like a schoolteacher. There was no way that they could do this to us.

The pale lad sprang at my bag, grabbed it and tried to pull it off my wrist. We were nose-to-nose, wrestling for it and I was still shouting "No!". All those years on the squash court or in the gym or wheeling barrows of debris were paying off. I was prepared to fight for my medical card, my precious shoes and my principles. Steve loomed over the gunman, much taller than him, his tattooed forearms clearly visible, and the combination of our responses must have surprised and frightened them. Perhaps they were beginners and their confidence was low. At any rate, by some unspoken agreement, they suddenly backed off, jumped on the motorbike and revved away. It was over so quickly that we stood there in disbelief. Had that actually happened?

My next thought was that we needed to get out of there as rapidly as possible, that we needed a taxi. Of course no such vehicle existed in the area, which was still ominously deserted.

"Come on," Steve echoed my thoughts. "Let's get somewhere more public."

We walked briskly back the way we had come, towards La Boca. Down a side- street we heard a motorbike again. If they came back, we were ready for another fight.

"I'll pull them off it," Steve muttered. "Bloody little shits."

Luckily for them, or for us, they did not return. We found the route to the harbour area with its cafés and shops, and dived into a tango bar for some coffee. We were shaken by the experience, but relieved to have come off unscathed. All cities have their rough areas and danger zones and we had, literally as it turned out, crossed some old railway lines that were barely visible in the stony road, and gone 'the wrong side of the tracks.' Even the police hesitate to go into that locale in Buenos Aires and many crimes go undetected. As Dino and Chloë said later, we were lucky not to have been shot. Had there been three or four of them, or had Steve said to me, "Give them your bag," they would have succeeded with the theft. We had reacted instinctively to the situation and our anger, on this occasion, may have saved our lives.

As we drank our coffee, the humid storm clouds burst above our heads and down came the rain. The street vendors scattered and the bars filled up. We watched a young couple dance a sleek tango or two, but felt that the performance was marred by the bored expression on the girl's face and her incessant chewing of gum. When the hat came around we were less generous than we might have been. After a while, when it was clear that this downpour could last for hours, we decided to head for home. We got off the Metro too soon, walked a long way and got somewhat lost again, but finally arrived back, soaking wet and full of our adventures. Dino produced a bottle of wine and our first day ended, appropriately, in a tired and hazy blur.

I had known before we left Spain that I would need my Faslodex injections during this week, and Chloë kindly rang round to find a private nurse who would come to the house and do this. Mid-morning, the bell rang and an improbable blonde of about 55, named Peggy, stood on the step. Efficiently and quickly she delivered the jabs, telling me while she did so about her family, the economic crisis, and how the medical system worked there. If my Argentinian Spanish had been better, I might have learned a lot from her; as it was, I was glad simply to keep my medication going.

Chloë took us on a short bus tour that included a café with delicious empanadas, similar to Cornish pasties, thence to another café, nestled beneath an enormous carob tree, for ice creams at vastly inflated prices and, finally, to the equivalent of Highgate Cemetery. Here lay many famous or wealthy Argentinians, entombed within small-scale pyramids, mock Grecian temples, tiny, imitation houses and larger, decorative palace facades. A simple, black marble mausoleum contained the remains of Eva Peron, garlanded with fresh white lilies and surrounded by eager tourists, cameras in hand.

The rest of the day passed rapidly until it was time to get to my pre-arranged tango class. Steve, nobly, accompanied me as far as the door and then went off to watch billiards in a converted, brick-built wine store. I went into a large bar-cum-nightclub, where several couples were navigating smoothly around the dance floor. My teacher, Lucia appeared, a slender, dark-skinned woman from the north-west of Argentina, together with a middle-aged Californian couple who seemed to be circumnavigating the world, dance shoes in hand. We went downstairs into the basement, which had been converted into a dance classroom, lined with mirrors. Was it going to be just the three of us and Lucia?

It turned out that, sadly, the father of Lucia's partner Gerry had died suddenly, in Ireland, so she was obliged to take on both the men's and women's teaching roles. Fortunately, she was expert enough for this not to matter very much. To gauge my expertise, she took me in a close embrace and we danced for about 3 minutes.

"You need to relax more," she commented, "and lower your shoulders. Take longer steps, especially when you go backwards. Only put a little weight into your right hand, but give a bit more resistance to your partner at the same time. You have as much control over the dance as he does."

The first part of this was not was new to me and it was curiously reassuring to find that I was making the same mistakes on both sides of the Atlantic, but the control element was contrary to the more traditional 'leader' and 'follower' arrangement that I had been taught in Spain. As the lesson progressed, it was additionally clear that Argentinian tango danced in its country of origin is more sensuous, more intimate, than anything Europe has to offer.

When we went back to the bar upstairs, where a *milonga* was in progress, I found Steve waiting, much amused.

"As soon as I came in," he laughed, "all the women stared at me, thinking I might be a potential partner. They looked really hungry.

Terrifying. Thank goodness I was still in shorts and flip-flops - not quite dago dancing style."

"Let's go and find something to eat," I suggested, "I'm starving."

We looked at various glass-fronted and impressive restaurants, but settled for a student's hang-out called Angelito's where almost every table, inside and out, was occupied and the prices looked cheap. A young couple next to us had some appetising-looking food on their plates, so we simply ordered the same and a carafe of wine, for about 60 pesos (£7.00 or 8 Euros) for two. It was so good that we went back there another evening for our supper.

Over the next few days, we continued to explore Buenos Aires, either on foot or using the Metro (the Subte) or via the frequent buses. Chloë had armed us with a plastic card to pay for our journeys, a couple of bus timetables and more of her unique, decorative maps. Gradually we began to understand the layout and street life of this vibrant Latin American city, by day and by night.

One very hot afternoon we wandered through the city zoo, worrying about the threadbare camels and bored elephants, yet fascinated, as one always is, by large snakes and threatening crocodiles. We admired the flocks of native llamas and alpacas, and some delicate hare-like creatures that grazed, without barriers, at the sides of the grassy pathways.

We took a mainline train from the impressive Art Deco railway station, with its Nile-green tiling and high glass roof, in order to visit Las Barrancas de Belgrano, a distant suburb containing sports arenas, equestrian and athletics centres, tennis clubs and, somewhere, I felt sure, the Pumas' rugby ground. We flashed past a Crossfit gym and caught glimpses of various military academies, until we reached our stopping point and the Chinese quarter of the city.

The shops were indistinguishable one from the other, cheap and cheerful just as they are elsewhere, so we concentrated on eating Chinese street food until we were stuffed, then went to the park to lie in the shade, idly watching passers-by and, in Steve's case, having a snooze. He had discovered some really bad American movies on the TV in our room and, insomniac that he is in the wee small hours, had plugged in the headphones and watched 1970s detectives chase after a happy blend of UFOs, government crooks and mysterious Russian spies, whilst making use of entirely spurious forensic evidence. Now, he was shattered and desperate for sleep. I, meanwhile, tried to read my book, a poor translation into Spanish of Henry James' *The Turn of the Screw*, pausing frequently to observe the students, yoga practitioners, young cellists and, of course, lovers, who were scattered around under the trees.

One of these trees, though alive and in leaf, had a vertical slit in its trunk that ran from ground level up to about 5 metres. This seemed to have occurred naturally and the edges of the bark had rolled inwards, trying to close up the wound. An inner pith was exposed, perhaps 30 centimetres wide and the whole piece had been treated as an art form. The 'wound' had been stained red, and a narrow, woven cord criss-crossed its way up the slit, like a form of corsetry. It reminded me of the work of Frida Kahlo, the Mexican painter whose physical agony and artistic virtuosity produced equally strange 'magic realism.' Elsewhere in Buenos Aires we came across instances of impressive graffiti, sometimes official and sometimes controversial. Alongside the buskers and street artists, this city is full of colour and sound, a blend of many nations and many cultures, resounding with creativity.

Another day, we spent a happy hour with Chloë at a very up-market shoe shop, Comme Il Faut, which specialises in tango shoes. She had brought along her watercolour paint-box, some heavy-duty paper and her superb eye for detail. The shop was in the best part of town, tucked away in a small courtyard and up a flight of stairs. Admission could only be gained after ringing the door bell. The atelier consisted of one long, dove-grey room, lined with mirrors, where individual shoes were placed on shelves and pillars, each one offset by a spray of flowers or a complimentary swathe of cloth. Dance posters and photographs adorned empty wall spaces. This was a temple to all things tango.

We were guided to a seating corner and I was asked for my shoe size. Politely, no one appeared to notice Steve's unusual city attire - the ubiquitous shorts and flip-flops. The assistant began to bring out dozens of boxes, removing the lids and holding out, one by one, enough podiatric gems to satisfy most shoe fetishists. Chloë immediately busied herself with her brushes, which no one seemed to mind, while Steve gazed with some bemusement at this female emporium of elegance and desire.

Two other women were trying on glinting numbers in silver and gold, and what appeared to be open-toed white satin with high, shiny, red heels. I had already decided that I wanted something more discreet, perhaps in snakeskin or black patent, but my main priority was the fit. It's not much fun dancing for several hours if your shoes are killing you.

Chloë admired a vibrant shoe of yellow, purple and turquoise leather and began to paint it, but I knew that it was too extreme for me. We all liked some black velvet shoes tied with a pale pink satin bow, looking rather like ballet slippers, but they turned out to be a strange fit. A pair of two-tone bronze shoes with 9cm spiked heels, open-toes and a diagonal, wrap-over strap were the strongest candidates, but not quite right. I began to dither.

Perhaps through close observation, perhaps just excellent stock knowledge, the manager came over carrying a single box in her hand.

"These are the next size down, but I think they will fit you," she smiled. She produced a silver-grey, leather shoe, open-toed and absolutely plain, with a single ankle strap and high, metallic silver heels. Immediately, I longed for them to be the right size; the colour, design and sophistication were all that I had been hoping for. Like Cinderella, I slipped one on and it fitted perfectly.

"You shall go to the ball," murmured Steve.

"These are the ones," I said, pirouetting.

"They're just right," responded Chloë with a grin.

"There's an extra discount if you pay in cash and a bit more off if you pay in US dollars," explained the manager. I looked at Steve, knowing that I was only carrying a Visa card and Argentinian pesos.

"I think I might have that," he responded magnificently, and took out his wallet. For a man whose entire wardrobe usually costs less than 20 litres of petrol, he certainly has his moments.

The manager nodded admiringly. "So useful to come shopping with a man like that," she said.

"Yes, indeed," I replied, with heartfelt sincerity.

That evening, Dino and Chloë invited some friends round and prepared a *parilla* on the rooftop terrace. We ate grass-fed beef steaks, luscious lamb cutlets, and juicy pork chops, accompanied by a simple salad and more excellent Argentinian wine. Although there are many vegetarian options in the restaurants and street outlets, this is a country for carnivores, where the meat has a flavour and texture not available in British or Spanish outlets. We yielded to our Paleolithic ancestors in every way and ate with our hands.

Around about midnight, we could hear loud drumming a couple of blocks away.

"Carnaval," said Dino. "You ought to go and have a look."

We dashed off and found a procession of people, perhaps two hundred, arranging themselves into an open rectangle in one of the wider streets. In the centre, taking their turn, were small groups of men, women and children, all in matching costumes and representing their particular barrio, who were performing a series of gymnastic dance routines to loud drums, whistles and singing. Each solo piece was loudly applauded, each collective set greeted with cheers and shouts. At the back of the crowd, the children ran about with water bombs and plastic bottles; it was just like the Ferreirola water festival and if we weren't careful, we would get a soaking yet again.

"Let's get back to that barbecue," we agreed and slipped away. In fact, the evening culminated in a massive, localised thunderstorm with its own display of forked lightning, drum-rolls and heavy rain, so everyone got to see a carnival of some sort.

No one can visit his great city without spending a Sunday at the San Telmo street market, a seemingly endless succession of colourful stalls with innovative and unusual goods for sale, impromptu music, tango dancing on the pavements, interesting arcades of antique shops and probably, though we did not see them, the inevitable pickpockets.

We watched a man from Uruguay crouching low on the pavement as he wove hats from a type of green bamboo leaf, each one identical to the last and each one destined to dry out to a bleached sand colour; we paused to chat with a Bolivian making beautiful jewellery from an elaborate type of crochet work containing either semi-precious stones or shark's teeth or shells; an illustrator was selling his own witty postcards and T-shirts; and somewhere I purchased a black straw trilby and danced a sidewalk tango with a small, fat man, no longer in his youth but expert with his steps.

Inspired by this, we decided to go back to Las Barrancas de Belgrano and dance tango under the stars. I say 'we,' but of course this was all for my benefit, with Steve acting as escort and protector, and 'under the stars' meant a large open-sided, floodlit bandstand. As it was teeming with people, certainly more women than men, we agreed that I should stand on my own and Steve would lurk out of sight, so as not to put off any potential dance partners. Much to my delight, a youngish man, Argentinian, drew me onto the circular floor and we had several, progressively improving dances. The first one is always a test, to find out how each other moves and what level of experience each one has. Subsequent dances can only get better. I think he was getting himself warmed up for more ambitious and experienced dancers, but I didn't care. For me, to be dancing tango in Argentina, on a warm summer's night, was pleasure enough.

As we returned to the city centre on the bus, round about midnight, we passed close to another football stadium just after a match had finished. Spectators in their preferred strip were pouring out onto the streets, some walking calmly, others clearly preparing for trouble. The police, it seemed, were also prepared: a group of them swept past on motorcycles, each one carrying a pillion passenger armed with a shotgun. This would be, we agreed, unusual for a match between Barcelona and Madrid, or even Millwall versus Chelsea, but clearly normal practice in Argentina.

Finally, it was time to leave South America and head back to Europe. Our month was up. We would be returning to winter and a chilly Andalucía, wiser in our fleeting understanding of a different continent, or at least of one or two small corners of it. We knew that we had strayed onto paths less frequently travelled and had some unique experiences along the way, notably at Arturo and Gemilia's farm in Chile and fending off the young *pistoleros* in the city. Yet, as always, we longed to be back in our own bed, in our own home, in our own little village.

Chapter 17

Blizzards and a Buena Noche

We arrived back to the cold nights and wet days of early spring, when the Alpujarra usually acquires sufficient snow on the mountain tops to benefit the valleys for the rest of the year. Sometimes there are deep pockets of snow, 18 or 20 metres thick, most of which eventually filters through the rock and down into the underground aquifers. As the drier, brighter days develop, skiers flock to their dedicated resort above Granada and backpackers begin to traverse the lower slopes.

In late March, our friend Anne suggested a snow-shoeing expedition. "Fernando organises half-day outings," she said. "Shall I book us a session?"

We took Scottish Joyce with us, a quietly-spoken, experienced fell runner, and kitted ourselves out in suitable clothing (waterproof jackets or ski suits, hats, and gloves) before we set off for Granada in Anne's car. As we neared the city we could see dark clouds obscuring Mulhacén, Veleta and El Caballo and the occasional drop of rain fell on the car windscreen.

"This could be an interesting adventure," commented Joyce, dryly.

The road up to the resort at Pradollano (meaning a flat meadow in English) takes about an hour, winding its way up the northern flanks of the Sierra Nevada, above the village of Pinos Genil. The altitude changes from 600 to 2000 metres over about 20 kilometres and by the time we reached the 1500 metre level we were into the snow line; at first just a dusting, then a few centimetres that banked a little by the roadside, then sections of the road began to disappear under a fine, white layer. Snowflakes were falling in increasing amounts.

"Oh dear," said Anne anxiously, "I don't like the look of this."

By the time we reached Pradollano (*prado* means meadow in English), a continuous light snow was coming down; not enough to deter us, but a handful of traffic controllers had appeared also and were starting to advise people where to park. It was only 9 a.m., so we were surprised at their presence. Then we noticed the flags and banners.

"Of course," I remembered, "it's the World Snowboarding and Freestyle Skiing Championships! It should have finished by now, but it's probably been delayed by the weather. There must be loads of spectators on their way."

"Maybe not," commented Steve, "if this keeps chucking down."

We turned uphill, above the resort and drove as close as we could to our destination, the old *albergue* hut, once the centre of all skiing activities but now used mainly as a hostel. A few people scurried past, heads down, hoods and hats on. The wind whipped at us as we collected our backpacks and walked the last half-kilometre to the *albergue*. Even then, we were not sure that the car would have made it up the narrow roadway, made smaller by the encroaching snow on either side.

However, our leader, the self-styled Buitre (pronounced Vuitre and meaning vulture), was reassuringly upbeat about the conditions and introduced us to another, bigger group from Cadiz who were going to follow the same route, leaving just after us. We were kitted out with boat-shaped, plastic snow-shoes (the days of tennis racquet-style footwear are long gone) and walking poles, and our gloves and headgear got checked. A quick cup of tea or coffee and we were all set.

Our route lay uphill, parallel to one of the ski runs, but the falling snow and low cloud meant that we could have been within 20 metres of a slalom run and not known about it. A few bare rocks loomed up on either side, the rest was a white curtain.

We formed a crocodile - Buitre, then Steve, followed by Anne, myself, and with Joyce bringing up the rear.

"Do you want to go in front of me?" I asked, "I'm bound to be slower than you."

"No, you're fine," she replied. "Besides, I think we're going at a fair pace already."

This was true. Buitre, a youngish man and very fit, was stepping out in fine form and Steve was able to go with him quite comfortably. However, this began to prove difficult for the rest of us.

"I can't keep this up!" breathed Anne, "I'll have to stop for a minute."

The wind and snow were beginning to lash our faces and all exposed hair was stiffening up with frost. Although our exertions made us very warm, the air temperature was about -15 Centigrade.

"Buitre," I called, "Buitre!"

He stopped and turned around, cheerful enough.

"We aren't all 25," I jested. "Us girls need to have a pause."

Five minutes later, we continued up the mountain, although now Steve took up a place at the rear. We reached a large cairn of dressed stone, about 10 metres high, with a statue of the Virgen de las Nieves, the Virgin of the Snows, placed in a niche half-way up, her hands pressed together in prayer. We may need her assistance before too long, I thought, the way this weather is going.

As we moved on, Buitre pointed over to our left.

"We need to keep away from that edge!" he shouted into the wind. "It's quite a dangerous spot, with a steep drop. Someone had a fatal accident there a few years ago."

Probably in swirling snow and strong winds, I thought. In fact, we were getting close to a complete white-out situation. Rocks had disappeared and only the occasional slalom pole indicated that we were in the correct location. Some skiers appeared from above, heading rapidly downhill; no international competitions today, we were sure.

After about 3 hours, Buitre decided that we should make our way back. No one dissented and we knew that we would travel much faster on the return leg. I noticed that our footprints had disappeared already under the drifting blasts and by now we could have been in Antarctica or the Himalayas for all we knew.

We met the other group still ascending, and the two guides conferred for a moment. One of this group, a youngish man named Juan, was struggling with the altitude and his own lack of fitness, so he elected to join us and go down. As we descended, I noticed that Buitre was looking about in a much less confident manner and was not surprised when he stopped altogether.

"I want to make sure we are on the right path," he explained to Steve and I, who were standing nearest to him. "We should get to the *Virgen* again soon, she's somewhere over on our right."

"Do you think he's lost?" whispered Steve to me.

"Well," I replied, "I'm pretty sure the *Virgen* should be below us on our left!"

By good fortune, a sudden blast of wind cleared the landscape for a few moments and revealed a few extra metres. A black rock stood out, clear as a beacon, below and to our left.

"We need to head for that," called Buitre, sounding relieved.

We slid and slithered our way down the slope and soon found other familiar landmarks. The *Virgen* came into view, also on our left and later on, a military training building. The dangerous precipice had been averted, thanks to a gust of wind and, perhaps, the beneficent influence of a blue-robed woman carved in stone.

By the time we reached the *albergue*, everyone was chilled and hungry. We unclipped our snowshoes and put on extra layers. I found that although my ski-suit had kept me dry and reasonably warm, especially the hood over my beanie, it was the merino thermal layer underneath everything that had completed the job. Bought half-price in LIDL's seven years earlier, this base layer has proved invaluable. My spare sweater, in my little, non-waterproof rucksack, was soaked, as were my feet, clad in hiking boots that had long since lost their proofing qualities.

Out came bars of chocolate and various types of sandwiches. Juan looked particularly wobbly and pale.

"Eat this," I said, offering him one of our snack bars. "Get some sugar inside yourself."

This did seem to help him and he perked up quite a lot. Everyone had a hot drink in the little bar, where Buitre advised us that we would be driven back down to our car in their 4x4 as the snow was so deep.

Linda Caine

"What about the other group?" we asked. "Shouldn't they be down by now?"

"Oh, they're with Manuel, they'll be fine. He's a very experienced mountaineer. Juan can wait for them in the bar."

Trusting that he was correct, the rest of us piled into the 4x4 and set off over the shifting dunes of white powder. 50 metres along the little road we were confronted by a wall of snow about a metre high and six metres long.

'We'll walk," we chorused and would have got out there and then, but the driver wanted to park his vehicle again first and began to reverse towards the *albergue*. Whether he looked on the wrong side, or his mirrors were misleading him, he somehow managed to reverse into the tail of a blue van, up to its axles in snow. Everyone jumped out to check the damage, fortunately not too severe although the van would need a new rear light.

On foot this time, we made our way down to Anne's car and the ski centre, and managed to get ourselves onto the road down to Granada. By then my feet were freezing as well as wet, but luckily I had had the foresight to chuck spare socks and trainers into the car, so comfort was soon restored. It was about four in the afternoon, with another couple of hours of daylight.

As we descended, the falling snow eased and then stopped, but the air temperature was beginning to drop too, despite a lower altitude. We were in a slow-moving trickle of vehicles, everyone keeping a moderately safe distance. Gradually we became aware of more and more cars coming the other way, climbing up to Pradollano, which perplexed us.

"What can they be doing," we wondered. "Why come up here now?"

We noticed that many cars, Audi's, Mercedes and BMW's, had Polish or Italian number plates and were driven by smartly-dressed people in *après-ski* type clothes.

"Got it!" I exclaimed. "There hasn't been any competing today, so everyone, all the teams and spectators and supporters, who are staying at the resort, have had a day shopping in Granada and are now on their way back to their hotels or holiday flats."

This seemed to be the explanation, but as the traffic slowed to a crawl in both directions and then a standstill, we became mystified once more. People were parking off the road to fit chains, but not sufficiently to one side, on the invisible 'kerb,' for others to get past. One or two

276

cars going up had begun to slide across the carriageway. Anne was nervous.

"The traction doesn't feel very good," she said. "Steve, do you want to drive?"

He willingly agreed and, as soon as it was sensible and the traffic queue stationary, he and Anne opened their respective doors and attempted to change places. Anne got as far as the bonnet before her feet slid away. She hauled herself around the front wing and grabbed the passenger door handle. Steve, going in the other direction round the rear bumper, ended up on his hands and knees. This was not tarmac, this was sheet ice.

The journey down became tortuous in the extreme. No one seemed to care where they stopped or what the repercussions might be for other drivers, up or down. The light was going and we began to speculate on how we would cope after dark. Granada was 20 kilometres away and the resort at least two hours uphill on foot.

Then we had some good luck. A coach driver and a JCB digger driver, both in the 'up' lane, put on their padded jackets, had a discussion in the middle of the road, nodded to one another and very decisively began to take charge. People pulling over to put on chains were told to get as far off the carriageway as they could. Spaces were opened up in each direction so that careful overtaking became possible. The middle section, where snow had been piling up, gradually became compressed and more useable. Traffic began to flow again, quite rapidly on our side, going down.

Of course, by the time we reached the main Guadix-Granada highway, all snow had vanished, there were rainbows in the late afternoon sky and one might never have guessed that only 1200 metres above us, people were struggling and swearing as they inched their way to their smart hotels and apartments. No *après-ski* tonight we guessed, just a hot bath and a double whisky. For ourselves, we had enjoyed our snow-shoeing, but next time we wanted sunshine, a view of the whole of Spain and the energy of 25 year olds!

That was the last of our close encounters with snow for that year. We welcomed it and enjoyed gazing up at it, but we didn't get up into the mountains and put our feet in it for another few seasons. I was pleased that I had managed the uphill sections without too much trouble and felt remarkably energetic throughout. Perhaps the new infusion, designed to counter bone mineral loss and weakness, was proving its worth. Most of the time, except when I looked in the mirror and bemoaned my pre-adolescent body, I forgot entirely that I was a woman with terminal cancer.

***

Well, by contrast, the year has come around again and last night the men were out in the *plaza* putting up the flags, the bunting, the lights and the illuminated banners, all proclaiming *Buenas Fiestas*. Despite the fact that not much water is flowing from the fountain because of the summer drought and many people have lost their jobs due to the global financial crisis, the village will have its annual fiesta this weekend. The car park is already full, some of the otherwise empty houses have been occupied and the celebrations will soon begin.

At midnight last night we were sitting around in the *plaza*, enjoying the cooler air, the girls with bare arms, the men in shorts, the children running about. Light streamed from the doorway of our little bar; inside a quartet of older men were playing their obscure version of whist. A few teenage boys whizzed through on their bikes and vanished down one of the narrow streets; an 80 year old tottered past, on her way to bed. A music centre appeared and was positioned on a window ledge, the speakers 'hot-wired' into an electricity box on someone's wall. Small chairs were scattered around on the sloping stone walkway under the *tinao,* a gardening mattock and a finely-sharpened hook leaned companionably together against the wall, a bucket of ripe tomatoes beside them. Work was definitely over for a couple of days.

A crescent moon peeped over the rooftops and somewhere out there I imagined that the annual Perseid meteorites were beginning to fly past. Or we were flying through them. Perhaps we should go down to the land, into the darkness and watch as the universe slowly revolved around us, not worrying if we simply drifted off into the stratosphere.

Eventually, however, two women set up a bingo game and as the caller shouted out the numbers, the children repeated them in their shrill voices, making sure that everyone heard. Small groups shrieked and yelled, encouraging each other on; friendly rivalries began to form.

"Time for a late supper?" I asked Steve.

"I think so," he replied, gathering up our glasses and taking them into the bar.

"*Buenas noches,*" we called as we left. A few heads came up, briefly.

"*Buenas noches,*" chorused the reply, "*hasta mañana.*"

Printed in Great Britain
by Amazon.co.uk, Ltd.,
Marston Gate.

13024667R00159